Driving Business Transformation with Modern Data and AI Strategies

A Leader's Guide to Turning Data and AI into Business Value

Rahat Yasir
Kasam Shaikh

Apress®

Driving Business Transformation with Modern Data and AI Strategies: A Leader's Guide to Turning Data and AI into Business Value

Rahat Yasir
Montreal, QC, Canada

Kasam Shaikh
Kalyan, Maharashtra, India

ISBN-13 (pbk): 979-8-8688-2624-5
ISBN-13 (electronic): 979-8-8688-2625-2
https://doi.org/10.1007/979-8-8688-2625-2

Managing Director, Apress Media LLC: Welmoed Spahr
Acquisitions Editor: Smriti Srivastava
Editorial Assistant: Jessica Vakili

Cover designed by eStudioCalamar

Cover image designed by Freepik (www.freepik.com)

Distributed to the book trade worldwide by Springer Science+Business Media New York, 1 New York Plaza, New York, NY 10004. Phone 1-800-SPRINGER, fax (201) 348-4505, e-mail orders-ny@springer-sbm.com, or visit www.springeronline.com. Apress Media, LLC is a Delaware LLC and the sole member (owner) is Springer Science + Business Media Finance Inc (SSBM Finance Inc). SSBM Finance Inc is a **Delaware** corporation.

For information on translations, please e-mail booktranslations@springernature.com; for reprint, paperback, or audio rights, please e-mail bookpermissions@springernature.com.

Apress titles may be purchased in bulk for academic, corporate, or promotional use. eBook versions and licenses are also available for most titles. For more information, reference our Print and eBook Bulk Sales web page at http://www.apress.com/bulk-sales.

Any source code or other supplementary material referenced by the author in this book is available to readers on GitHub. For more detailed information, please visit https://www.apress.com/gp/services/source-code.

If disposing of this product, please recycle the paper

This book is dedicated to my beautiful wife, Claudia,
and our newborn son, Miles Laliberte Yasir, with all my love.
—Rahat Yasir

This book is dedicated to my father, the late
Mr. Ahmed Kasam Shaikh, who is always a source of
inspiration for me. And to my mentor, Mr. Sabarinath Iyer.
—Kasam Shaikh

Table of Contents

About the Authors

Rahat Yasir was named one of Canada's *Top 30 Software Developers Under 30* in 2018 and is a 12-time Microsoft Most Valuable Professional in Artificial Intelligence. He holds a bachelor's degree in computer science and engineering and a master's degree in computer science with a specialization in artificial intelligence and has completed multiple executive education programs focused on enterprise data, AI policy, strategy, and leadership.

He brings extensive experience across artificial intelligence, cloud, data analytics, cross-platform system development, and large-scale enterprise systems. Rahat authored the first eBooks on Windows Phone 8.1 and Universal Windows Platform development and has held a range of senior technical and research roles, including AI Researcher at the University of Saskatchewan's P2IRC, Lead AI Developer at Immersive Design Studios, and AI Engineer at Intact Financial Corporation. He has also led AI initiatives at OSEDEA, CAE, and ISAAC Instruments.

Currently, Rahat serves as Head of Data Insights & Advanced Analytics at IATA, where he leads global data, analytics, and AI initiatives supporting aviation safety and security use cases. In 2025, he was recognized with the *AI100 Early Adopters in North America* award. His work has also been honored with the *DataIQ Data & AI for Good Hero Organisation Award* and the *Grand Prix Award at DataIQ North America 2025.*

Kasam Shaikh is a four-time recipient of the prestigious Microsoft Most Valuable Professional (MVP) Award in AI—and the first and only Indian professional under the age of 40 to earn this honor consecutively for three years. A recognized global AI speaker, published author, and tech influencer, Kasam is widely known for his contributions to the AI ecosystem through his YouTube channel, mentoring initiatives, and thought leadership. He currently serves as a Cloud Solutions and Generative AI Architect at the Associate Director level, driving digital transformation and AI adoption across business units. As the founder of Dear Azure - Az-INDIA, the largest Azure AI community in the region, he plays a key role in nurturing AI talent and fostering innovation. Additionally, he is acknowledged as a career expert in AI by Rediff Gurus and leads the Gen AI Expert Community at the practice level within his organization.

About the Technical Reviewer

Shailesh is a global technology leader enabling client success driven through technology enablement, having more than two decades of experience. He is currently working with Capgemini India as a CTO and chief architect. Shailesh works with clients across the globe to drive large-scale transformations and help define IT vision and roadmap for enterprises. He is passionate about and specializes in turning cutting-edge AI/ML, blockchain, IoT, and cloud convergence—like generative AI, agentic AI, and autonomous agents—into enterprise-grade, real-world solutions that drive enterprises end to end.

Shailesh is also a published author and regular speaker in academia, conferences/summits, and industry and has written articles on artificial intelligence, big data, information retrieval, blockchain, and IOT.

Acknowledgments

I would like to thank all my friends, family members, relatives, teachers, mentors, and colleagues who have supported and guided me, helping shape me into who I am today. I am also deeply grateful to Apress for making this book a reality.

—Rahat

I would first like to thank Almighty ALLAH, my mother, my better half, and especially my daughter Maryam, for motivating me throughout the process. I am highly thankful to Apress for considering me for this opportunity and for believing in me.

—Kasam

Endorsements

Having hired Rahat as our Director of AI at ISAAC Instruments, I saw firsthand his exceptional ability to define a clear AI vision, build a high-performing team, and translate innovation into tangible business value. This book reflects that same practical expertise, giving leaders a clear framework for turning complex data ecosystems into measurable results. Any executive serious about leading real AI transformation—not just talking about it—should have this on their desk.

David Brillon, M.Sc.A., Eng.
ISAAC Instruments
Strategist – Advanced Technologies Innovation, Cofounder

This book highlights an important shift: data and AI must be treated as enterprise assets that require disciplined management. By introducing practical frameworks for AI road map, capability assessment, and responsible AI, the authors show how organizations can translate these assets into measurable business outcomes. A thoughtful guide for leaders looking to make data and AI a real driver of business transformation.

Wilson Mok
Director, AI & Business Intelligence
SMS Equipment

Introduction

In today's digital-first world, data is no longer merely a technical asset, it is a strategic superpower. *Driving Business Transformation with Modern Data and AI Strategies* is a practical guide for forward-thinking business leaders seeking to make informed, confident decisions powered by data, analytics, and artificial intelligence (AI).

This book is designed to demystify complex data technologies and explain their relevance in clear, accessible language. It empowers C-level executives, department heads, and transformation leaders to align data, analytics, and AI initiatives with tangible business outcomes.

Over the past few decades, we have observed that organizations embracing data-centric decision-making are consistently outpacing their competitors. They are launching innovative products, enhancing customer understanding, and unlocking new sources of competitive advantage. In contrast, those clinging to traditional, intuition-led approaches often struggle to meet market demands, lose relevance, and might become obsolete.

This book is intended for both technical and nontechnical leaders—whether you are already working within the data and AI space or planning to enter it. The era where data and AI were confined to technologists is over. Increasingly, domain experts across industries are stepping into this field by acquiring complementary data literacy and AI understanding.

We've written this book to support

- Senior executives seeking a clear and comprehensive overview of the domain
- Leaders preparing to make strategic investments in data and AI
- Technical professionals transitioning into leadership roles in data strategy
- Digital transformation leads and data executives building the future of intelligent enterprise

Whether you are new to this journey or have been immersed in it for years, this book offers a practical roadmap, real-world insights, and a powerful refresher on key principles.

What You Will Learn

Key takeaways include—but are not limited to—the following:

- How to unlock business value through efficiency, insight, and innovation leveraging data and AI
- Strategies for democratizing data, analytics, and AI across your organization
- Core concepts in data analytics and AI and their business use cases
- How to design a modern, cloud-native data platform
- Steps to assess and build analytics maturity
- How to identify and implement traditional AI and generative AI (GenAI) use cases
- Ethical, regulatory, and operational considerations for responsible AI
- How to define Return on Investment (ROI) and lead data and AI initiatives with clarity and confidence
- Building a sustainable and impactful data and analytics roadmap

Structure of the Book

The content is organized into four parts:

Part 1: The Data-Driven Business Landscape
Introduces the transition from legacy systems to modern cloud-based platforms, outlining the essential components of a model data ecosystem. This part also explores the pivotal role of business leaders in driving data strategy and securing ROI.

Part 2: The Advanced Analytics and AI Ecosystem
Provides a maturity model for analytics, covering the progression from descriptive to prescriptive insights. Readers will explore business intelligence, data storytelling, and how to embed insights into day-to-day decision-making. Even seasoned data leaders will discover new ideas to enhance their current strategy.

Part 3: AI in Action
Explores the practical application of AI—traditional machine learning (ML), generative AI, AI agents, and more. It covers frameworks for responsible AI, team building, and future-looking strategies for organizations of all sizes. Packed with domain-relevant use cases, this part makes AI approachable and actionable for business leaders.

Part 4: Strategy, Culture, Execution, and Future-Proof Next Steps
Focuses on creating a data-first culture, aligning cross-functional teams, managing change, and measuring business impact. The section concludes with a practical checklist for leaders to assess organizational readiness and define next steps with confidence.

Throughout the book, we aim to maintain a light, engaging tone supported by real-world examples, humorous dialogues, and memorable quotes from industry leaders. These moments are designed to bring context to key ideas and make the reading experience both insightful and enjoyable.

Whether you're embarking on your first data transformation or scaling established AI initiatives, this book will equip you to lead with clarity, courage, and conviction in a data-driven future.

PART I

The Data-Driven Business Landscape

CHAPTER 1

Introduction: Why Data Is Your Business Superpower

Who has the data has the power.

—Tim O'Reilly

Part 1 of this book explores the foundation of becoming a data-driven enterprise. It focuses on the data ecosystem, the modern data stack, the key components leaders must consider, and the evolving business landscape in today's data driven world.

Chapter 1 sets the stage for the rest of the book by articulating the **urgency and strategic relevance of a robust data strategy**. In an increasingly competitive and dynamic economy, data is no longer optional—it is mission-critical. This chapter highlights why business leaders can no longer afford to overlook data as a core enabler of growth, efficiency, and innovation.

We examine the **value of demystifying data**, removing the technical and operational fog that often clouds decision-making, and presenting data as a clear, strategic lever for business outcomes. Readers will gain insight into how to extract tangible value from data and understand who benefits most—and how—in a data-led environment.

We also address the profound shift taking place in organizational decision-making: from *gut instinct* to *graph-driven insight*. This transformation is reshaping industries, redefining leadership, and exposing the high cost of inaction for those slow to adapt.

R. Yasir and K. Shaikh, *Driving Business Transformation with Modern Data and AI Strategies*,
https://doi.org/10.1007/979-8-8688-2625-2_1

This opening chapter establishes the tone and purpose of the book. Its content is structured into six clear and interconnected sections:

1. The Rise of the Data-Driven Enterprise
2. Business Value from Data: Efficiency, Insight, Innovation
3. Competitive Advantage in This Data-Driven World
4. Shift in Decision-Making from Gut to Graph
5. What Data Really Is and Isn't
6. High Cost of Ignoring Data

Based on a recent survey [1] conducted by **Carruthers and Jackson** across the UK and US markets, **26% of organizations** still operate without a formal data strategy, while **39% report having little to no data governance framework** in place. In the absence of a clear strategy, these organizations struggle to adopt data-driven decision-making and continue to rely heavily on instinct and intuition.

Figure 1-1 demonstrates a familiar scenario in many businesses today—where one leader must persuade another of data's role as a true business superpower.

To bring these concepts to life, we introduce an ongoing conversation (Figure 1-1) between two business leaders, **Miles** and **Clara**. In this chapter, Clara questions whether data is simply a fleeting trend. It doesn't take long, however, for Miles to demonstrate that data is far more than hype—it is a catalyst for competitive advantage, smarter decision-making, and operational efficiency.

Figure 1-1. *Conversation between two leaders on data as a business superpower*

The Rise of the Data-Driven Enterprise

> *Information is the oil of the 21st century, and analytics is the combustion engine.*
>
> —Peter Sondergaard, former SVP at Gartner

The rise of the data-driven enterprise represents one of the most significant transformations in modern business. Organizations have shifted from intuition-based management to a model in which **data forms the backbone** of strategy, product development, operations, and innovation.

What Is a Data-Driven Enterprise?

A data-driven enterprise is one that treats **data as a strategic asset**. It establishes a long-term data vision, recognizing that the benefits of data require time, discipline, and investment to realize.

Such organizations

- Use analytics and insights to inform decisions across all levels.
- Embed data into daily workflows and operational practices.
- Promote a culture in which data is trusted, shared, and actively used.

A data-driven enterprise builds its own **data ecosystem**, aligned to its business domain. This ecosystem enables the organization to gain a holistic view of its operations, connect insights across data sources, understand user behavior, anticipate market shifts, and identify emerging product needs.

At maturity, data-driven enterprises are anchored by a **robust data strategy** and leverage advanced analytics and artificial intelligence to unlock measurable benefits—such as efficiency, insight, innovation, and speed.

Throughout this book, we will explore the critical elements of a data-driven enterprise and provide a practical framework to help you build one within your own organization.

Key Characteristics of a Data-Driven Organization

- Decision-making is both **top-down and bottom-up**—empowering all levels of the organization to contribute to strategic and operational decisions.
- **Democratization of data** enables employees to work at 2–5× speed and deliver greater impact.
- A data-driven culture provides a **clear view of current performance** and highlights areas for improvement.
- **KPIs are transparent**, easy to track, and guide continuous improvement.
- **Analytics and AI serve as copilots**, helping employees deliver better, faster, and more consistently.
- A **data flywheel effect** helps the business uncover customer needs, identify new features, and explore innovative use cases.

- A well-defined **governance framework** ensures security, compliance, and cost control.
- The organization becomes increasingly **customer-centric**, guided by data on market trends, user behavior, and future opportunities.

While this section does not explore the benefits of becoming data-driven in detail, the remainder of the chapter will highlight them through practical examples and lighthearted conversations. These will cover themes such as business value, competitive advantage, shifts in decision-making, and the cost of inaction—similar to the discussion illustrated in Figure 1-2, where two leaders reflect on the benefits of a data-driven decision-making process.

Figure 1-2. *Conversation between two leaders on data-driven decision-making benefits*

Key Challenges in Becoming a Data-Driven Organization

- **Data silos** persist across departments, limiting integration and value realization.

- **Lack of visionary leadership**—leaders who fail to recognize the opportunity cost of inaction or take bold, strategic decisions—can stall progress.
- A shortage of **skilled talent** capable of developing impactful, real-world use cases.
- **Data quality issues** undermine the effectiveness of even the most sophisticated platforms; poor-quality data often leads to failed strategies.
- **Reliance on legacy systems** limits an organization's ability to execute modern data initiatives.
- Initial underinvestment in building the **data ecosystem** can result in platforms that fall short of expectations.
- **Lack of a composite knowledge base**—organizations often stop at isolated data products rather than building a surrounding data ecosystem that reveals deeper patterns and enables root-cause analysis.
- **Cultural resistance** to change remains a significant barrier. Becoming data-driven requires effective change management, continuous training, and a mindset shift. Data, analytics, and automation must be seen not as threats, but as enablers of greater productivity and decision-making excellence.
- **Privacy and compliance risks** can derail initiatives. A robust **data governance framework** and an active **data governance council** are essential to ensuring trust, accountability, and sustainability in all data-related activities.

Business Value from Data: Efficiency, Insight, Innovation

> *Data is what you need to do analytics. Information is what you need to do business.*
>
> —John Owen, IT executive

One of the key issues we have observed in recent years is that certain organizations invest in building platforms, centralizing their data, and creating comprehensive repositories—yet, once this is achieved, they lack a clear plan for **extracting business value** from that data. Simply holding vast volumes of data delivers limited benefit beyond meeting regulatory and compliance requirements, such as retention and governance policies.

To truly leverage data as a strategic asset, an organization must establish a robust **data and AI strategy**. This is the essential first step in becoming a data-driven enterprise. Once in place, the next stage is to apply advanced analytics to the collected data—using descriptive and statistical analysis to gain deeper business understanding and unlock a range of practical use cases.

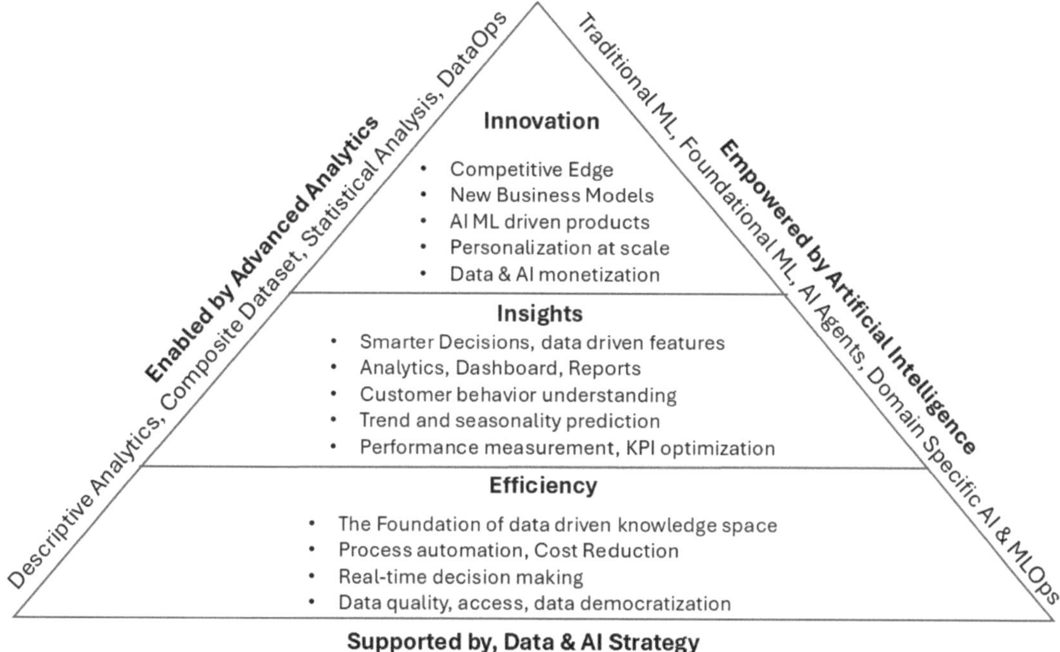

Figure 1-3. *Diagram of driving business value through data, analytics, and AI*

Following this, artificial intelligence algorithms can be deployed to maximize outcomes, turning raw data into actionable insights, predictive capabilities, and innovative business solutions. Executed effectively, this process creates a **data flywheel**—a self-reinforcing cycle in which more data enables richer analytics and

AI, which in turn attract more customers, generate new opportunities, and deliver a sustained competitive advantage.

Figure 1-3 illustrates the complete journey of a **data and AI strategy**—from advanced analytics and artificial intelligence to the extraction of business value in the form of **efficiency, insights, and innovation**.

Efficiency represents the first stage of value an organization can derive from data. Achieving this requires a well-defined **data and AI strategy** encompassing data governance, an integrated ecosystem, and a robust platform architecture. At this stage, organizations consolidate data—whether in batch or real time—from multiple systems to drive process automation, reduce costs, enable real-time decision-making, implement alerting and monitoring mechanisms, and democratize access to data across the enterprise.

Insights form the second stage of value creation. Here, data is transformed into dashboards, analytics outputs, and **composite datasets**—where multiple sources are integrated to reveal deeper narratives. This enables compelling storytelling, root-cause analysis, KPI optimization, trend identification, seasonality understanding, and forecasting. These insights equip leaders to anticipate developments and make more precise strategic choices.

Innovation is the third and most transformative stage. At this level, data and AI strategies combine with advanced analytics and artificial intelligence to create entirely new business models, establish competitive advantage, and develop innovative, data-backed products. This stage also unlocks fresh monetization opportunities, informed entirely by reliable, actionable information.

In this section, we explore these ideas through a conversation (Figure 1-4) between **George** and **Leonie**, two senior leaders debating whether data can genuinely fuel product innovation within their organization. Their exchange sparks a new wave of possibilities—captured in the accompanying comic illustration.

Figure 1-4. *Conversation between two leaders on innovation using data*

Competitive Advantage in This Data-Driven World

> *Without big data analytics, companies are blind and deaf, wandering out onto the web like deer on a freeway.*
>
> —Geoffrey Moore

As business leaders, one of our primary objectives is to gain **competitive advantage** through the strategic use of data in today's data-driven world. Data should not merely serve as a supporting tool—it must sit at the heart of all core strategies, enabling organizations to outperform their rivals in **time to market, speed, decision-making, innovation, customer engagement, and the understanding of market sentiment and trends**.

Below are key principles for using data to secure and sustain competitive advantage:

- **Treat data as an organizational asset** and elevate it to a board-level priority.

- Ensure the **data and AI strategy** is fully aligned with the corporate and organizational strategy, with clearly defined business outcomes linked to growth, profitability, and market share.
- Assign **ownership and accountability** to a chief data officer (CDO) or chief data and AI officer (CDAIO) to ensure strategic alignment, governance, and effective execution.
- Build a **unified, high-quality data ecosystem** that enables all parts of the business to contribute to and benefit from shared data resources.
- Actively **discourage non-data-driven decision-making**, as it undermines organizational focus and strategic coherence.
- Move beyond basic reporting—**leverage advanced analytics and AI** for diagnostic, predictive, and prescriptive insights that drive smarter, faster decision-making.
- **Embed AI and automation** across every business unit. Establish dedicated **rapid-action analytics teams** within business functions or innovation and digital departments to accelerate time-to-market strategies.
- **Democratize data and AI** throughout the organization, empowering teams from the bottom up and the top down to maximize resource utilization and operational efficiency.
- Explore **data monetization opportunities**—for example, adopting Data-as-a-Service models, selling anonymized insights to partners or industry players, and integrating analytics into product offerings to create new revenue streams.
- Treat **data privacy, ethics, and compliance** as competitive differentiators, building trust with customers and stakeholders.
- Recognize that in the digital era, **speed is critical**. Shorten the cycle from data collection to action and move quickly from pilot to production for AI-driven initiatives to stay ahead of the competition.

In this section, we explore these ideas through a conversation (Figure 1-5) between **Mitchel** and **Christin**, two senior leaders reflecting on how competitors are accelerating through data-driven decision-making—and how strategic use of data is enabling them to win decisively in their markets.

Figure 1-5. *Conversation between two leaders on data-driven competitive advantage*

Shift in Decision-Making from Gut to Graph

> *Most of the world will make decisions by either guessing or using their gut. They will be either lucky or wrong.*
>
> —Suhail Doshi, founder of Mixpanel

For decades, traditional organizations have relied on **gut-based decision-making**. But the business landscape has changed dramatically. Organizations that persist with this approach are increasingly **falling behind competitors**, becoming less innovative, losing market share to agile new entrants, failing to understand customer needs, and, ultimately, risking obsolescence. Over the past two decades, we have seen once-dominant market leaders lose their position and value due to an inability to anticipate "what's next." Notable examples include Yahoo, AOL, Netscape, Kodak, and Nokia—brands that once defined their sectors but were overtaken by those who adapted faster.

In today's **digital-first world**, the shift is clear: we have moved from **gut-based decision-making** to **graph-based decision-making**—where insights are driven by data, analytics, and measurable evidence rather than instinct alone.

Figure 1-6 illustrates examples of both gut- and graph-based approaches and why this transformation is taking place. If you are a business leader still relying primarily on gut instinct, take this as a **clear signal to act**. It is time to modernize your approach, redesign your decision-making processes, and embrace data-led strategies to remain relevant, competitive, and resilient in the market.

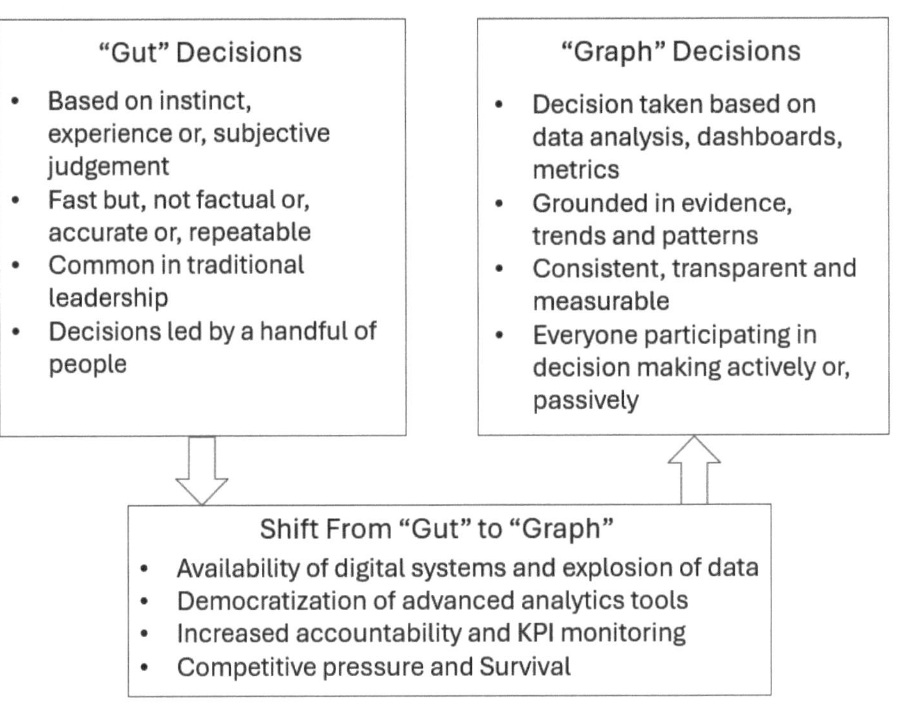

Figure 1-6. *Shift from "gut" to "graph" decision-making*

The question for any business leader is this: **how do you transition your organization from gut-based to graph-based decision-making?**

Below are key actions you can take to lead this change effectively:

- **Build data literacy** and upskill your existing workforce through both strategic and tool-based training programs.
- **Empower business units** by providing self-service tools, robust platforms, targeted training, and easy access to relevant knowledge.

- **Lead by example**—select a single business unit to run data-driven experiments and use its success as a case study to expand similar initiatives across the organization in stages.
- Provide **change management training** and help employees understand that AI, automation, and analytics are here to enhance—not threaten—their roles. Position these tools as enablers of efficiency, effectiveness, and job security.
- **Make data visible** via dashboards and reports and embed data-driven decision-making into every process—from hiring and performance measurement to strategic growth initiatives.
- Foster a **culture of experimentation and measurement**. Inspire teams to prepare for the future using evidence-based strategies rather than reacting to market hype.
- **Track ROI** rigorously, reward tangible business outcomes, and use these achievements to inspire others. Promote leaders who champion innovation and recognize those who deliver measurable impact.

In this section, we introduce a conversation (Figure 1-7) between **John** and **Emily**, two senior leaders debating a common misconception: that producing more reports automatically strengthens decision-making. They explore why it is not the quantity of reports that matters, but their relevance, adoption, and ability to deliver actionable insights. They also discuss how to design smarter, more valuable reports that genuinely serve customers and drive business performance.

Figure 1-7. *Conversation between two leaders regarding gut-based decision-making to graph*

What Data Really Is and Isn't

> *That's all data is. A gift from yesterday that you receive today to make tomorrow better.*
>
> —Jon Acuff

We have observed that some traditional leaders continue to struggle with understanding **what constitutes data in a business context—and what does not**.

Here is a clear, concise definition:

What is data?

- Raw facts, figures, observations, or signals that can be measured, collected, recorded, and analyzed.
- It may be **quantitative** or **qualitative**, **structured** or **unstructured**.
- Examples include sales figures, website metrics, social media activity, email engagement, behavioral logs, datasets purchased from different sources, and employee records.

In a business context, a single data point, a single source, or an isolated dataset provides only **fragmented information**. To generate deeper insights and create an **unbiased, evidence-based narrative**, leaders must connect multiple relevant data sources—sometimes as many as possible. Doing so allows the organization to understand

- **What** has happened
- **What** is happening
- **What** may happen next
- **Why** events are occurring
- **What actions** will lead to the desired outcome
- **Which factors** are influencing those outcomes

What is not data?

Many things are not data because they cannot be reliably measured, recorded, or accessed for analysis. Examples include

- Intuition and gut feelings
- Opinions or rumors
- Anecdotal stories without supporting evidence
- Unrecorded observations
- Vague goals such as “increase efficiency”
- Outdated information that no longer reflects current reality

It is important to distinguish between **data** and **insight**. Data is the raw material; insight is the value we extract from that data to inform decisions and strategies in a business context.

In this section, we introduce a conversation (Figure 1-8) between **Martine** and **Claudia**, two senior leaders discussing a common misconception—that data alone is the answer to everything. They agree that there is no "magic" in data by itself. Instead, data provides **direction and clarity of approach**, but it does not make the decision for us. It is the leader's role to use those insights wisely to navigate toward the organization's destination.

Figure 1-8. *Conversation between two leaders on data usage for business context*

High Cost of Ignoring Data

Things get done only if the data we gather can inform and inspire those in a position to make [a] difference.

—Michael Schmoker

One critical question always arises: **what is the cost of ignoring data?**

Whether an organization persists with traditional **gut-based decision-making** or adopts a **hybrid approach**—where leaders use their experience as a reason to downplay or bypass data—the risks are significant.

Earlier in this chapter, we have already highlighted how competitive advantage can be eroded, how organizations can drift toward obsolescence, and how market value can be lost. Here, we offer a different perspective—one that quantifies the **high cost of ignoring data** in today's digital-first world:

- **Poor organizational decision-making** - Without accurate, timely data, decisions rely on intuition, assumption, or outdated information, leading to missed market opportunities, inefficient operations, and misaligned strategies.
- **Revenue loss** - Failing to understand customer behavior, trends, preferences, and sales patterns results in missed opportunities to grow revenue and capture market share.
- **Operational inefficiency** - Redundant processes, misallocation of resources, and rising costs become persistent challenges.
- **Heightened risk exposure** - Increased vulnerability to fraud, compliance violations, cyber threats, anomalies, and governance failures.
- **Customer attrition** - Slow service, unmet expectations, and poor experiences lead to frustration, declining retention, reduced loyalty, and an eventual loss of competitive position—potentially leading to irrelevance in the market.
- **Wasted investment** - Poorly informed initiatives underperform, ROI remains unclear, and marketing campaigns fail to deliver intended results.

- **Cultural stagnation** – A lack of innovation, diminished accountability, and stalled improvement cycles hinder long-term growth.

The accompanying comic (Figure 1-9) captures this scenario vividly: a traditional leader, **Nelson**, remains reluctant to use data in decision-making, while a younger, well-informed leader, **Eloise**, challenges this mindset—making a compelling case for the value at stake and the true cost of ignoring data.

Figure 1-9. *Conversation between two leaders on cost of ignoring data*

Chapter Summary

As the world embraces the AI boom, the real opportunity lies in approaching it with intention and structure. To fully leverage this trend, organizations must have a clear data strategy, commit to becoming truly data-driven, build data literacy across the workforce, understand and track ROI, and harness the benefits of data and AI in an iterative, value-focused manner.

It is never too late to start. This book is written for business leaders who are already on this journey but want to accelerate their progress—and for those seeking the clarity to take the next decisive steps. There is no magic formula here; however, by engaging with the principles in these chapters, you will gain a comprehensive guide to the actions required to move forward with confidence.

You have not "missed the train" nor are you "too late" to the AI boom (Figure 1-10 representing a stressful scenario). Transformation is a process, and it is ongoing. If you start today, your organization could be in a significantly more advanced and revenue-generating position within the next two to three years. But the key is to start now.

If you are already on this path but have not yet seen meaningful transformation, it may be time to reassess your approach—whether by refining your strategy, bringing in new leadership, broadening involvement across the organization, or ensuring that progress is measured and managed in a truly data-driven way. If you are on the right track, you should be able to observe tangible progress quarter by quarter—both in your operational capabilities and in the measurable business outcomes you deliver.

***Figure 1-10.** Leaders are panicking whether they missed the AI train or not!*

Reference

[1] Survey by Carruthers and Jackson 2025, Data maturity survey finds a quarter of organisations with no strategy | Computer Weekly

CHAPTER 2

The Modern Data Stack: Explained Simply

Data is a precious thing and will last longer than the systems themselves.

—Tim Berners-Lee

Why Read This Chapter?

Modern enterprises generate and consume data at unprecedented speed and variety. Traditional data architectures, while reliable in their time, are too rigid, slow, and costly to meet today's demands. This chapter explains what a Modern Data Stack (MDS) is, why it matters, and how leaders can implement it strategically—anchored in Microsoft Azure, yet flexible enough for multi-cloud realities.

Key Takeaways

- **Faster insights** – From days to near real time, enabling quicker decisions.
- **Elastic scalability** – Pay for what you use; scale instantly when needed.
- **Modular design** – Choose the right tool for each function without vendor lock-in.

R. Yasir and K. Shaikh, *Driving Business Transformation with Modern Data and AI Strategies*,
https://doi.org/10.1007/979-8-8688-2625-2_2

- **Governance baked in** – Compliance and trust at every stage.
- **AI readiness** – High-quality data pipelines for machine learning and automation.

Introduction

Monday Mornings, Metrics, and Missed Opportunities

As illustrated in Figure 2-1, this leadership exchange captures the urgency many enterprises feel when struggling with outdated data systems.

Figure 2-1. *Conversation between teams on the Modern Data Stack*

It is 9:07 a.m. on a crisp Monday in Mumbai, India.

It's a rainy Monday morning in Mumbai. Mr. Shailesh A, the chief operating officer (COO) of ISkillSetu, a rapidly expanding e-learning company, is visibly frustrated in a leadership sync call.

"Why does it take ten days to get a reliable sales forecast? We're drowning in data, but it feels like we're back in 2005!"

Next to him sits Ms. Maryam S, the principal solution architect, who has just returned from an industry summit. She gently intervenes.

"Shailesh, we don't have a data problem. We have a data stack problem. It's time we adopt the Modern Data Stack—modular, scalable, real time."

Nilesh chimes in, "And it takes us two days to make schema changes propagate across reporting systems. That's just not acceptable anymore."

It isn't the first time ISkillSetu is hitting bottlenecks. But this time, there is consensus in the room: the company's data architecture needs a serious rethink.

This chapter begins here, at a realization many enterprises face. The traditional data landscape, while functional, can no longer support the agility, scale, and intelligence modern businesses demand. This chapter lays the groundwork by explaining, in simple terms yet with depth, what a "Modern Data Stack" is, why it matters, and how to approach it as a strategic architecture.

What Is the Modern Data Stack?

The Modern Data Stack (MDS) is not just a collection of new tools, it is an architectural approach that embraces modularity, cloud-native services, API (Application Programming Interface)-first integration, and scalable pipelines. At its core, the MDS enables teams to collect, process, store, analyze, and activate data with reduced friction.

Core Layers of the Modern Data Stack

1. **Data ingestion**
   Tools - Azure Data Factory, Azure Synapse Pipelines.
   Purpose - Seamless extraction of data from a variety of sources—
   APIs, databases, SaaS apps, logs.

2. **Data storage (lake or warehouse)**
   Tools - Azure Data Lake Storage (ADLS) Gen2, Azure Synapse Analytics.
   Purpose - Centralized, scalable storage supporting structured, semi-structured, and unstructured data, with decoupled compute and storage.

3. **Data transformation (ELT (Extract, Load, Transform), not ETL (Extract, Transform, Load))**
   Tools - Azure Synapse Spark Pools, Azure Dataflows, Spark Structured Streaming.
   Purpose - Transform raw data within the analytics platform using SQL-based and distributed processing models.

4. **Data orchestration**
   Tools - Azure Data Factory, Azure Synapse Pipelines.
   Purpose - Manage pipeline execution, dependencies, failure handling, and observability.

5. **Business intelligence and analytics**
   Tools - Azure Synapse SQL Pools, Power BI, Tableau.
   Purpose - Data exploration, dashboarding, operational reporting.

6. **Reverse ETL and activation**
   Tools - Census, Hightouch, Azure Synapse Link.
   Purpose - Push transformed data back into CRM, marketing platforms, or operations tools.

7. **Data governance, cataloguing, and observability**
   Tools - Azure Purview, Collibra, Alation, Monte Carlo.
   Purpose - Data discovery, lineage tracking, data quality, and policy enforcement.

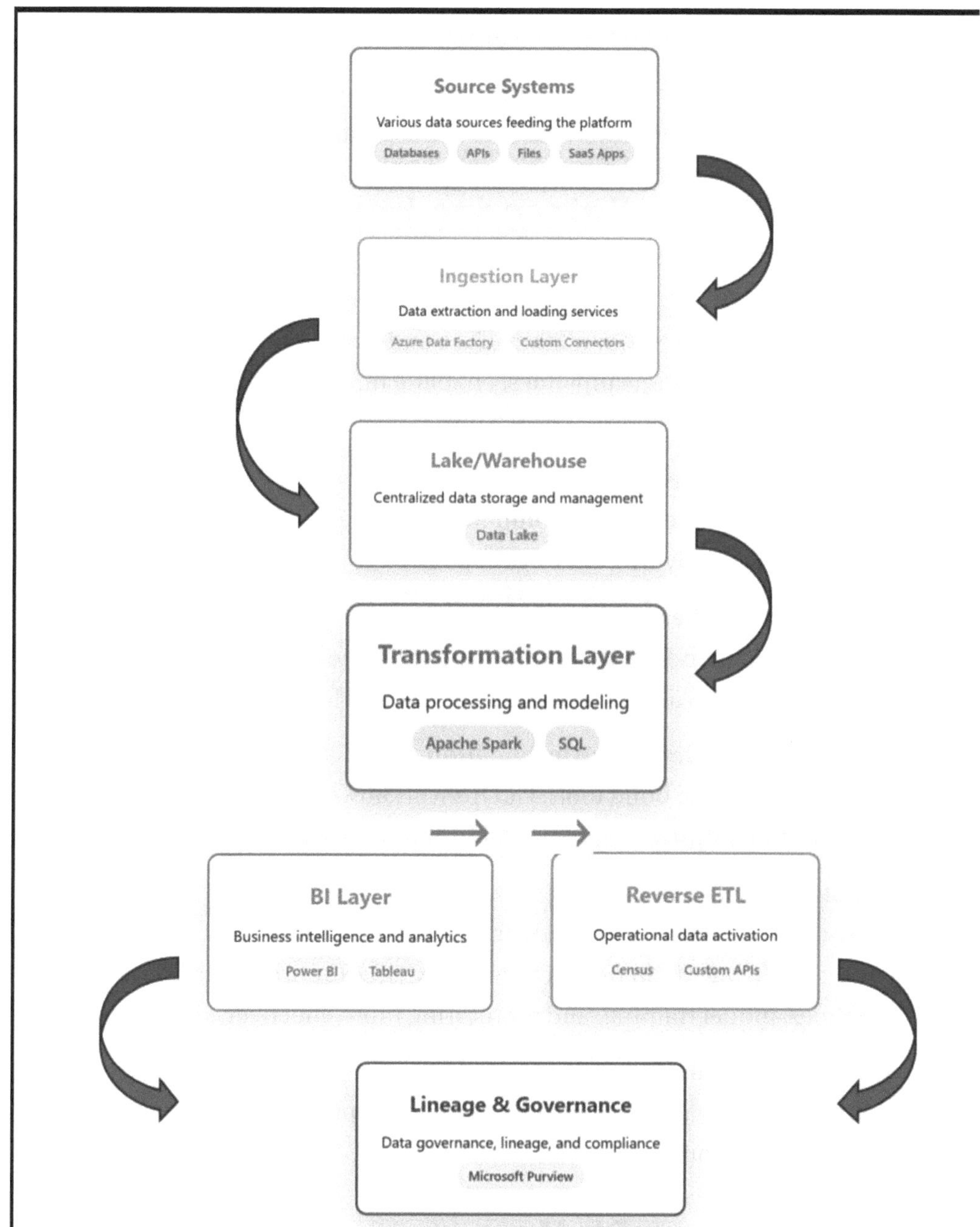

Figure 2-2. *Visual presentation of the core layers of the Modern Data Stack*

Figure 2-2 illustrates how the Modern Data Stack is organized into its core layers, each with a clear role in the flow from ingestion to activation.

Conceptual Architecture Diagram

The MDS isn't a rigid prescription; it's a framework. It prioritizes loosely coupled services, clean contracts between systems, and interoperability over monoliths.

Why the Shift? The Enterprise Imperatives

1. **Speed to insight**
   Legacy stacks often rely on nightly ETLs and static reports. MDS supports near-real-time pipelines, enabling rapid experimentation and decision-making.

2. **Scalability and elastic compute**
   Cloud-native tools decouple compute and storage, allowing teams to scale horizontally without huge capex.

3. **Modularity and best-of-breed**
   Rather than depending on a single vendor for the entire data lifecycle, the MDS allows choosing the best tool for each layer.

4. **Developer experience and automation**
   Tools like dbt (data build tool), GitOps workflows, and declarative orchestration improve maintainability and reduce human errors.

5. **Enablement of AI/ML**
   High-quality, well-modeled data is foundational for operationalizing ML in production. The MDS supports feature pipelines, model training, and monitoring more effectively.

6. **Governance by design**
   With built-in lineage tracking and metadata capture, the MDS ensures better compliance and auditability.

Legacy vs. Modern Platforms

> *These legacy systems now stand resolutely in the way of progress. They're big, rigid, change-resistant, costly to run, and lock-in-place practices that are long overdue for change.*
>
> —Geoffrey Cann, energy industry consultant; source [1]

Transitioning from legacy data platforms to a Modern Data Stack—particularly in the Microsoft ecosystem—entails a shift from rigid, monolithic architectures to agile, service-oriented, and cloud-optimized systems. This section outlines the core contrasts to help decision-makers and architects grasp the gravity and benefit of the change.

As shown in Figure 2-3, the leadership exchange highlights the sharp contrast between legacy data platforms and the modern stack.

Figure 2-3. Conversation between teams on legacy vs. modern platforms

Architecture

- **Legacy** - Monolithic BI systems like SQL Server Reporting Services (SSRS) connected via tightly coupled ETL jobs. Scaling required manual intervention or hardware upgrades.
- **Modern (Microsoft)** - Azure Synapse unifies warehousing, big data analytics, and integrated notebooks. Azure Data Factory offers orchestrated pipelines decoupled from compute. Scaling is automatic and horizontal.

Data Movement

- **Legacy** - Scheduled ETL processes with nightly jobs and intermediate file storage.
- **Modern** - Streaming ingestion through Azure Event Hubs or Data Factory triggers. ELT model preferred to load raw data into the lake and then transform using Spark or SQL engines.

Tooling and Development

- **Legacy** - GUI-based tools with poor versioning and deployment overhead.
- **Modern** - Infrastructure-as-code (Bicep, ARM), integration with Azure DevOps or GitHub Actions, and support for modular pipelines.

Governance and Metadata

- **Legacy** - Disconnected systems without lineage tracking or data cataloguing.
- **Modern** - Microsoft Purview automatically scans, classifies, and links datasets across the stack. Business and technical users can search for trusted data assets.

User Enablement

- **Legacy** – Central IT owns and controls data delivery.
- **Modern** – Power BI enables self-service exploration, with row-level security and shared certified datasets. Domain users can be trained to build their own insights.

Performance and Scaling

- **Legacy** – Performance tuning through indexing, archiving, and vertical hardware scaling.
- **Modern** – Compute scaling via serverless options, workload isolation, and performance tiers. For example, Azure Synapse supports on-demand queries on Parquet files in ADLS.

Decision-Making Guide: When to Use What

Objective	Recommended Approach	Example Tools
Quick dashboarding for business teams	ELT + Cloud warehouse + BI tool	Snowflake + Power BI
Building ML-ready datasets	Lakehouse architecture with Spark	Delta Lake + Azure ML
Governed reporting for finance	SQL-first transformation + Cataloguing	Azure Purview + Synapse
Multi-source ingestion with semi-structured data	Schema-flexible ingestion with validation	Data Factory + Lakehouse

Heuristic Tip If your business users are struggling with inconsistent metrics, start with a robust semantic layer and clear data contracts across tools.

Multi-cloud Ecosystem: Why and How

> *81 % of organizations are working with two or more public cloud providers. A multi-cloud strategy gives companies the freedom to use the best possible cloud for each workload.*
>
> —Urs Hölzle, SVP Cloud Infrastructure, Google; source [2]

In today's data landscape, the question for enterprises is no longer *if* they will adopt the cloud, but *how many*. With growing regulatory complexity, vendor risk management, and the need to serve global operations, multi-cloud strategies have become increasingly relevant—especially for data and AI workloads.

Why Multi-cloud Matters

Shailesh recalls an urgent board-level request from the previous quarter: "What if one of our cloud providers experiences a regional outage or a service breach? Can our analytics stay operational?"

Maryam, ever focused on business resilience, has made it clear: "We need to architect for portability, not dependency."

Here's why more enterprises are leaning toward multi-cloud data platforms:

- **Risk mitigation** - Relying solely on a single provider can amplify vendor lock-in and systemic risks. Diversifying across Azure, AWS, and/or GCP can offer redundancy and compliance advantages.
- **Data residency and sovereignty** - Different countries enforce unique data storage laws. A multi-cloud strategy allows workloads and datasets to stay compliant across jurisdictions.
- **Cost optimization** - By leveraging pricing differences for compute-intensive tasks (e.g., model training or large-scale transformation jobs), enterprises can reduce total cost of ownership.
- **Tool specialization** - Some teams might favor Azure for analytics, but prefer another platform for specialized AI frameworks or open source compatibility.

How to Build a Multi-cloud Data Strategy (with Azure at the Core)

While enterprises can architect in a multi-cloud manner, it's critical to retain a *core data backbone*. For organizations committed to the Microsoft stack, Azure can act as this centralized platform, with integrations to other cloud platforms as needed.

Key Architectural Approaches

- **Data federation via Azure Synapse Link** - Connect on demand to external data sources—including those hosted on AWS S3 or GCP BigQuery—without needing to ingest all data into Azure up front.
- **Interoperability using Azure Arc** - Extend governance, security policies, and even services like Azure SQL or Kubernetes across hybrid and multi-cloud environments.
- **Cross-cloud pipelines** - Azure Data Factory allows creation of pipelines that fetch and push data across heterogeneous environments. Pre-built connectors simplify integration.
- **Central governance via Microsoft Purview** - Regardless of where data lives, Purview can serve as the metadata catalogue and classification engine across clouds using REST APIs and scanning rules.
- **AI/ML portability** - Models trained on Azure Machine Learning can be exported in ONNX or containerized formats and deployed on other cloud runtimes like SageMaker or Vertex AI if needed.

Conceptual Diagram

Figure 2-4 provides a high-level view of how a multi-cloud ecosystem can be structured, with Azure at the core and interoperability across other platforms.

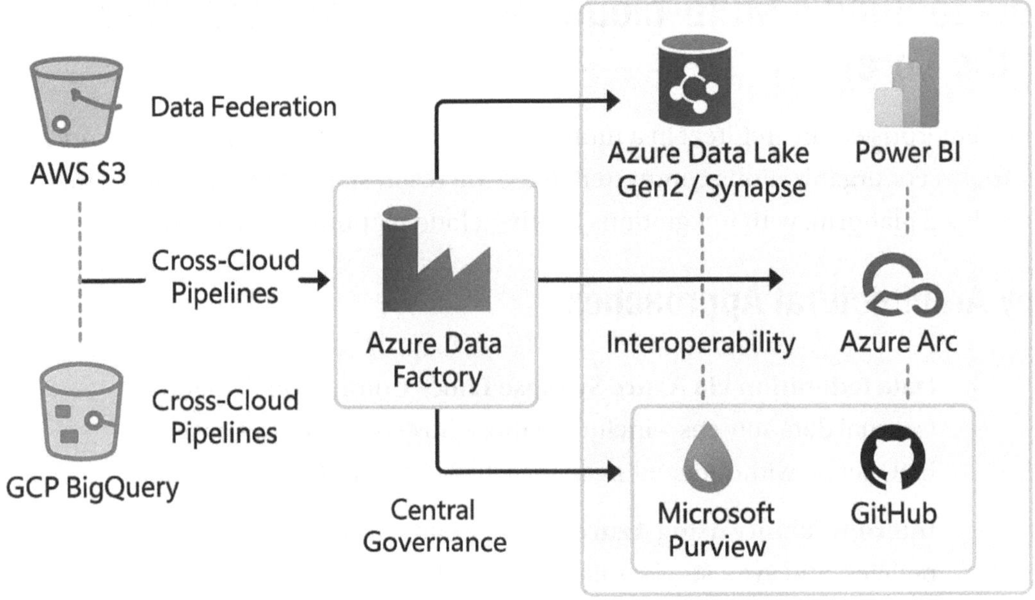

Figure 2-4. *Conceptual diagram of a multi-cloud ecosystem*

Common Multi-cloud Use Cases

- **Disaster recovery (DR) across regions** – Synapse and Data Lake Storage geo-replicated with failover triggers to secondary cloud.
- **Hybrid retail deployment** – Transaction data processed on Azure; streaming IoT data from physical stores routed through edge to another cloud.
- **Model training optimization** – Training on cost-effective GPU instances in one cloud, while serving from Azure-hosted endpoints integrated with Power Platform.

Design Considerations and Pitfalls

- **Network latency** – Minimize real-time cross-cloud queries unless cached or pre-aggregated. Keep ML serving close to users.

- **Identity federation** - Use Azure AD B2B/B2C and hybrid identity models to enable seamless access across cloud tenants.
- **Cost transparency** - Employ tools like Azure Cost Management + third-party cloud spend optimizers to avoid budget overruns.

Best practice - Anchor data governance and cataloguing in one platform—preferably Microsoft Purview—and then extend interoperability outward.

Decision heuristic - If >60% of operational and analytical workloads already sit in Azure, consider keeping transformation and orchestration centralized in Azure while federating data access and AI inferencing outward.

Cloud-Native Architectures

> *We're trying to bring a perceived conflict into balance: software-driven business agility vs. software system resiliency. We want to move fast and yet not break things. In order to do this, we're going to change how we build software, not necessarily where we build software.*
>
> —Matt Stine, Global CTO at Pivotal; source [3]

At the heart of the Modern Data Stack lies a foundational principle: **cloud-native design**. This is more than just "running things in the cloud"—it refers to an architecture that is purpose-built to leverage the elasticity, scalability, modularity, and automation capabilities of cloud platforms like Microsoft Azure. For organizations aiming to stay competitive and resilient, embracing cloud-native is no longer optional—it is strategic.

A cloud-native architecture decouples data components, enabling independent scaling, granular cost control, and composability. Traditional on-premise systems often required full-stack provisioning for every analytics workload; in contrast, Azure's serverless offerings like Synapse serverless SQL pools or Azure Functions allow architects to pay only for what is used and scale with demand automatically.

Take the example of **data ingestion**. A cloud-native approach employs event-driven pipelines using services like Azure Event Grid, Logic Apps, or Stream Analytics to process changes in real time. This removes delays and reduces complexity in managing static file drops or polling-based mechanisms.

In **data transformation**, cloud-native systems leverage distributed engines like Azure Databricks or Spark pools in Synapse. These engines can be spun up on demand, scaled out during heavy loads, and terminated automatically when idle—significantly optimizing both performance and cost.

Another defining aspect is **containerization and microservices**. Microservices can be deployed using Azure Kubernetes Service (AKS) or Azure Container Apps, allowing each service—say, data quality validation or enrichment logic—to evolve independently. This modularity brings agility to the engineering teams and accelerates time-to-insight.

Cloud-native architectures also embed **observability and automation** from the ground up. Services like Azure Monitor, Log Analytics, and Application Insights provide deep visibility into pipeline health and performance. Integration with GitHub Actions or Azure DevOps automates deployment, testing, and rollback, ensuring high-quality delivery cycles.

Security and compliance are first-class citizens in cloud-native design. Identity is managed through Azure AD with role-based access control (RBAC), while Microsoft Defender for Cloud ensures threat detection across data services.

As shown in Figure 2-5, the layered flow captures the modular, cloud-native nature of the architecture—scalable, loosely coupled, observable, and governed end to end.

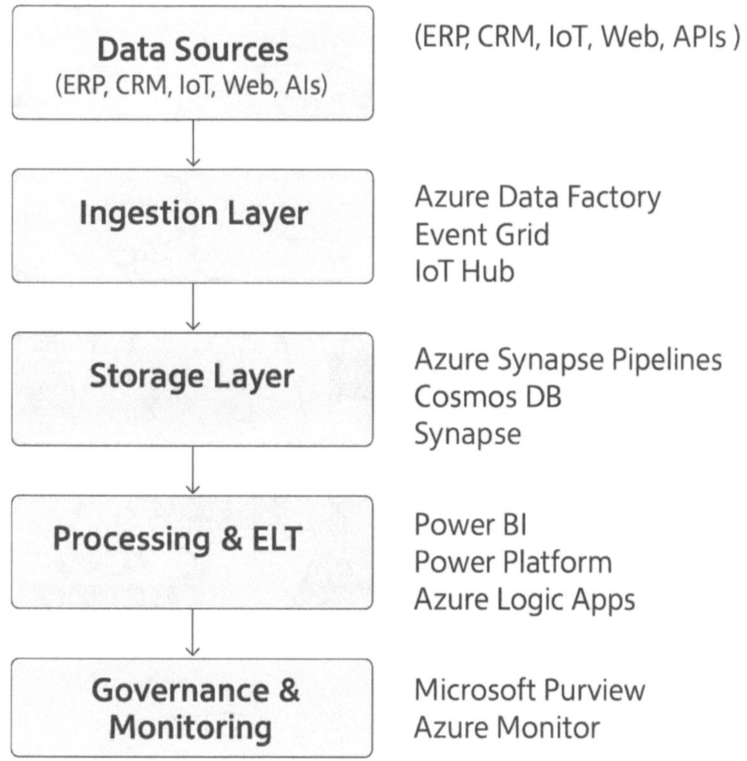

Figure 2-5. *Cloud-native architectural flow*

Cloud-native is not just a technical upgrade—it's an operational evolution. By treating data services as composable, automated, and observable units, enterprises can meet the needs of modern analytics with confidence, speed, and sustainability.

Overview: Data Ingestion, Storage, Processing, Analytics, and Governance

> *A data platform is an integrated and scalable system that combines technologies, processes, and governance to support the end-to-end lifecycle of data within an organization.*
>
> —Mohan R. Gupta, Acumen Velocity, source [4]

Figure 2-6. *Visual representation of analogy*

This analogy, illustrated in Figure 2-6, compares the data stack to a kitchen, where ingestion brings the ingredients, storage is the pantry, processing is the cooking, analytics is the plating, and governance is the hygiene check.

To build a resilient, scalable, and insight-driven organization, one must understand the essential flow of data—from its origin to its impact. The Modern Data Stack, particularly in a Microsoft-centric architecture, is designed to streamline this journey across five foundational pillars: ingestion, storage, processing, analytics, and governance. Each pillar plays a distinct role but together they form a continuous, orchestrated loop.

1. **Data ingestion**
   Purpose – *Collect data from diverse sources, batch and streaming, and land into the data lake of the organization in raw, untransformed form.*

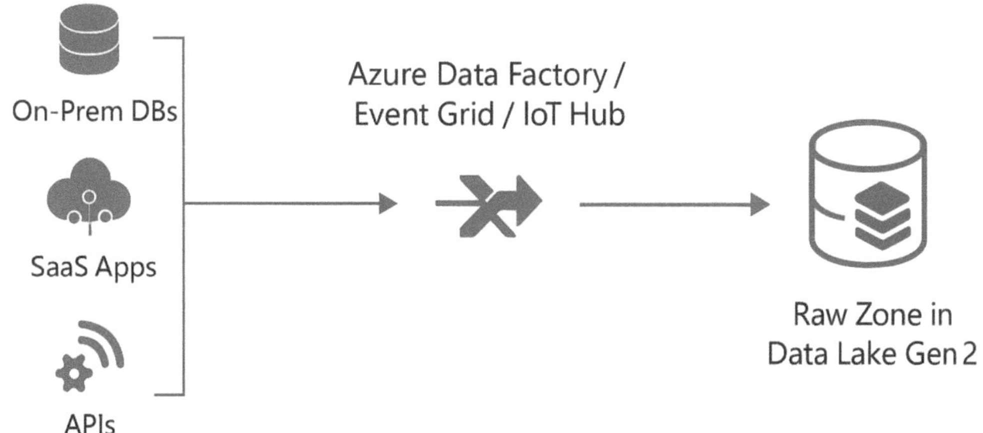

Figure 2-7. *Conceptual view of data ingestion*

As depicted in Figure 2-7, data ingestion is the entry point. It encompasses all the mechanisms through which raw data—be it structured, semi-structured, or unstructured—enters the ecosystem. Microsoft Azure offers flexible options for batch, real-time, and event-driven ingestion.

For example, Azure Data Factory excels at orchestrating data pipelines from legacy SQL systems, SaaS APIs, or flat files, while Azure Event Hubs and IoT Hub specialize in high-velocity, streaming telemetry. The aim is to ensure a frictionless, secure, and scalable way to ingest data from diverse endpoints into the central platform without manual intervention.

2. **Data storage**

   Purpose - *Unified storage of raw and curated data, regardless of type or format, optimized for scale and access.*

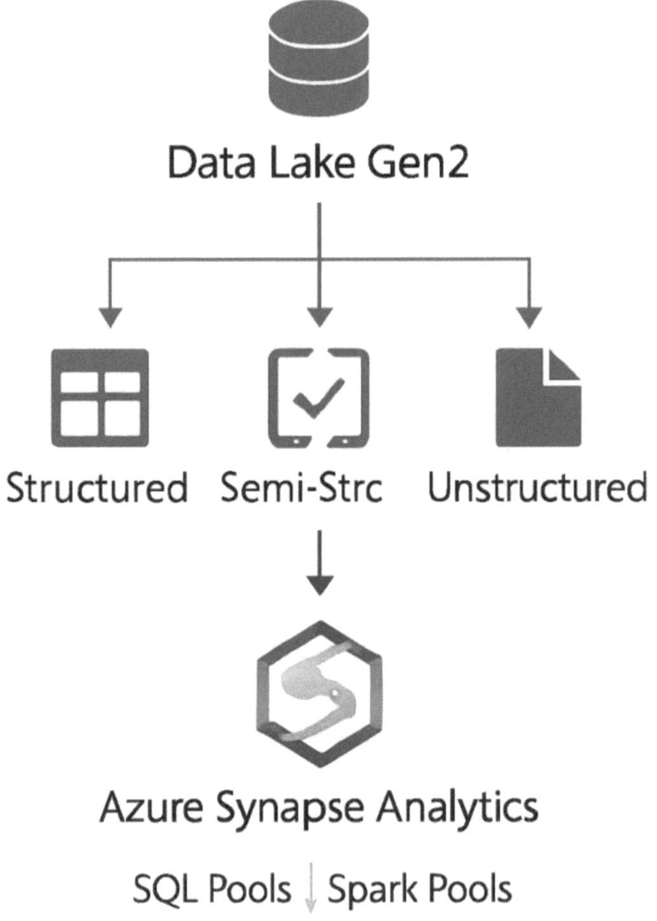

Figure 2-8. *Conceptual view of data storage*

As shown in Figure 2-8, once ingested, data must be stored securely and efficiently. Here, architectural decisions hinge on workload patterns. Azure Data Lake Storage Gen2 serves as the foundation for cost-effective storage of raw, semi-structured, and unstructured data. Azure Synapse Analytics and Azure SQL Database provide structured storage for curated, query-optimized datasets.

The lakehouse pattern—combining the flexibility of a data lake with the performance of a data warehouse—is increasingly the default choice. With support for Parquet, Delta Lake formats, and hierarchical namespace, organizations can separate raw, cleaned, and curated layers for better lineage and access control.

3. **Data processing**

   Purpose – *ELT-style processing inside cloud-native tools—transforming raw data into business-ready datasets.*

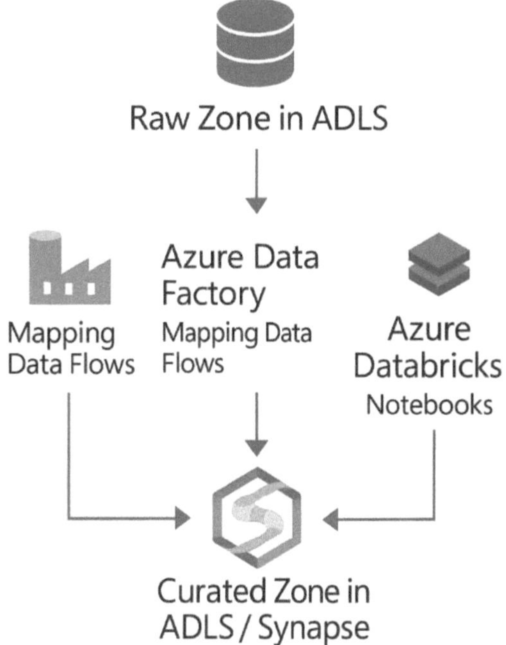

Figure 2-9. *Conceptual view of data processing*

As illustrated in Figure 2-9, processing transforms raw input into valuable, queryable formats. This can involve cleansing, enrichment, business logic application, and more. Azure Synapse Pipelines and Azure Data Factory offer GUI-based and code-first pipeline development for scheduled or event-driven data flows.

For scalable, distributed transformations, Azure Databricks and Spark pools in Synapse allow data engineers and data scientists to apply ML models, SQL scripts, or Python notebooks at petabyte scale. Processing can follow the ELT model—load data first and then transform it within the data lake or warehouse—leveraging scalable compute closer to the data.

4. **Analytics and visualization**

   Purpose – *Delivering trusted, timely, and interactive insights to decision-makers via self-service BI and advanced models.*

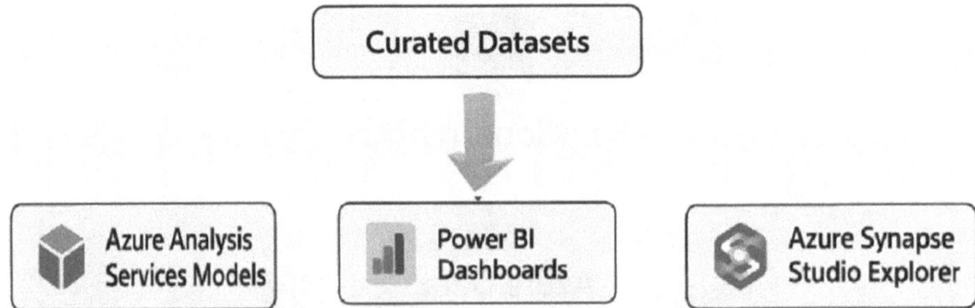

Figure 2-10. *Conceptual view of analytics and visualization*

As shown in Figure 2-10, the goal of any data platform is insight. Power BI sits at the forefront of Microsoft's analytics layer, offering business-friendly dashboards, real-time scorecards, and ad hoc exploration. Users can interact with datasets governed via Azure Analysis Services or Synapse SQL Pools, blending self-service agility with enterprise-scale security.

Whether it's operational reporting, executive dashboards, or AI-driven predictions, this layer is where data becomes a strategic asset. Features like DirectQuery, composite models, and natural language queries further democratize analytics.

5. **Data governance and observability**

   Purpose – *Enforce compliance, ensure observability, and provide end-to-end data discovery and control across the stack.*

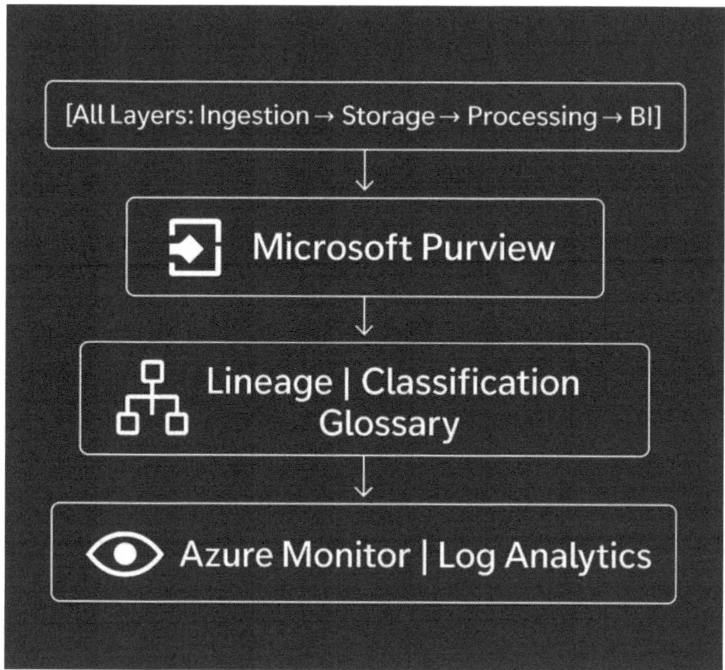

Figure 2-11. *Conceptual view of data governance and observability*

As highlighted in Figure 2-11, a Modern Data Stack without governance is a liability. Microsoft Purview provides a unified platform for data cataloguing, classification, access policies, and lineage tracking. It connects to all major Azure data services and supports compliance efforts like GDPR (General Data Protection Regulation), HIPAA (Health Insurance Portability and Accountability Act), and ISO standards.

Meanwhile, Azure Monitor and Log Analytics enable observability—ensuring data flows are healthy, pipelines are performant, and issues can be debugged quickly. This observability extends to cost monitoring, audit trails, and anomaly alerts.

Strategic insight - *Organizations that treat data governance as a core enabler, not an afterthought, reduce risk, build trust, and accelerate data adoption across domains.*

Real-World Case Study: Modernizing Retail Insights at ISkillSetu

ISkillSetu started with batch ETL jobs running on SSIS and nightly reports on Excel. By mid-2023, product analytics took three days to load. The customer churn model was being trained on two-month-old data.

Transformation Path

- Introduced Fivetran for ingestion from ERP, POS, and Shopify
- Moved the data warehouse to Azure Synapse
- Used dbt for modeling and transformations, version-controlled via GitHub.
- BI moved to Power BI embedded into business apps
- Built data lineage and policies in Azure Purview

Outcome

- Latency dropped from three days to under four hours.
- Self-service BI enabled across operations, marketing, and HR.
- Product team launched ML-powered recommendations based on fresh purchase history.

Best Practices for Implementing a Modern Data Stack

- **Start small; scale smart** – Avoid big-bang migrations. Begin with a pilot domain like sales or supply chain.
- **Choose cloud-native first** – Pick managed services where possible; it reduces operational overhead.

- **Implement GitOps** - Use CI/CD pipelines for data models and transformation logic.
- **Design for observability** - Add monitoring for data freshness, pipeline failures, and schema drift.
- **Prioritize documentation** - Invest early in data cataloguing and metric definitions.
- **Treat data as a product** - Assign owners, define SLAs, and measure usage.

Looking Ahead: From Stack to Strategy

As the Monday meeting at ISkillSetu wraps up, Shailesh turns to Maryam and says, "We're not just retooling systems, we're rearchitecting how data powers decisions."

Maryam smiles. "And this time, let's ensure data is not a bottleneck, but a bridge. So what's next after the modern stack?"

Shailesh replies, "We need to go deeper. The tools are in place. But now we must focus on what cloud-native data components we *must* have to make this vision resilient, secure, and future-ready."

As Shailesh and Maryam step out of the boardroom, the gravity of their discussion lingers. It is no longer about fixing a broken report or tweaking an old ETL job—it is about transforming how ISkillSetu approaches data itself. The Modern Data Stack isn't just a tech upgrade; it is a strategic enabler for scale, speed, and smarter decisions.

Yet, a powerful stack alone isn't enough.

Choosing the right cloud-native components, those that play well together, that scale with business growth, and that embed governance by design, is the next critical step.

Figure 2-12. *Conversation between teams on planning "stack to strategy"*

As reflected in Figure 2-12, the discussion signals a shift from simply adopting tools to shaping a forward-looking data strategy.

In the next chapter, we'll go deeper into these building blocks. From secure storage and scalable compute to integration-ready services and low-code accelerators, we'll break down the *must-have cloud data components* that every enterprise architecture should consider when designing for the future.

References

[1] Is Your Digital Transformation Effort Lagging The Competition? - Geoffrey Cann—Energy News, Top Headlines, Commentaries, Features & Events | EnergyNow.com

[2] The future isn't just cloud—it's multi-cloud | Google Cloud Blog

[3] Defining Cloud Native: A Panel Discussion | InfoQ

[4] The Executive Guide To Modern Data Platforms | Acumen Velocity

CHAPTER 3

Must-Have Cloud Data Components

> *The cloud services companies of all sizes ... The cloud is for everyone. The cloud is a democracy.*
>
> —Marc Benioff, CEO of Salesforce.com

Introduction

Every organization that aspires to become data-driven eventually asks the same question: what does a modern data platform actually look like? For a company like ISkillSetu, scaling rapidly across geographies and industries, the answer is not about adopting the latest tool or following a single vendor's playbook. It is about assembling the must-have components that enable trust, agility, resilience, and compliance. This chapter takes a practical, executive-level view of those components; it's about building the *foundation*.

It is late afternoon at ISkillSetu's headquarters in Mumbai. The boardroom carries the energy of both urgency and ambition. The leadership team has just wrapped up their review of the Modern Data Stack in the previous session.

Shailesh, the chief operating officer, looks at the group thoughtfully.

"Maryam, we've agreed that the modern stack is the right direction. But which components are truly essential for us to invest in? I don't want a bloated architecture. I want clarity—what must we have to grow at scale, remain compliant, and keep costs under control?"

R. Yasir and K. Shaikh, *Driving Business Transformation with Modern Data and AI Strategies*,
https://doi.org/10.1007/979-8-8688-2625-2_3

Maryam, the principal solution architect, adjusts her notes. With her characteristic calm, she replies:

"Not every component is optional. Some form the backbone of trust, resilience, and speed. If we miss them, we'll pay heavily later—either in penalties, downtime, or lost customer confidence."

Nilesh, the data evangelist, leans forward. "We need to align these components with the types of data we actually generate and consume. If we don't categorize and understand our data, we risk building the wrong foundation."

Vijay, the tech lead, adds his perspective. "From a technical lens, we need to consider variety. It's not just structured data anymore—our systems log semi-structured events, and our learners generate unstructured data like videos and reviews."

The room nods in unison. The consensus is clear: before choosing architectures, the leadership has to begin with **data types**, because every subsequent decision, storage, processing, compliance, would depend on this foundation.

As shown in Figure 3-0, this leadership exchange highlights the core question of which cloud data components are truly essential for growth, compliance, and resilience.

Figure 3-0. *Conversations between leaders on "must-have cloud data components"*

This chapter begins with that exploration, before moving into architectural patterns, governance, ingestion methods, and compliance guardrails.

Different Data Types Based on Your Business

The goal is to turn data into information, and information into insight.

—Carly Fiorina, former CEO of Hewlett-Packard

A narrative starting point

At the Monday morning steering committee, Shailesh poses a simple question:

"If a learner uploads a video, a faculty member submits a course plan in Word, and our finance system generates invoices in Excel, are these all the same kind of data?"

Maryam smiles. "Technically, no. Each falls under a different type of data—structured, semi-structured, and unstructured. How we treat them determines cost, accessibility, and insight potential."

This realization often marks the beginning of data maturity: recognizing that not all data is created equal.

Structured Data

Definition – Structured data is highly organized, typically residing in relational databases. Rows, columns, keys, and schemas provide predictability.

Examples at ISkillSetu

- Enrolment records (student IDs, names, course codes)
- Financial transactions (invoices, payments)
- Operational KPIs (number of active learners per day)

Tools and services

- Azure SQL Database, Azure Synapse Dedicated Pools, Amazon RDS, Google BigQuery

Executive insight – Structured data is the easiest to query, secure, and govern. For compliance-heavy areas like finance, it remains indispensable.

Heuristic for leaders – If the business demands **auditability, standard reporting, and transactional accuracy**, structured data should be the anchor.

Semi-structured Data

Definition – Data that carries some organizational tags (like JSON, XML, or logs) but lacks rigid schemas.

Examples at ISkillSetu

- Web clickstream logs from the learning portal
- JSON responses from APIs tracking learner behavior
- Event telemetry from mobile apps

Tools and services

- **Azure Data Lake Storage Gen2** for raw ingestion
- **Azure Event Hubs/AWS Kinesis** for streaming
- **Databricks** for schema-on-read flexibility

Challenge – Semi-structured data can balloon storage and processing costs if not managed well.

Best practice – Apply schema-on-read for agility but define schema-on-write when insights are stable and repeatedly used.

Unstructured Data

Definition – Data with no predefined schema, often multimedia or free text.

Examples at ISkillSetu

- Recorded video lectures (MP4)
- Learner feedback in natural language
- PDF study material uploads

Tools and services

- **Azure Blob Storage** or **Amazon S3** for low-cost archiving
- Azure AI Search or Elasticsearch for text-based search
- **Document Intelligence, Speech Services, and Azure OpenAI** for extracting meaning from media

Executive consideration – Unstructured data is 80% of enterprise data but underutilized. Monetization comes from applying AI/ML for discovery, personalization, and insights.

Streaming Data

Definition – Data generated continuously by systems, sensors, or applications.

Examples at ISkillSetu

- Real-time learner engagement (quiz attempts, video pauses)

- System telemetry for uptime monitoring
- Clickstream during live virtual classes

Tools and services

- **Azure Stream Analytics, Databricks Structured Streaming, Kafka on Confluent Cloud**

Key use cases

- Detecting student drop-off patterns live
- Triggering recommendations in real time
- Proactive system monitoring and alerting

Every company is now a data company. But in the age of streaming, every decision can be made in real time.

—Satya Nadella

Decision Heuristics for Leaders

Business Objective	Recommended Data Type	Example
Regulatory reporting (compliance)	Structured	Finance and HR data
Tracking learner engagement	Semi-structured	JSON clickstream logs
Personalized learning recommendations	Unstructured + AI transformation	Video transcripts analyzed with natural language processing (NLP) models
Operational monitoring	Streaming	Uptime telemetry, system health

Leadership Tip Start by classifying your enterprise data assets into these categories. Only then can you align them with the right storage, processing, and governance model.

Figure 3-1 illustrates how structured, semi-structured, and streaming data each play a distinct role in shaping business decisions.

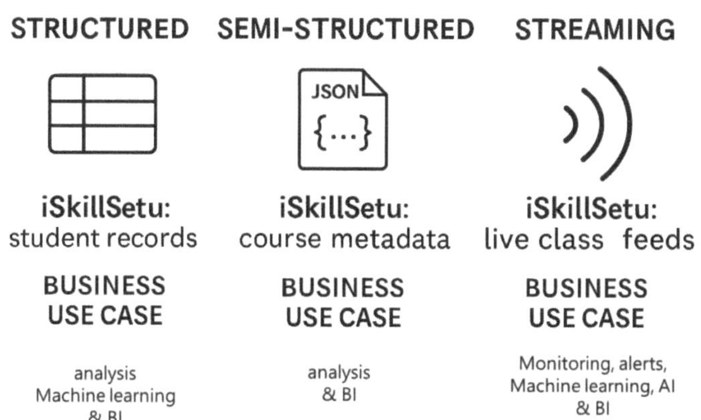

Figure 3-1. *Conceptual diagram of data types in an enterprise*

Takeaway

- **Not all data is the same**: business leaders must categorize first.
- **Structured data** powers compliance and finance.
- **Semi-structured data** reveals user behavior.
- **Unstructured data** holds innovation potential when combined with AI.
- **Streaming data** drives agility and real-time interventions.

Data Lakes, Warehouses, and Lakehouses

The world is one big data problem.

—Andrew McAfee, MIT Sloan School of Management

The following day at ISkillSetu, Shailesh opens the leadership huddle with a dilemma.

"Our finance head insists on a warehouse for structured data, but the product team wants a lake to handle video and clickstream data. Then yesterday, someone mentioned a *lakehouse*. Are we just adding buzzwords?"

Maryam, the principal solution architect, leans forward with clarity.

"Not at all. These are architectural choices, each designed for specific needs. A data lake is flexible, a warehouse is optimized for analytics, and a lakehouse blends the two. The question is not which is better universally, but which aligns with *our* business workloads."

Nilesh, ever the evangelist, adds, "This decision will shape how fast we generate insights, how much we spend on storage, and how seamlessly we integrate AI."

The discussion illustrates a common challenge: leaders often hear these terms interchangeably but miss the nuance. In reality, the choice is context-dependent—and sometimes, enterprises need more than one.

Data Lakes

A **data lake** is a central repository designed to store raw data in its native format, structured, semi-structured, and unstructured. It follows a schema-on-read model, meaning data is stored first and structured later when needed.

For ISkillSetu, a data lake becomes indispensable for

- Video content uploaded by educators
- Raw learner clickstream and interaction logs
- Semi-structured event data from APIs and mobile apps

Key characteristics

- **Low-cost, scalable storage** - Azure Data Lake Storage Gen2 or Amazon S3
- **Flexibility** - No upfront schema definition, enabling experimental use cases
- **AI readiness** - Provides training datasets for ML and GenAI models

Limitation - Without governance, a data lake can easily devolve into a "data swamp," filled with unusable, undocumented datasets.

Data Warehouses

A **data warehouse** is built for structured, curated, and query-optimized datasets. It enforces schema-on-write, making it ideal for repeatable analytics and compliance reporting.

For ISkillSetu, the warehouse houses

- Financial transactions for regulatory reporting
- Learner enrolment records with relational integrity
- Standardized KPIs for executive dashboards

Key characteristics

- **Performance-oriented** – Highly optimized for SQL queries and aggregations.
- **Governed** – Tight data quality and consistency enforcement.
- **Business-friendly** – BI teams can build dashboards without data engineering complexity.

Limitation – Less flexible for unstructured or rapidly evolving data. Transformations must occur before loading, increasing latency and operational effort.

Lakehouses

The **lakehouse** is a modern pattern that combines the strengths of both. It builds analytical capabilities on top of a lake, offering flexibility and governance simultaneously.

For ISkillSetu, this is particularly powerful:

- Raw video and clickstream data lands in the lake.
- Delta Lake or Apache Iceberg layers provide transactional consistency.
- Curated datasets can be queried directly in BI tools like Power BI.

Key characteristics

- **Unified storage + analytics** - Reduces need for dual platforms.
- **Supports structured + unstructured data** equally well.
- **AI-friendly** - Data scientists can access raw data, while BI teams use curated layers.

Executive consideration - Lakehouses reduce duplication and simplify architecture, but they require investment in modern tools like Databricks, Snowflake, or Synapse with Delta Lake support.

Decision Heuristics for Leaders

- **If the primary need is regulatory reporting and financial accuracy ➤ choose a warehouse.**
- **If flexibility and raw data capture matter most ➤ build a data lake.**
- **If the organization needs both agility and governance at scale ➤ invest in a lakehouse**.

A growing enterprise like ISkillSetu often requires **all three**—with a lake for raw capture, a warehouse for reporting, and a lakehouse as the unifying analytical layer. The art lies in deciding which layer takes precedence in each domain.

As shown in Figure 3-2, the comparison highlights the distinct strengths and trade-offs between lakes, warehouses, and lakehouses, helping leaders match architecture to business needs.

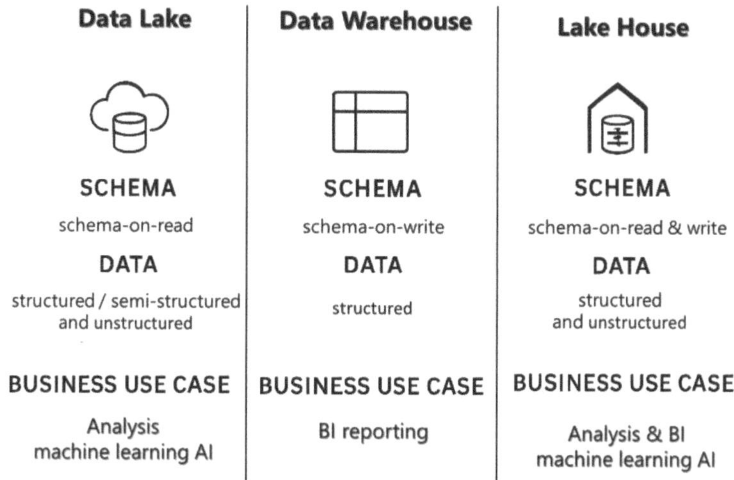

Figure 3-2. *Conceptual comparison: data lake vs. data warehouse vs. lakehouse*

Takeaway

- **Data lakes** - Best for raw, varied, large-scale data storage—flexible but risky without governance
- **Data warehouses** - Optimized for structured, repeatable, and compliance-driven analytics
- **Lakehouses** - Emerging hybrid, blending flexibility with governance—ideal for enterprises scaling advanced analytics and AI

The decision is not binary. In practice, enterprises combine these components into a layered strategy.

Choosing the Right Storage for Your Needs

Data engineering isn't about perfect data; it's about building the perfect environment for data to thrive.

—Benjamin Rogojan

By mid-week, ISkillSetu's leadership team convenes again. Shailesh opens with a challenge that many executives face:

"Maryam, yesterday we agreed on the differences between lakes, warehouses, and lakehouses. But as a business leader, how do I actually decide what to invest in? I don't want to waste money on storage we don't need or, worse, pick the wrong one and slow us down."

Maryam replies with precision:

"The choice depends not on technology first, but on your business use case, cost sensitivity, and compliance needs. Think of it like choosing between a warehouse for standardized products, a garage for raw material, and a hybrid hub for both storage and assembly. The wrong choice means inefficiency, duplication, or compliance risk."

Nilesh, the data evangelist, adds:

"This is where decision frameworks come in. Leaders need heuristics, not jargon. You don't need to be an architect to make the right call, but you must understand the trade-offs."

Business-Led Storage Decisions

Storage decisions are not purely technical. They hinge on business questions:

- Do we need speed and consistency for financial reporting?
- Do we need flexibility to store unpredictable or raw learner data?
- Do we expect to run AI models on unstructured sources like video or voice?
- How critical is compliance with regulations in our operating markets?

The answers guide whether a lake, warehouse, or lakehouse should be prioritized.

Cost Considerations

Shailesh raises a CFO's perspective: "Show me the cost impact."

Maryam responds with a framework ISkillSetu now uses:

- **Data lakes** - Lowest storage cost (Azure Data Lake Storage Gen2), but higher compute cost for queries
- **Data warehouses** - Higher storage cost (Synapse Dedicated Pools or Snowflake credits), but optimized query performance
- **Lakehouses** - Balanced approach, mid-range costs with reduced duplication, but require additional platform investments (Databricks, Delta Lake)

Executive heuristic – If storage cost is the bottleneck, start with a lake. If query performance for business intelligence is critical, invest in a warehouse. If both matter, consider a lakehouse.

Compliance and Data Residency

For ISkillSetu, which serves learners in India, Europe, and North America, storage decisions also involve where the data lives. There are regulations as follows:

- **GDPR** (Europe) demands storage within specific jurisdictions.
- **HIPAA** (US healthcare data) mandates controlled environments.
- **India's DPDP (Digital Personal Data Protection) Act (2023)** requires localization for certain sensitive data.

Here, a **warehouse** often offers stronger compliance tooling (audit trails, access logs), while **lakehouses** need added governance layers like Microsoft Purview.

Flexibility vs. Performance

Vijay, representing the technical team, summarizes it well:

"If you want agility for experimental data science, pick a lake. If you want consistent, fast dashboards for executives, pick a warehouse. If you want both, consolidate into a lakehouse."

This captures the essence of **flexibility vs. performance**: a balance each enterprise must strike.

Decision Framework

Business Priority	Best Fit	Rationale
Regulatory compliance and audit	Warehouse	Strong governance and schema-on-write ensure trust.
Experimental data science	Lake	Schema-on-read, raw format access for ML/AI.
Unified analytics and AI	Lakehouse	Combines scale of lakes with speed of warehouses.
Cost minimization	Lake	Cheap storage, pay-as-you-go compute.
Business dashboards	Warehouse/ lakehouse	Optimized queries, governed access for BI.

Figure 3-3 presents a decision framework that links business priorities with the most suitable storage choice—lake, warehouse, or lakehouse.

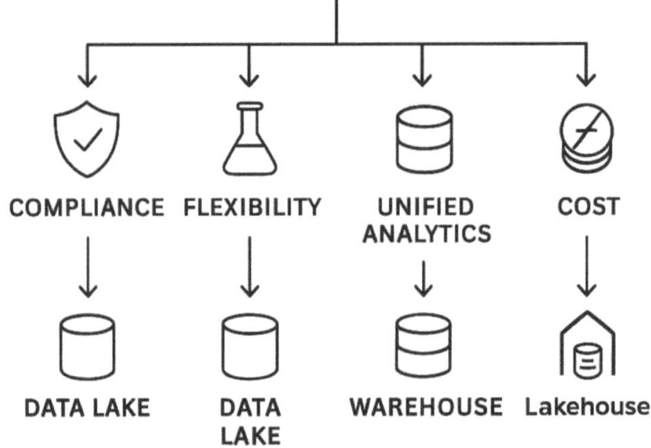

***Figure 3-3.** Framework for choosing the right storage*

Takeaway

- Storage decisions must begin with business priorities, not tools.
- Costs, compliance, and performance are the three pillars of decision-making.

- Leaders should use frameworks and heuristics, not vendor pitches, to decide.
- Often, enterprises adopt a layered approach, using lakes, warehouses, and lakehouses together, but with clarity on *when to use what.*

Model Data Platform

> *Data really powers everything that we do.*
>
> —Jeff Weiner, former CEO of LinkedIn

Later that week, ISkillSetu's boardroom buzzes with a different energy. Shailesh leans over the table and asks:

"We've spent time dissecting lakes, warehouses, and lakehouses. But how do they come together into something tangible? What does our *ideal platform* look like?"

Maryam, as always, translates complexity into clarity:

"Think of it as building a city. Lakes are your raw reservoirs, warehouses are your regulated commercial zones, and the lakehouse is the hybrid hub. But to run a city, you need roads, utilities, governance, and resilience. That's what a **Model Data Platform (MDP)** represents: a blueprint that ensures all components connect logically and serve business needs."

Nilesh adds, "Without a model platform, we risk ad hoc decisions. We'll end up with siloed projects, ballooning costs, and duplication. A reference model helps us standardize, scale, and communicate a clear vision across teams."

This discussion marks a crucial pivot for many enterprises: moving from individual technology choices to a **holistic architecture** that unifies them into a consistent, governed, and future-ready platform.

What Is a Model Data Platform?

A **Model Data Platform (MDP)** is not a product but a **reference architecture** that integrates the essential cloud-native components needed to collect, store, process, analyze, and govern data.

It ensures that

- Business requirements drive technology choices.

- Components are modular yet interoperable.
- Governance and compliance are built in, not bolted on.
- AI/ML readiness is embedded from the start.

For ISkillSetu, the MDP aligns with the need to scale rapidly while remaining compliant with global regulations and providing personalized experiences to learners.

Core Layers of a Model Data Platform

1. **Ingestion layer**
    - Handles structured, semi-structured, unstructured, and streaming data
    - **Tools** - Azure Data Factory, Event Hubs, AWS Glue, Kafka
    - **Key feature** - Schema flexibility, reliability, monitoring for freshness
2. **Storage layer**
    - Provides a unified, cost-effective repository for raw and curated data
    - **Options** - Data lakes (ADLS Gen2), warehouses (Synapse, Snowflake), lakehouses (Databricks, Delta Lake)
    - **Key feature** - Tiered storage (hot, warm, cold) to optimize cost vs. performance
3. **Processing and transformation layer**
    - Converts raw data into analytics- and AI-ready formats
    - **Tools** - Azure Databricks, Synapse Spark Pools, dbt
    - **Key feature** - ELT-first approach with scalable compute
4. **Analytics and consumption layer**
    - Enables BI, dashboards, predictive models, and operational insights

- **Tools** - Power BI, Tableau, Azure ML, Looker
- **Key feature** - Self-service for business teams, governed access for sensitive data

5. **Governance and security layer**
    - Ensures compliance, lineage, cataloguing, and monitoring
    - **Tools** - Microsoft Purview, Collibra, Alation
    - **Key feature** - Metadata-driven governance that spans multi-cloud environments

6. **Integration and activation layer**
    - Pushes insights back into business systems (CRM, LMS, HR tools)
    - **Tools** - Reverse ETL platforms, APIs, Synapse Link
    - **Key feature** - Closing the loop—data is not just analyzed but also activated in workflows

Reference Architecture (Conceptual Flow)

A typical MDP at ISkillSetu would look like this:

- **Data sources** - LMS logs, finance systems, HR apps, student feedback forms, video libraries
- **Ingestion** - Batch via Azure Data Factory, streaming via Event Hubs
- **Storage** - Raw data in ADLS, curated layers in Synapse, unified access via a lakehouse
- **Processing** - Databricks for enrichment, dbt for modeling
- **Analytics** - Power BI dashboards for executives, ML models for personalization
- **Governance** - Purview cataloguing, RBAC via Azure AD, compliance audit logs
- **Activation** - Insights fed into the CRM for marketing, into the LMS for adaptive learning journeys

This model ensures **traceability from source to consumption**—a hallmark of maturity.

Business Benefits of a Model Data Platform

- **Clarity for leaders** - A standard blueprint avoids confusion and conflicting priorities.
- **Scalability** - Modular design allows incremental adoption.
- **Risk reduction** - Compliance and governance embedded from the start.
- **Cost control** - Tiered storage and on-demand compute prevent overruns.
- **AI enablement** - By design, the platform ensures readiness for predictive and generative AI use cases.

Decision Heuristics for Leaders

- If your **data strategy feels fragmented**, push for a reference model.
- If **costs are spiraling**, enforce tiered storage and compute governance.
- If **AI is on the roadmap**, ensure processing and storage are designed for flexibility (lakehouse-first approach).
- If **regulators are asking tough questions**, invest early in metadata cataloguing and data lineage.

As illustrated in Figure 3-4, the conceptual architecture brings together ingestion, storage, processing, analytics, governance, and activation into a unified model.

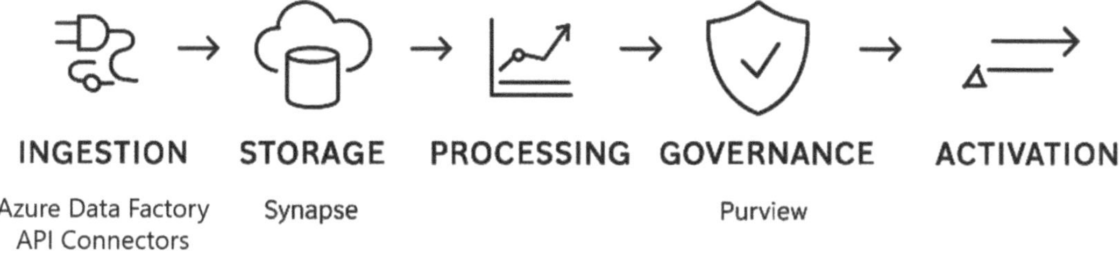

Figure 3-4. Conceptual architecture of a Model Data Platform

Note Governance is shown as a distinct block for clarity; however, in practice it is a cross-cutting capability applied across all layers of the data platform.

Takeaway

- A **Model Data Platform** is not about tools—it is a reference architecture that unites ingestion, storage, processing, analytics, governance, and activation.
- It ensures clarity, scalability, and AI readiness.
- For leaders, it provides a north star to evaluate technology proposals against business priorities.
- For ISkillSetu, it means moving beyond piecemeal solutions to a coherent, future-ready platform that supports rapid growth.

Real-Time vs. Batch Ingestion

Torture the data, and it will confess to anything.

—Ronald Coase, Nobel Prize–winning economist

On Thursday morning, Shailesh receives an urgent message from the customer success team: "We need to know immediately if learners are dropping out of live sessions due to connection issues. Waiting for daily reports isn't good enough."

Frustrated, he walks into the meeting room.

"Maryam, this is exactly what I mean. Yesterday's reports are history. Our decisions must be made as things happen."

Maryam nods.

"You're absolutely right, Shailesh. This is the difference between batch ingestion and real-time ingestion. Batch has its place—finance, compliance, consolidated reporting. But when agility and instant action matter, real-time ingestion is non-negotiable."

Nilesh interjects, "The challenge for ISkillSetu is balancing both. Over-engineering everything for real-time can drain budgets and add unnecessary complexity."

This tension is universal. Every enterprise struggles to balance the reliability and cost-efficiency of batch pipelines with the immediacy and responsiveness of real-time ingestion.

Batch Ingestion

Batch ingestion collects and processes data in chunks at scheduled intervals.

How it works

- Data is moved periodically (hourly, daily, weekly) from source systems into the platform.
- **Example** – Nightly jobs pulling enrolment and finance data into Synapse.

Business fit

- Regulatory reporting.
- Consolidated dashboards (e.g., daily learner engagement summaries).
- Historical analysis where immediacy is not required.

Advantages

- Cost-effective (compute is used only during load).
- Simpler to manage with existing ETL/ELT tools.
- Predictable schedules and performance.

Limitations

- Latency—insights are outdated by hours or days.
- Not suitable for operational decisions or interventions.

Real-Time Ingestion

Real-time ingestion streams data continuously, enabling immediate availability for analytics or automated actions.

How it works

- Event-driven pipelines capture and process data the moment it is generated.
- **Example** - Streaming learner activity during a live quiz to detect disengagement instantly.

Business fit

- Monitoring platform uptime and system health.
- Personalized recommendations as learners interact.
- Fraud detection in financial transactions.

Advantages

- Near-zero latency—data available within seconds.
- Enables proactive and adaptive decision-making.
- Essential for AI-driven use cases (e.g., churn prediction).

Limitations

- Higher infrastructure and compute costs.
- Increased complexity in design and monitoring.
- Requires specialized skills (Kafka, Event Hubs, Stream Analytics).

Hybrid Reality: When to Use What

Maryam explains it succinctly to the group:

"Real-time isn't about replacing batch; it's about complementing it. Leaders must decide which use cases justify the complexity and cost."

Decision heuristics for leaders

- If **regulators** require consistent, auditable data ➤ choose **batch**.
- If **operations** demand immediacy (e.g., platform uptime) ➤ go **real-time**.
- If **customer experience** depends on responsiveness (e.g., adaptive learning) ➤ blend **real-time for key events + batch for history**.

At ISkillSetu, this translates into

- **Batch** for finance, HR, and compliance
- **Real-time** for learner engagement analytics
- **Hybrid** for marketing campaigns (streaming triggers + nightly rollups)

Tools and Services

Batch pipelines

- Azure Data Factory, AWS Glue, Google Dataflow

Real-Time pipelines

- Azure Event Hubs, Azure Stream Analytics, Kafka, Confluent Cloud

Hybrid orchestration

- Databricks Structured Streaming (handles both batch + streaming)
- Azure Synapse pipelines with triggers

Figure 3-5 contrasts batch and real-time ingestion, showing how each approach aligns with different business needs and decision speeds.

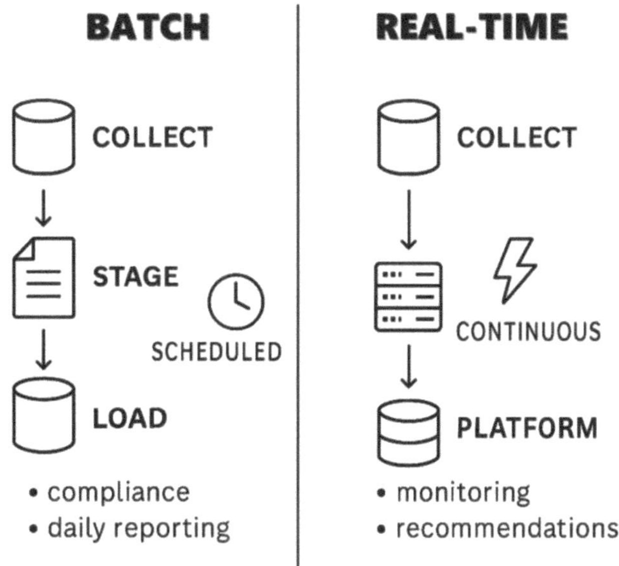

Figure 3-5. *Conceptual view: real-time vs. batch ingestion*

Takeaway

- **Batch ingestion** is cost-effective and reliable for compliance and periodic analysis.
- **Real-time ingestion** enables agility, adaptive learning, and proactive decision-making.
- Enterprises rarely pick one over the other—hybrid ingestion strategies balance cost and responsiveness.
- Leaders should decide based on business criticality, not technical enthusiasm.

ETL vs. ELT

Big data is at the foundation of all the megatrends that are happening.

—Chris Lynch

By Friday morning, the ISkillSetu leadership team has just settled into their discussion when Vijay, the tech lead, raises a critical operational pain point:

"Last night's ETL job failed again." He sighs. "The finance data pipeline broke because a single column changed in the source system. It took us four hours to debug and rerun. We can't keep operating this way."

Shailesh frowns. "Why are we still struggling with something as basic as moving data? Aren't we supposed to have solved this years ago?"

Maryam responds calmly:

"This is the difference between **ETL** and **ELT**. ETL is yesterday's approach—transforming data before loading it. ELT is today's model—load raw data first, and transform later in the cloud where compute is elastic. The choice determines agility, cost, and resilience."

Nilesh adds, "For ISkillSetu, shifting from ETL to ELT isn't just a technical upgrade—it's about enabling faster experimentation, reducing downtime, and preparing for advanced AI workloads."

What Is ETL?

Extract, Transform, Load (ETL) is the traditional method:

1. **Extract** data from source systems.
2. **Transform** it into a structured, standardized format.
3. **Load** it into the target data warehouse.

Advantages

- Clean, consistent data enters the warehouse.
- Processing load is kept outside the warehouse, conserving resources.
- Works well for small, stable datasets.

Limitations

- Transformation happens before loading—slows down ingestion.
- Sensitive to schema changes (fragile pipelines).
- Doesn't scale easily for modern semi-structured or unstructured data.

What Is ELT?

Extract, Load, Transform (ELT) flips the order:

1. **Extract** raw data.
2. **Load** it directly into a data lake or warehouse.
3. **Transform** it inside the platform using scalable cloud compute.

Advantages

- Faster ingestion—data is loaded immediately.
- Greater flexibility—transformations can be defined or revised later.
- Scales seamlessly for big data, streaming, and AI use cases.

Limitations

- Requires cloud-native platforms (Synapse, BigQuery, Snowflake).
- Storage costs can rise if raw data is not managed well.
- Governance is critical—otherwise, raw data becomes messy.

ETL vs. ELT: Strategic Trade-Offs

Maryam summarizes the trade-offs for the leadership team:

- **ETL** is like a customs checkpoint—goods are standardized before they enter the country.
- **ELT** is like free trade zones—goods are admitted quickly and then organized later based on demand.

For ISkillSetu, this means as follows:

- **ETL** remains relevant for highly regulated, repetitive pipelines (finance, HR).
- **ELT** powers flexible, exploratory, and large-scale workloads (learner engagement analytics, AI models).

Tools and Services

- **ETL tools** - SSIS, Talend, Informatica
- **ELT tools** - dbt (data build tool), Azure Synapse SQL Pools, Databricks, Snowflake native transformations

Modern platforms like **Azure Data Factory** and **Databricks** allow hybrid models, orchestrating ETL where needed and enabling ELT for scale and agility.

Decision Heuristics for Leaders

- If **compliance and predictability** are paramount ➤ favor **ETL**.
- If **scalability and flexibility** are required ➤ prefer **ELT**.
- For most modern enterprises ➤ adopt a **hybrid** model: ETL for core finance/HR, ELT for analytics, AI, and experimentation.

As shown in Figure 3-6, the comparison makes clear how ETL and ELT differ in sequence, agility, and suitability for modern workloads.

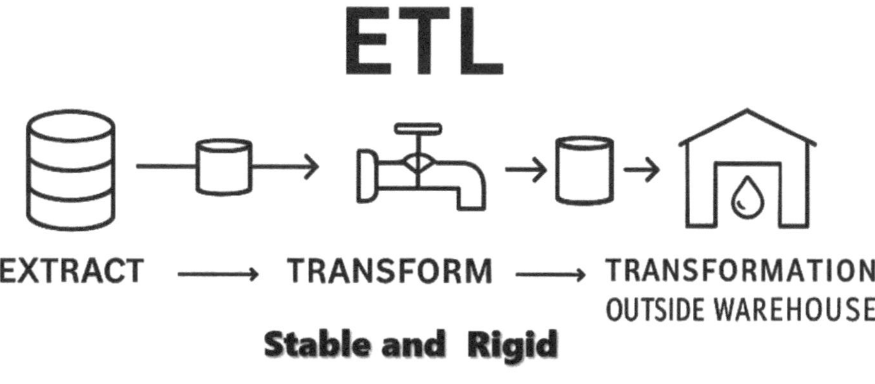

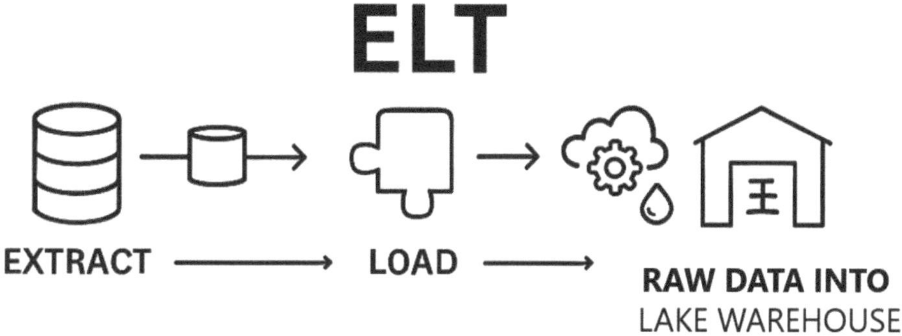

Figure 3-6. *Conceptual comparison: ETL vs. ELT*

Takeaway

- **ETL** – Still relevant for compliance-heavy, repetitive workloads.
- **ELT** – Dominant model for cloud-native, scalable, and AI-driven use cases.
- Leaders must embrace a **hybrid strategy**, using the right model for the right workload.
- For ISkillSetu, ELT ensures agility and scale, while ETL safeguards critical compliance domains.

APIs, Connectors, and Integration Tools

Data is a precious commodity and not everyone has equal access to it.

—Tim Berners-Lee

Friday afternoon, Shailesh walks into the boardroom with a problem statement from the marketing team.

"They've signed up with a new email automation tool, but it doesn't connect with our data warehouse. Now they're exporting CSVs, cleaning them in Excel, and manually uploading into the system. This is slowing campaigns and risking errors. Why can't we just connect everything seamlessly?"

Maryam smiles knowingly.

"This is where APIs, connectors, and integration tools come into play. They are the plumbing that ensures our data flows freely across systems without bottlenecks or risky manual work."

Nilesh leans in. "Think of it this way: without connectors, even the best data platform is like an island. APIs are the bridges that make it part of a thriving ecosystem."

Vijay adds with a laugh, "And every time we avoid CSVs being emailed around, we reduce compliance risk too."

APIs: The Universal Language of Integration

An **Application Programming Interface (API)** is a contract that allows different systems to talk to each other. Modern APIs, often REST or GraphQL, enable real-time, secure, and standardized data exchange.

Use cases at ISkillSetu

- Fetching learner activity from the LMS into the analytics platform
- Connecting the CRM with marketing tools for unified campaigns
- Integrating payment gateways with finance systems

Executive insight - APIs reduce vendor lock-in. Instead of being tied to a single vendor's ecosystem, APIs allow businesses to choose the best tool for each function while still integrating seamlessly.

Connectors: Pre-built Shortcuts

While APIs provide the language, **connectors** are pre-built integrations that save engineering time.

Examples

- Azure Data Factory offers 100+ connectors (Salesforce, SAP, SQL, SaaS platforms).
- Fivetran and Stitch provide managed connectors for popular SaaS and database systems.
- Power BI has built-in connectors for hundreds of enterprise applications.

Business value

- Faster time-to-value—integrations can be established in hours, not weeks.
- Reduced need for custom code, lowering maintenance overhead.
- Better reliability as connectors are vendor-supported.

Limitation - Connectors may not support every custom use case, so APIs still remain critical.

Integration Tools: Orchestration and Governance

Integration tools manage the **movement, scheduling, and monitoring** of data across APIs and connectors.

Cloud-native tools

- **Azure Data Factory** - Enterprise-grade orchestration
- **Azure Logic Apps** - Low-code workflows for business processes
- **MuleSoft** - Cross-cloud, enterprise integration platform
- **Informatica** - Strong governance and master data management features

Role in a Model Data Platform

- Handle **data pipelines** (batch and streaming).
- Manage **dependencies and retries**.
- Provide **observability** to track errors and data freshness.

Strategic Considerations for Leaders

Shailesh asks bluntly, "How do I know if we're over-engineering integration?"

Maryam replies:

"Focus on three principles:

- **APIs for flexibility** - Build them when the integration is unique to your workflows.
- **Connectors for speed** - Use pre-built ones when they meet 80% of the need.
- **Integration tools for governance** - Orchestrate flows to ensure reliability and compliance."

Nilesh adds, "And never allow shadow integrations—teams building their own unsanctioned pipelines. That's a recipe for compliance breaches."

Decision Heuristics for Leaders

- If the integration is **common and well-supported** ➤ choose **connectors.**
- If the integration is **unique or customized** ➤ invest in **APIs.**
- If **multiple pipelines and dependencies** exist ➤ enforce **integration tools with governance.**

This blended approach keeps agility without sacrificing reliability.

Figure 3-7 maps out the integration ecosystem, showing how APIs, connectors, and orchestration tools together enable seamless data flow across platforms.

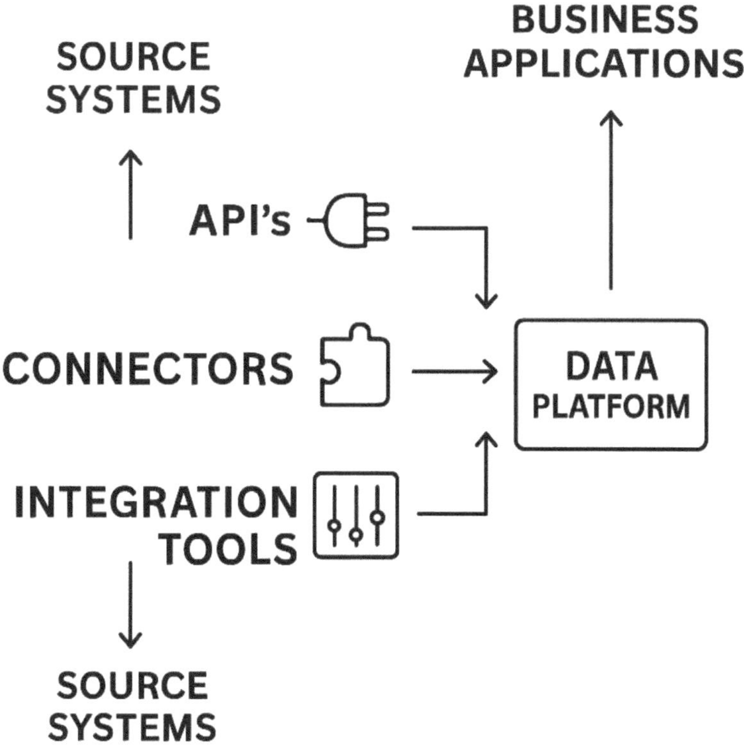

Figure 3-7. *Data integration landscape*

Takeaway

- APIs, connectors, and integration tools are the arteries of a data platform.
- APIs give flexibility, connectors deliver speed, and integration tools ensure governance.
- A balanced approach prevents manual work, reduces errors, and supports multi-cloud, multi-vendor ecosystems.
- For ISkillSetu, these choices mean faster campaign execution, reduced compliance risks, and greater agility in integrating new SaaS tools.

Data Residency, Redundancy, Cost, and Accessibility

> *Data are just summaries of thousands of stories.*
>
> —Chip and Dan Heath (authors, *Made to Stick*)

On Monday morning, Shailesh walks into the executive briefing with a concern that came directly from the legal team.

"Our new European clients are asking where their learners' data is stored. They want confirmation that it never leaves the EU. Meanwhile, our operations team complains that costs are creeping up with redundant copies across regions. How do we balance compliance, cost, and accessibility?"

Maryam replies without hesitation.

"This is the classic data residency and redundancy trade-off. Leaders need to balance three competing forces:

1. **Regulatory requirements** - Where data must reside
2. **Resilience** - Ensuring availability even in outages
3. **Cost vs. accessibility** - How much redundancy is affordable while keeping data usable across regions"

Nilesh adds, "It's not only a compliance issue. Poorly designed redundancy strategies can double costs while providing little value. The challenge is knowing when to replicate, where to store, and how to govern access."

Data Residency

Definition - Data residency refers to the physical or geographical location where data is stored and processed.

Regulatory drivers

- **GDPR (EU)** - Personal data must remain within European Union (EU) or approved jurisdictions.
- **DPDP Act (India, 2023)** - Mandates localization of sensitive personal data.
- **HIPAA (US)** - Strict controls for healthcare data.

Executive consideration

- Residency decisions are legal and contractual, not just technical.
- Multi-cloud and hybrid strategies often emerge from residency obligations.

Case at ISkillSetu: For its European learners, ISkillSetu hosts data in Azure's West Europe region while ensuring anonymized analytics datasets can still be federated globally.

Data Redundancy

Definition – Data redundancy involves maintaining multiple copies across locations to ensure reliability and disaster recovery.

Models

- **Geo-redundancy** – Copying data across regions (e.g., Azure GRS replication).
- **Zone redundancy** – Within a region, data is mirrored across multiple data centers.
- **Custom replication** – Enterprises replicate specific datasets across clouds or regions for resilience.

Business value

- Protects against outages or disasters
- Ensures continuity for critical workloads
- Builds trust with clients who demand high availability

Challenge – Redundancy can double or triple costs if implemented without careful design.

Cost Considerations

Shailesh raises the CFO's concern again: "How do I keep redundancy without spiraling costs?"

Maryam explains with a layered approach:

- **Hot storage** for frequently accessed operational data
- **Cool storage** for less-used but compliance-critical data
- **Archive storage** for rarely accessed but mandatory retention data

Tools

- Azure Blob tiers (Hot, Cool, Archive)
- AWS S3 Intelligent-Tiering
- Google Cloud Nearline/Coldline

This tiering reduces cost while keeping redundancy intact.

Accessibility

Accessibility ensures that authorized users and systems can get to the data they need—without compromising security.

Business context

- Learners expect seamless access to personalized recommendations.
- Executives demand dashboards without latency.
- Regulators require audit trails on who accessed what.

Strategies

- Role-based access control (RBAC) via Azure AD
- Federated identity across regions/clouds
- Content Delivery Networks (CDN) for global access to media (e.g., video lectures)

Balance - Too much restriction hinders agility, while too little creates compliance and security risks.

Decision Heuristics for Leaders

- If **regulators dictate storage location** ➤ enforce **data residency** strictly.

- If **system downtime is unacceptable** ➤ invest in **geo-redundancy**.
- If **cost pressures dominate** ➤ adopt **tiered storage strategies**.
- If **global access is critical** ➤ design for **regional replicas + RBAC**.

At ISkillSetu, this means: EU learners' personal data is localized, redundant copies are stored regionally for resilience, and anonymized analytics are shared globally to support innovation.

As shown in Figure 3-8, the balance between residency, redundancy, cost, and accessibility highlights the trade-offs leaders must manage in global data strategies.

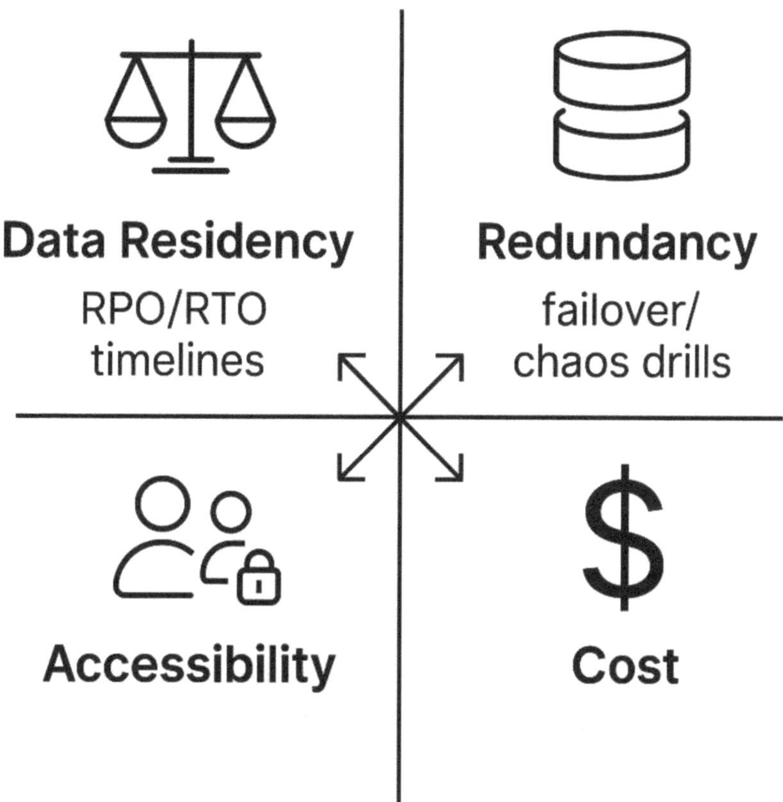

Figure 3-8. *Balancing data residency, redundancy, cost, and accessibility*

Takeaway

- **Residency is non-negotiable**—defined by law and contracts.
- **Redundancy protects business continuity** but must be balanced against cost.
- **Tiered storage strategies** are critical for cost optimization.
- **Accessibility requires strong governance**—enabling agility without compromising compliance.
- For ISkillSetu, balancing these factors ensures global expansion without regulatory or financial setbacks.

Things to Consider: Disaster Recovery, Testing, Latency

> *We're entering a new world in which data may be more important than software.*
>
> —Tim O'Reilly (founder, O'Reilly Media)

That same week, Shailesh receives a call from the CIO of a large corporate client. Their learners have faced downtime during a critical leadership development course. The cause? A regional outage at one of ISkillSetu's cloud providers.

At the boardroom table, Shailesh's frustration is clear.

"If one outage can stop thousands of learners mid-session, we're risking our reputation. How do we make sure this never happens again?"

Maryam replies calmly, "This is exactly why disaster recovery, testing, and latency planning must be embedded into our data platform strategy. Redundancy isn't enough—we need rehearsals, automation, and proactive monitoring."

Nilesh adds, "Think of it as insurance. You don't just own a policy—you also run drills to make sure your people know what to do when disaster strikes."

Disaster Recovery (DR)

Definition - Disaster recovery is the set of policies, tools, and processes that ensure critical systems and data can be restored quickly after an outage or catastrophic event.

Key considerations

- **Recovery Point Objective (RPO)** - How much data loss is tolerable? Minutes, hours, or days?
- **Recovery Time Objective (RTO)** - How quickly must systems recover to avoid business disruption?
- **Multi-region deployment** - Replicating workloads across geographies.
- **Failover mechanisms**: Automated switching to secondary systems when the primary fails.

Example for ISkillSetu: For live virtual classes, RTO must be <5 minutes; for monthly finance reporting, a 24-hour RTO may be acceptable.

Testing and Rehearsals

Shailesh asks bluntly, "How do we know our DR plan will actually work?"

Maryam explains, "Testing is not optional. We need simulated failovers, chaos engineering, and regular drills to validate our assumptions."

Practices

- **Tabletop exercises** - Business leaders walk through hypothetical outage scenarios.
- **Failover drills** - Simulated regional outages with automatic failover validation.
- **Chaos testing** - Tools like Azure Chaos Studio or Gremlin inject controlled failures to measure resilience.

Executive insight - Testing is not about perfection—it is about **confidence** that when disaster strikes, the team can respond seamlessly.

Latency Considerations

Definition - Latency is the time delay between a user's action and the system's response. In a global, cloud-native environment, latency can significantly impact user experience and data freshness.

Sources of latency

- **Network distance** - Data traveling across regions
- **Pipeline design** - Inefficient queries or transformations
- **Concurrency limits** - Too many simultaneous users

Mitigation strategies

- **Edge and CDN deployment** - For video lectures, replicate content closer to learners.
- **Regional data processing** - Perform transformations locally instead of centralizing everything.
- **Pipeline optimization** - Use partitioning, caching, and indexing in data warehouses.

Example for ISkillSetu - Live quiz results should update in seconds globally. Video-on-demand can tolerate slight buffering. Finance dashboards can update nightly.

Strategic Balance

Maryam summarizes the leadership dilemma:

"We can't afford infinite budgets for zero latency and zero downtime. The question is: **what level of risk is acceptable for each workload?** Leaders must define this, not engineers."

Decision Heuristics for Leaders

- If **downtime directly impacts customers** (e.g., live sessions) ➤ design **active-active redundancy with near-zero RTO/RPO**.
- If **the workload is critical but not time-sensitive** (e.g., finance) ➤ adopt **cost-efficient backup-first DR**.

- Always **test failover plans**—an untested plan is a liability.
- Treat **latency budgets** as business requirements—define them per workload.

As illustrated in Figure 3-9, disaster recovery, testing, and latency trade-offs must be balanced to align resilience investments with business priorities.

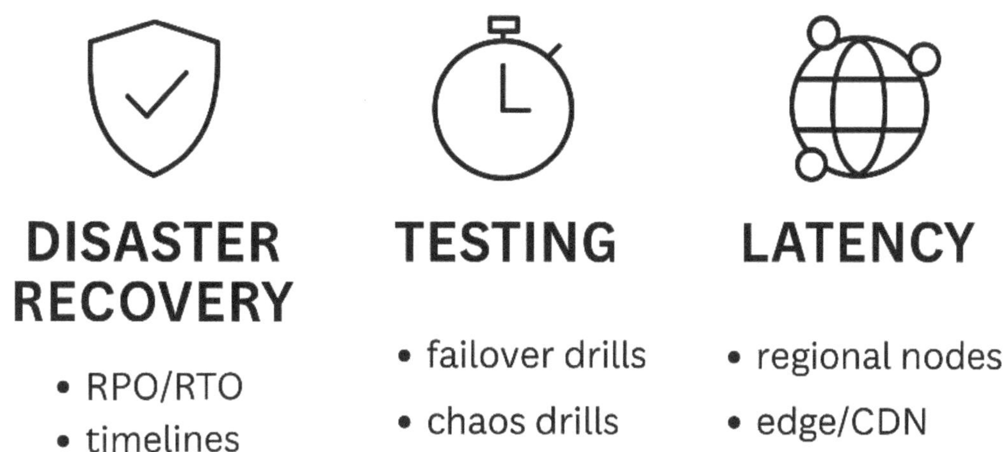

Figure 3-9. *Disaster recovery, testing, and latency trade-offs*

Takeaway

- **Disaster recovery** requires clarity on RTO/RPO and automated failover mechanisms.
- **Testing** validates resilience—without rehearsals, plans remain theoretical.
- **Latency** directly impacts user experience and must be treated as a business requirement, not just a technical metric.
- Leaders must **balance risk, cost, and customer expectations**, aligning resilience investments with business priorities.

Metadata, Lineage, and Catalogues

Data will talk to you if you're willing to listen.

—Jim Bergeson

It is a rainy evening in Pune when Shailesh receives a late call from a strategic partner. The partner wants access to learner engagement datasets for a joint research project. The simple request turns into an ordeal—Vijay's team spends two days just figuring out which dataset is the most accurate version.

At the next leadership meeting, Shailesh vents his frustration.

"How can we run a digital-first company when it takes days to find the right dataset? Shouldn't this be at our fingertips?"

Maryam responds firmly.

"This is a metadata and lineage problem. We are collecting terabytes of data, but without a proper catalogue, we don't know what we have, who owns it, or whether it can be trusted. Metadata, lineage, and catalogues aren't technical luxuries—they are the foundation of trust and speed in data-driven decisions."

Nilesh adds, "Without governance, our data platform is like a library without a catalogue. Books may exist, but good luck finding the right one."

Metadata: The Data About Data

Definition - Metadata describes the attributes of data—its origin, structure, usage, and ownership.

Types of metadata

- **Technical metadata** - Schema, data types, size, creation date
- **Business metadata** - Meaning of fields, business rules, KPIs
- **Operational metadata** - Data freshness, access logs, performance metrics

Business value - Metadata provides **context**, turning raw datasets into assets that can be confidently used.

Example at ISkillSetu - A learner activity log without metadata is just a JSON dump. With metadata, it reveals that activity_type = "video_pause" belongs to the course "AI Foundations 101," updated hourly, owned by the product analytics team.

Data Lineage: Tracing the Journey

Definition - Data lineage tracks the **flow of data from its origin to its final use**, showing all transformations along the way.

Business value

- **Transparency** - Executives know where KPIs come from.
- **Compliance** - Regulators demand proof of data origin and transformation.
- **Troubleshooting** - If a dashboard metric looks wrong, lineage shows where the error was introduced.

Example at ISkillSetu - A revenue figure in Power BI can be traced back through lineage: ERP system ➤ ingestion pipeline ➤ Synapse ➤ transformation logic in dbt ➤ curated dataset ➤ Power BI dashboard.

Tools - Microsoft Purview, Collibra, Alation.

Data Catalogues: The Discovery Layer

Definition - A data catalogue is the front door to enterprise data, enabling users to search, understand, and request access.

Key features

- **Searchability** - Like Google for internal data.
- **Trust indicators** - Certifications, data quality scores, owner details.
- **Self-service** - Business users can find and use datasets without IT bottlenecks.

Example at ISkillSetu - The marketing team uses a catalogue to find "active learners by region" without waiting on engineering. Metadata tells them it is refreshed daily, certified by the analytics team, and suitable for campaigns.

Strategic Importance

Maryam explains the leadership perspective:

"Without metadata and lineage, we waste time and lose trust. Without catalogues, we centralize knowledge in a few engineers' heads. For a scaling company like ISkillSetu, that is unsustainable."

Nilesh adds, "This isn't just governance—it's an accelerator for innovation. If teams can discover and trust data quickly, they experiment faster and deliver insights sooner."

Decision Heuristics for Leaders

- If business users complain about slow access to data ➤ prioritize a data catalogue.
- If executives question metric accuracy ➤ enforce lineage tracking.
- If regulators demand proof of compliance ➤ strengthen metadata governance.
- If data engineering teams are firefighting constantly ➤ invest in an integrated solution like Microsoft Purview.

As shown in Figure 3-10, the ecosystem of metadata, lineage, and catalogues forms the foundation for data discovery, trust, and compliance across the enterprise.

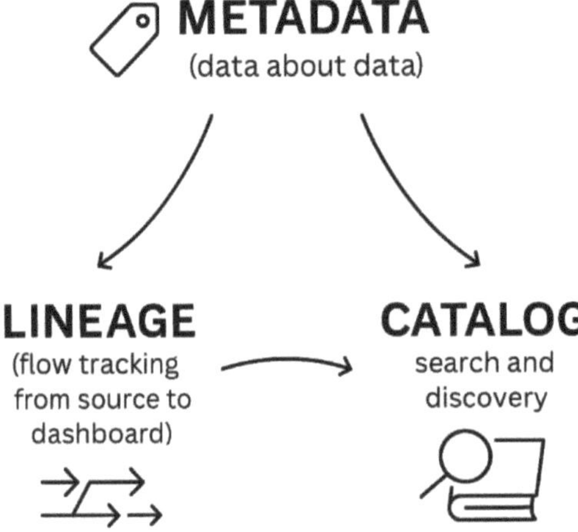

Figure 3-10. *Metadata, lineage, and catalogue ecosystem*

Takeaway

- **Metadata adds context** so data can be trusted and used effectively.
- **Lineage creates transparency**, showing the complete journey of data.
- **Catalogues enable self-service**, reducing bottlenecks and empowering business users.
- For ISkillSetu, investing in this trio means faster insight generation, regulatory compliance, and greater trust in data-driven decisions.

Data Quality Frameworks

Data quality problems become decision quality problems.

—Redman and Blanton

Late one evening, Shailesh receives a report claiming that 15,000 new learners have signed up in a single day. Excited, he calls the marketing head, only to be told that the real number is closer to 1,500. The dashboard has pulled from an unvalidated source.

The next morning's leadership meeting is tense.

"This is embarrassing," Shailesh says sharply. "If we can't trust our numbers, how can our clients, investors, or regulators trust us?"

Maryam replies calmly, "This isn't a tools problem. It's a data quality problem. Without a framework to validate, monitor, and govern data, we risk making poor business decisions, eroding trust, and damaging our reputation."

Nilesh adds, "Data quality is like the brakes in a car—it doesn't make you go faster, but without it, you can't drive safely."

Why Data Quality Matters

- **Business trust** – Leaders will ignore analytics if dashboards keep showing wrong numbers.
- **Operational efficiency** – Poor-quality data leads to rework, manual validation, and wasted hours.
- **Compliance** – Regulators expect accurate records, not estimates.
- **AI readiness** – Machine learning models trained on poor-quality data produce unreliable predictions.

For ISkillSetu, ensuring quality means avoiding embarrassing reporting errors and enabling reliable insights across teams.

Dimensions of Data Quality

A robust framework considers multiple dimensions, not just accuracy:

1. **Accuracy** - Is the data correct?
    - **Example** - Learner email addresses must be valid.
2. **Completeness** - Is all necessary data available?
    - **Example** - Enrolment forms must include country, age, and course ID.
3. **Consistency** - Is data uniform across systems?
    - **Example** - Revenue figures should match across finance and CRM.
4. **Timeliness** - Is the data up to date?
    - **Example** - Daily active users metric should refresh every 24 hours.
5. **Validity** - Does data conform to business rules?
    - **Example** - Course start dates cannot be later than end dates.
6. **Uniqueness** - Are duplicate records avoided?
    - **Example** - A learner should not appear twice in enrolment records.

Building a Data Quality Framework

Maryam proposes a layered framework for ISkillSetu:

- **Data profiling** - Analyze datasets to detect anomalies, missing values, or duplicates.
- **Validation rules** - Business-defined constraints (e.g., date ranges, mandatory fields).
- **Monitoring and alerts** - Automated systems flag issues in pipelines (e.g., freshness breaches).
- **Correction mechanisms** - Workflows for data stewards to fix or approve issues.
- **Ownership and accountability** - Assign responsibility for data domains (marketing, finance, learning).

Tools - Azure Data Factory validation, Great Expectations, Monte Carlo, Soda Core.

Embedding Quality into Culture

Shailesh asks, "How do we stop firefighting and make this systemic?"

Nilesh responds, "Data quality cannot be an afterthought. It must be part of our data culture. That means KPIs for data accuracy, accountability for data owners, and quality checks embedded into pipelines."

This shift requires leaders to treat quality not as an engineering task but as a shared organizational responsibility.

Decision Heuristics for Leaders

- If dashboards are mistrusted by executives ➤ prioritize accuracy and consistency checks.
- If pipelines often fail silently ➤ enforce monitoring and alerts.
- If compliance audits are upcoming ➤ focus on validity and completeness rules.
- If AI is a strategic priority ➤ invest early in a quality framework, as AI amplifies errors.

As illustrated in Figure 3-11, a structured data quality framework ensures accuracy, completeness, and timeliness, turning raw datasets into reliable business assets.

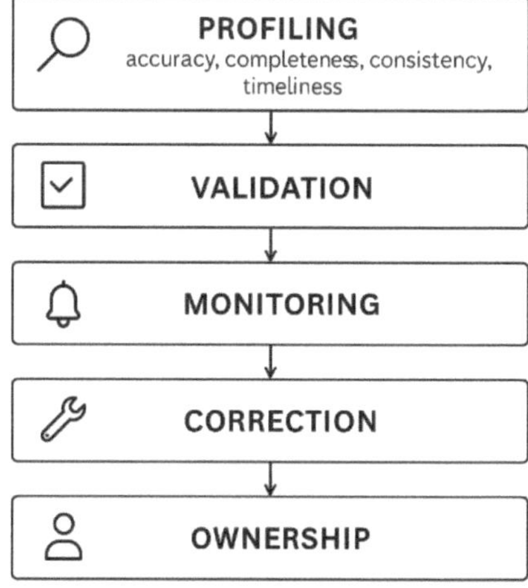

Figure 3-11. *Data quality framework*

Takeaway

- Data quality is foundational—without it, analytics and AI cannot be trusted.
- A framework approach ensures systematic monitoring across dimensions like accuracy, completeness, and timeliness.
- Embedding quality into culture and ownership prevents firefighting.
- For ISkillSetu, data quality frameworks mean reliable reporting for clients, consistent KPIs for leaders, and trustworthy datasets for AI models.

Regulatory Compliance (GDPR, HIPAA, etc.)

Data protection is not a barrier to innovation; it's a basis for trust.

—Giovanni Buttarelli

One Tuesday morning, ISkillSetu's sales team comes back from a pitch meeting with a European bank. The bank is interested in deploying ISkillSetu's platform for leadership development programs but has a non-negotiable demand: *prove compliance with GDPR and provide clear audit trails for learner data.*

Shailesh looks at Maryam and asks, "Can we guarantee this today?"

Maryam replies carefully, "We have pieces in place—data encryption, role-based access—but compliance is more than technology. It is about policies, accountability, and demonstrable governance. If we want to expand into regulated sectors like banking, healthcare, and government, compliance must become a core design principle."

Nilesh adds, "This isn't about slowing down innovation. It's about building trust. If we do compliance right, clients will see us as a safe pair of hands."

Why Compliance Matters

- **Client confidence** - Enterprises won't adopt platforms unless they are compliant with regional regulations.
- **Legal protection** - Avoid fines and reputational damage from breaches.

- **Market access** – Many contracts mandate certifications such as GDPR, HIPAA, or ISO standards.
- **Ethical responsibility** – Learners entrust ISkillSetu with personal and behavioral data; safeguarding it is part of the brand promise.

Key Global Regulations

1. **GDPR (General Data Protection Regulation; EU)**
    - Governs personal data processing of EU citizens.
    - **Requirements** – Lawful basis for processing, right to erasure, explicit consent, and breach notifications.
    - **ISkillSetu example** – Ensuring learners can request deletion of their training history.
2. **HIPAA (Health Insurance Portability and Accountability Act; US)**
    - Governs healthcare data privacy and security.
    - **Relevance** – ISkillSetu's healthcare clients may use training data alongside patient data—the platform must demonstrate secure handling.
3. **India's Digital Personal Data Protection (DPDP) Act (2023)**
    - Requires localization of sensitive personal data within India.
    - **ISkillSetu example** – Storing Indian learner data in Azure India regions.
4. **Other standards**
    - **FERPA (US)** – Protecting student records
    - **ISO 27001** – International information security certification
    - **SOC 2** – Widely used compliance report for service providers

Embedding Compliance into Architecture

Maryam stresses that compliance cannot be a bolt-on. It must be baked into architecture and operations.

Key practices

- **Data localization** - Hosting data in specific regions when required.
- **Encryption** - Encrypt data at rest and in transit with strong keys (AES-256, TLS 1.2+).
- **Role-based access control (RBAC)** - Ensure least-privilege access across users and systems.
- **Audit logging** - Capture who accessed what, when, and why.
- **Data minimization** - Collect only what is needed for business outcomes.
- **Consent management** - Transparent collection and honoring of learner consent.

Tools - Azure Purview for governance, Azure AD for access control, Key Vault for key management, Compliance Manager dashboards in Microsoft 365.

Organizational Responsibilities

Shailesh asks, "So is this just IT's job?"

Nilesh shakes his head. "No—compliance is shared responsibility."

- **Leadership** - Set tone at the top; prioritize compliance in strategy.
- **Data protection officer (DPO)** - Mandated under GDPR for certain organizations.
- **Engineering teams** - Implement encryption, monitoring, and access controls.
- **Business teams** - Collect only lawful data, respect consent, and train staff on privacy.

For ISkillSetu, compliance becomes a board-level KPI linked to client expansion strategy.

Decision Heuristics for Leaders

- If **targeting Europe** ➤ GDPR compliance is mandatory.
- If **working with US healthcare** ➤ HIPAA safeguards are required.
- If **operating in India** ➤ DPDP Act must guide localization.
- If **scaling globally** ➤ invest early in ISO 27001 and SOC 2 certification.
- If **regulators request proof** ➤ ensure auditability via automated logs and reporting.

Takeaway

As highlighted in Figure 3-12, compliance is non-negotiable—it determines market access and client trust.

- Regulations differ by geography, so global businesses must design for multi-jurisdictional compliance.
- Embedding compliance into architecture and culture is more sustainable than bolt-on fixes.
- For ISkillSetu, compliance maturity opens doors to highly regulated clients, from banks to hospitals.

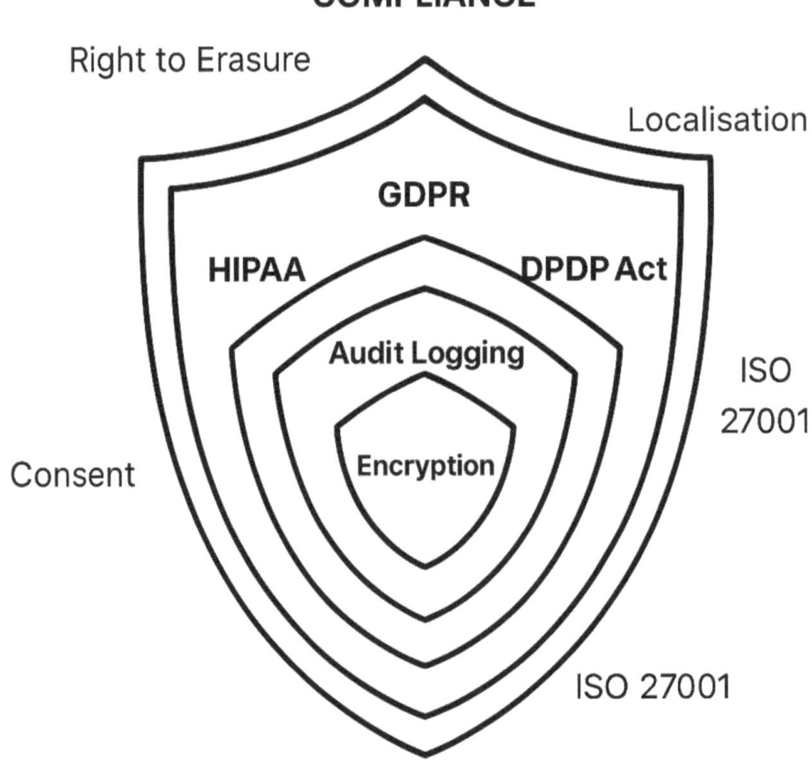

Figure 3-12. *Regulatory compliance in data platforms*

Chapter Takeaways

- A modern data platform is an ecosystem, not a single tool. It combines storage, integration, governance, and compliance in balance.
- Business leaders must make trade-off decisions between cost, resilience, accessibility, and compliance.
- Trust in data is established through lineage, quality frameworks, and governance mechanisms.
- Compliance readiness is not an IT concern alone—it is a board-level enabler of market expansion.

Chapter Summary

> *Every decision made using poor-quality data is a bad decision waiting to happen.*
>
> —Larry English

As the quarter closes, ISkillSetu's leadership team reflects on the lessons learned. Shailesh now understands that data strategy is not a technical side project; it is the foundation of credibility, growth, and client trust.

Maryam's architectural clarity shows the operational backbone required to make data usable. Nilesh's insistence on lineage and quality makes clear that without trust, insights are meaningless. Vijay's engineering perspective ensures that strategy remains executable at scale.

What began as a conversation about systems has transformed into a boardroom priority: the modern data platform is now central to business strategy.

Shailesh sums it up:

"We have the components. We have resilience, governance, and compliance. Now the question shifts: how do we, as business leaders, take ownership of this strategy—not just as technology, but as a driver of outcomes?"

Looking Ahead

As reflected in Figure 3-13, the leadership dialogue sets the stage for Chapter 4, where the focus shifts away from technology and toward executive responsibility.

Figure 3-13. *Conversation between leaders*

- What role should executives, not engineers, play in shaping data strategy?
- How do leaders balance ambition with governance?
- What frameworks help business leaders speak the same language as data architects and engineers?

If Chapter 3 answered "What must we build?", then Chapter 4 will answer: "Who must lead, and how must they act, to make data strategy succeed?"

CHAPTER 4

The Role of the Business Leader in Data Strategy

> *Successful data strategies begin with leadership clarity on value, accountability, and decision ownership.*
>
> —Andrew McAfee

The boardroom of ISkillSetu is unusually tense. The company has just finalized an ambitious plan to expand into Europe and Southeast Asia. Investor presentations highlight the potential of the e-learning market, but the questions from the board have shifted.

"Shailesh," the chairman asks the COO, "can we assure our clients that learner data will remain compliant with local laws? Will we have real-time insights to report on growth? And how will our technology investments align with our revenue forecasts?"

It is clear that these are not purely technical questions. They are business-critical, tied directly to revenue growth, regulatory risk, and reputation. Maryam, the principal solution architect, can explain how Azure regions, pipelines, and governance tools work. But unless Shailesh and his peers at the executive level own the mandate for data strategy, technology alone will not be enough.

This is where the role of the business leader becomes decisive. Data strategy is not just about what gets built, it is about who champions it, who funds it, who enforces accountability, who actively consumes it, and who ensures alignment with enterprise goals. Technology teams can design robust systems, but without executive sponsorship and leadership guidance, strategies stall.

R. Yasir and K. Shaikh, *Driving Business Transformation with Modern Data and AI Strategies*,
https://doi.org/10.1007/979-8-8688-2625-2_4

As depicted in Figure 4-0, the boardroom exchange captures how business leaders frame data not as a technical issue, but as a strategic mandate tied to growth, risk, and reputation.

Figure 4-0. *ISkillSetu boardroom discussion between leadership teams*

In this chapter, we will explore the mandate, roles, and responsibilities of business leaders in data strategy. We will examine the responsibilities of C-level executives and department heads, the challenge of bridging technology and business goals, the recognition of data as a strategic asset, the need for governance initiatives, and the importance of security in a regulated world. By the end of this chapter, executives will understand that owning the data strategy is not optional. It is a leadership responsibility that shapes growth, resilience, and reputation.

C-Level and Department Head Responsibilities

> *The primary role of the business leader in data strategy is to ask the right questions before approving the right technology.*
>
> —Bernard Marr

As ISkillSetu prepares for its international expansion, Shailesh gathers his leadership team. Present are the CIO, CFO, CMO, Head of Learning Operations, and Nilesh as Data Evangelist. The agenda is simple: define who owns what in the data strategy (Table 4-1).

"What worries me," Shailesh begins, "is that we talk about data as if it's everyone's problem, which often means it becomes no one's responsibility. We need to be clear."

Maryam nods. "If accountability isn't defined at the top, teams will keep waiting for instructions. We will keep firefighting instead of driving strategy."

The discussion that follows reveals a truth many organizations confront. Each member of the executive team has a distinct role to play in data strategy, and unless those roles are explicitly defined, strategy drifts. The CEO's responsibility lies in setting the strategic mandate. By treating data as a central enabler of growth, the CEO ensures it is not sidelined as an operational concern. When the chief executive speaks about data as an asset, the entire organization listens.

The COO's role is to translate this mandate into operational execution. At ISkillSetu, Shailesh carries the responsibility of ensuring that data practices build client confidence and enable scalability. For him, data is not an abstract concept—it is the foundation on which international clients will judge the company's credibility.

The CIO or CDO functions as the custodian of technology. Their role is not only to implement the architecture but also to act as a translator, ensuring IT priorities align with business goals. Without this translation layer, technology risks being optimized for efficiency at the expense of outcomes.

Beyond day-to-day custodianship, the CIO or CDO also carries the responsibility of setting a forward-looking vision for the organization's data and AI landscape. This vision typically spans a three-to-five-year horizon, while being reviewed and refined on a regular cadence, often quarterly, to remain aligned with business priorities, regulatory changes, and technology evolution. It integrates cloud adoption, data platform maturity, and AI enablement into a single strategic roadmap. Such a roadmap must articulate not only the target architecture but also the investment required, the sequencing of initiatives, and the expected return on those investments.

A well-crafted three-to-five-year vision ensures that data strategy is not reactive but anticipates regulatory demands, evolving customer expectations, and technological shifts. It provides the board with clarity on how today's investments in governance, platforms, and talent will translate into tomorrow's business value. For example, the roadmap might include milestones such as moving 80% of workloads to the cloud, deploying enterprise-wide data catalogues, enabling predictive analytics for customer retention, and embedding AI-driven personalization into core products. Without such a vision, enterprises risk fragmented projects and tactical spending; with it, they create alignment, consistency, and measurable progress toward long-term differentiation.

The CFO has a critical role as well. Data strategy is not cost-neutral. It requires funding for platforms, governance initiatives, and compliance. The CFO provides financial stewardship, weighing investment against return while also considering the cost of non-compliance, reputational damage, or inefficiency.

Department heads too cannot be passive consumers. Whether in marketing, HR, product development, or operations, leaders must take ownership of the data within their domains. If they abdicate this responsibility, silos form and shadow systems proliferate. In contrast, when functional heads define KPIs, monitor data quality, and embed analytics into their workflows, the enterprise gains a coherent strategy rather than fragmented initiatives.

Shailesh closes the meeting with a simple observation: "Data strategy cannot be an IT-owned initiative. It must be a joint accountability model where each leader has a mandate, and department heads carry domain responsibility. Without this clarity, we will never scale effectively." His words reflect a broader principle: data strategy succeeds when accountability is distributed but coordinated.

To make this explicit, the leadership team at ISkillSetu formalizes a **Responsibility Assignment Matrix (RACI)**. This framework clarifies who is accountable, who is responsible, and who needs to be consulted or informed for each key dimension of the company's data strategy.

Table 4-1. *CxO Responsibility Matrix for Data Strategy*

Data Strategy Dimension	CEO	COO	CIO/CDO	CFO	Department Heads	Data Governance Council
Vision and strategic mandate	A	C	C	C	I	I
Operational execution	I	A	R	C	R	C
Data platform architecture	I	C	A/R	C	C	C
Governance and stewardship	C	R	A	C	R	R/A
Data quality and KPIs	C	R	R	I	A	R
Regulatory compliance	A	C	R	R/A	I	R
Financial investment and ROI	A	C	C	R	I	I
Security and risk management	A	C	R	R/A	I	C
Analytics and business value	A	A	R	C	R	C

Legend

- **R – Responsible** (executes/delivers)
- **A – Accountable** (owns the outcome/final authority)
- **C – Consulted** (provides input/expertise)
- **I – Informed** (kept updated on decisions and progress)

Note The responsibilities outlined in the above matrix represent a general enterprise guidance model. Actual ownership and accountability may vary across organizations depending on operating model, regulatory environment, and organizational maturity. Business leaders should adapt this framework to reflect their specific context while preserving clear accountability.

Decision Heuristics for Leaders

- If data is treated as purely an IT problem, expect misalignment and underutilization.
- If executives do not own KPIs tied to data outcomes, accountability is missing.
- If functional heads ignore stewardship of their domain data, silos will persist.
- If CEOs and CFOs are disengaged, budgets and strategic alignment collapse.

Figure 4-1. *C-level and departmental responsibilities in data strategy*

Takeaway

As shown in Figure 4-1, data leadership is a shared responsibility. CEOs and COOs provide the mandate, CIOs and CDOs deliver execution, CFOs ensure funding and risk oversight, and department heads embed data into their functional goals. A clear responsibility model prevents the diffusion of accountability and ensures that data strategy drives measurable business outcomes.

Leadership Reflection

After reviewing the RACI matrix, Shailesh pauses and addresses the room:

> *"This isn't just a chart for documentation. It's a reminder that accountability lives here, in this room. If we don't own our parts, the strategy falls apart. When each of us stands behind our role, the organization can move with confidence."*

Maryam adds softly, adjusting her notes:

> *"The beauty of this model is its clarity. It tells every team where to look for direction and assurance. It removes ambiguity, which is often the biggest barrier in executing a data strategy."*

These reflections reinforce that the matrix is not a static document but a leadership tool—anchoring shared responsibility in the daily decision-making of ISkillSetu's executive team.

Bridging Tech and Business Goals

> *The role of leadership is to translate business ambition into technology priorities—not the other way around.*
>
> —Thomas H. Davenport

The meeting at ISkillSetu continues late into the afternoon. While the leadership team has clarified their individual responsibilities, a lingering issue remains: how to ensure that the company's technology initiatives are genuinely serving business objectives.

Vijay, the tech lead, shares an example. "We've built sophisticated learner analytics pipelines. The data is flowing; the dashboards look impressive. But unless these insights are used to make strategic decisions—like tailoring course recommendations or forecasting regional demand—it remains a technical showcase, not a business advantage."

This exposes a common trap. Too often, data strategies stall because they are treated as IT projects rather than enterprise initiatives. Architects and engineers may succeed in building scalable platforms, but if business leaders do not articulate the outcomes they expect—whether it is compliance readiness, faster customer onboarding, or improved retention—the technology risks being misaligned with business value.

At ISkillSetu, Shailesh knows that bridging this gap is now his responsibility. He works closely with Maryam to establish what he calls a "translation layer." This means that every major technology decision has to be reframed in terms of its business impact. For example, when Maryam proposes expanding into additional Azure regions, Shailesh translates it into board-level language: *this is not a technical choice; it is a compliance safeguard that allows us to expand into the European market without regulatory delays.*

Bridging tech and business goals requires discipline from both sides. Leaders must ask the right questions—*what outcomes will this enable? How does this improve customer trust? How does this create operational efficiency?*—while architects must express technical roadmaps in terms of risk, opportunity, and measurable return. It is a dual responsibility: executives cannot delegate understanding entirely to IT, and technologists cannot operate in isolation.

The value of this alignment becomes clear when ISkillSetu tests its AI-powered learning recommendation engine. The technical team has optimized it for accuracy, but from a business perspective, what matters is engagement. Nilesh demonstrates that even with slightly lower accuracy, if the recommendations increase learner interaction by 15%, it means higher retention rates and more predictable revenue. This reframing shifts the conversation from technical perfection to business relevance.

In many enterprises, this bridge is formalized through governance councils or steering committees that include both business and technical leaders. At ISkillSetu, Shailesh institutionalizes a quarterly "Data and Strategy Forum" where business KPIs are reviewed alongside technology roadmaps. This ensures that both perspectives influence decisions and that no major investment goes ahead without a clear line of sight to enterprise objectives.

The broader lesson is simple: technology is an enabler, but business leadership must shape its direction. When the two remain disconnected, data platforms risk becoming expensive infrastructure without impact. When they are integrated, however, every line of code and every pipeline directly serves a business purpose.

This principle is captured in Figure 4-2, which highlights how alignment between executives and technologists ensures that every data initiative connects directly to business outcomes.

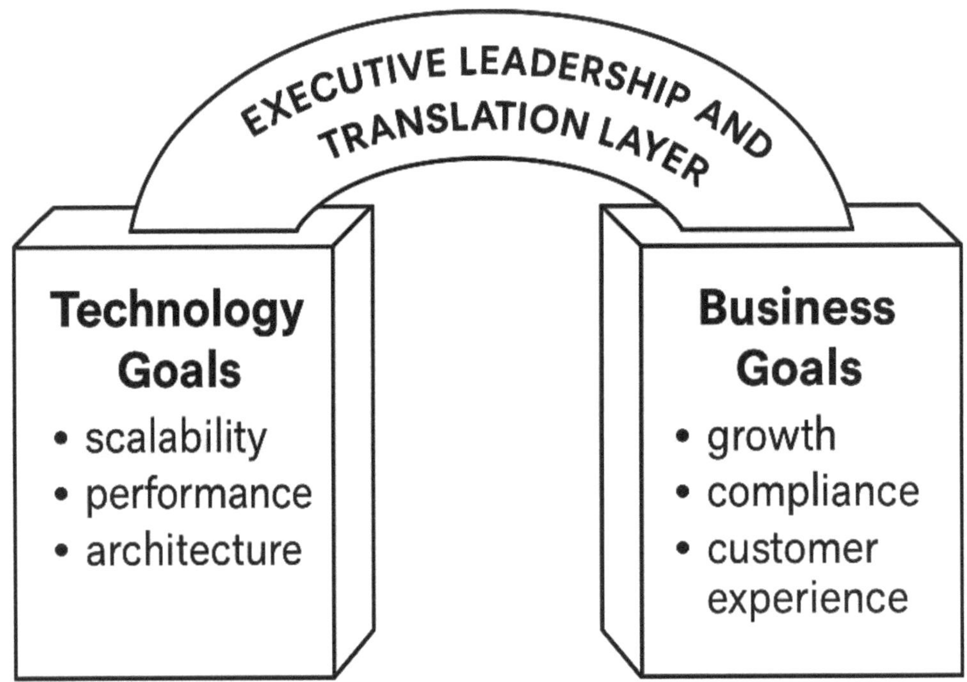

Figure 4-2. *Bridging technology and business goals*

Takeaway

Bridging technology and business is not the responsibility of a single role; it is a leadership discipline. Executives must learn to ask outcome-driven questions, while technologists must explain their work in terms of business value. Without this bridge, data strategy risks irrelevance; with it, every investment contributes directly to growth and resilience.

Leadership Reflection

As the team debates how to connect technical roadmaps with enterprise KPIs, Shailesh leans forward:

> *"We can't let technology run ahead of strategy. If we don't translate every technical choice into business outcomes, then we are just building systems, not value."*

Maryam follows with a practical reminder:

"Our architects should never speak in isolation, and neither should we as business leaders. The bridge is not a meeting—it's a way of thinking."

Data as a Strategic Asset

Data only becomes an asset when it is trusted, accessible, and actively used in decision-making.

—Bernard Marr

When ISkillSetu's leadership gathers for their quarterly strategy review, the conversation turns from operations to valuation. Investors have begun asking a different kind of question: "Beyond your revenue growth, what differentiates you from the dozens of other e-learning platforms in the market?"

Shailesh realizes that while ISkillSetu's product features are strong, the real differentiator lies elsewhere. The company has years of detailed learner data—preferences, engagement patterns, completion rates, geographic insights, and behavioral trends. Properly managed, this data is more than an operational by-product; it is capital. It can inform product design, improve learner outcomes, drive personalization, and even open new revenue streams through partnerships.

Maryam reinforces the point with a simple analogy. "In many industries, data is treated like exhaust—something produced as a side effect of operations. But here, it's fuel. If we treat it as a core asset, it powers growth."

This shift in perspective marks a critical step in leadership maturity. Enterprises that view data as an operational necessity tend to underinvest in governance, quality, and accessibility. Those that treat it as a strategic asset invest in its stewardship, much as they would with financial capital or intellectual property. For ISkillSetu, this means instituting data audits, creating a dedicated governance council, and tying executive KPIs directly to data outcomes.

Nilesh, as Data Evangelist, pushes the conversation further. He argues that ISkillSetu's learner data, when anonymized and aggregated, can provide insights valuable to universities and employers. This opens a potential new business line—licensing insights about skill demand trends across regions. Such thinking turns data into not only a strategic enabler but also a revenue generator.

However, treating data as an asset also demands rigor. Shailesh reminds the team that investors and regulators will scrutinize not just what they do with data, but how responsibly they manage it. Mishandling or overstating its value can erode trust. Hence, recognizing data as a strategic asset is not a marketing slogan; it is a governance principle backed by deliberate investment and accountability.

Beyond recognizing internal data as an asset, modern enterprises must also enrich it with external sources. Relying solely on organizational data is no longer sufficient to gain a sustainable competitive edge, as it reflects only internal activity and historical performance. Leading organizations build broader data ecosystems by acquiring, integrating, and in some cases having complementary datasets, such as market intelligence, demographic trends, behavioral insights, as well as consumer and partner data generated organically through digital channels, platforms, and business collaborations. These enriched sources expand the organization's perspective, connect fragmented signals, and enable a more holistic understanding of customers, markets, and emerging risks.

When these diverse data streams are unified, they form what can be described as a **data flywheel**, as presented in Figure 4-3. The cycle begins with data acquisition—collecting and purchasing relevant datasets. Integration then brings this information into the enterprise architecture, aligning it with existing systems. Enrichment transforms raw inputs into deeper knowledge, while application in products, analytics, and AI creates tangible business value. Crucially, this value generation attracts further data opportunities, reinforcing the cycle.

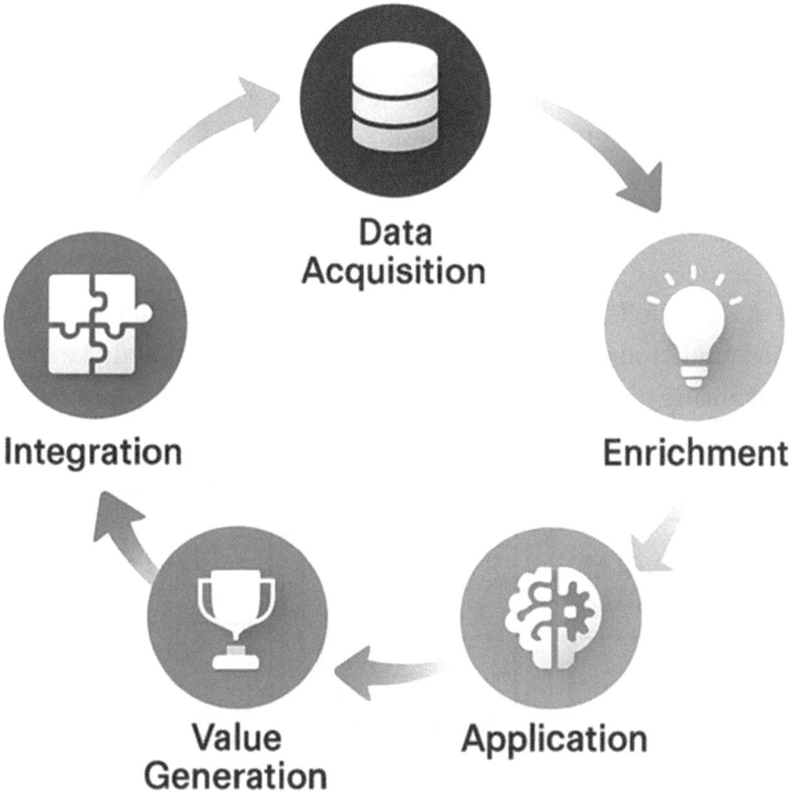

Figure 4-3. *Data flywheel—eagle view*

Note In Figure 4-3, *data acquisition includes initial ingestion, while integration is shown separately to highlight the ongoing harmonization, standardization, and alignment of data across systems throughout the data lifecycle.*

The power of the data flywheel lies in its compounding effect: each rotation makes the organization's knowledge base richer, sharper, and more defensible. Over time, this self-reinforcing loop helps enterprises not only understand what happened but also predict what is likely to happen, enabling them to outpace competitors. For ISkillSetu, combining its learner engagement data, such as course enrolment patterns, content consumption behavior, assessment outcomes, and drop-off signals, with external insights on regional skill demand, industry hiring patterns, and educational benchmarks can turn a strong dataset into a market-leading knowledge base that drives new products and partnerships.

The case for executives is therefore straightforward. Financial assets are managed with CFO oversight, intellectual property with legal guardianship, and brand with marketing stewardship. Data deserves the same level of care. It is a long-term differentiator, but only if leaders actively protect, enhance, and apply it.

Takeaway

As illustrated in Figure 4-3-1, for ISkillSetu, data becomes more than operational output; it becomes the foundation of differentiation, trust, and future growth. Leaders who treat data as an asset ensure it is governed, monetized, and valued appropriately. Those who neglect this mindset risk treating their greatest strategic resource as disposable.

Figure 4-3-1. *Data as a strategic asset*

Leadership Reflection

Reflecting on the conversation about data as capital, Nilesh shares his perspective:

> *"For too long, companies treat data as an exhaust pipe. Here, we must treat it like an investment portfolio—managed, protected, and expected to deliver returns."*

The CFO adds:

> *"When investors ask what makes us different, the answer isn't just our platform. It's the insight our data gives us about skills, trends, and learner behavior. That is the real value."*

Data Governance Initiatives

> *The purpose of data governance is to enable trust, scale, and accountability across the organisation.*
>
> —Jeanne Ross

The decision to treat data as a strategic asset soon leads ISkillSetu's leadership team to a practical challenge: governance. With expansion into new regions, different departments pulling data into their own silos, and regulatory scrutiny intensifying, the lack of structured governance is becoming a visible risk.

During one board review, Shailesh presents learner engagement metrics to the investors. To his surprise, Maryam interrupts, "These numbers don't align with what our operational dashboards show. We're counting the same learner differently across systems." The room falls silent. What seems like a minor discrepancy in reporting immediately raises doubts about data reliability and, more importantly, the company's credibility.

It is at that moment that Shailesh proposes establishing a **data governance council** chaired at the executive level. "This is not a back-office issue," he tells the team. "If we can't vouch for our own numbers with consistency and confidence, our investors and clients won't trust us."

Governance, in this context, goes far beyond cataloguing or classification. It is about defining **ownership, accountability, and processes** that ensure data is accurate, consistent, secure, and compliant across the enterprise. For ISkillSetu, this means creating clear data stewardship roles within departments, implementing data quality checks as part of every pipeline, and standardizing definitions for key metrics like "active learner" or "course completion."

Maryam reminds the team that modern governance is not about slowing things down with bureaucracy. Instead, it should operate as an enabler, providing guardrails so innovation can scale safely. When developers know where to source the right data, when compliance officers trust automated lineage reports, and when executives receive consistent dashboards, governance shifts from being a burden to being a competitive advantage.

Nilesh takes a cultural angle. He argues that governance needs not only rules but also advocacy. "People in the business must understand why definitions matter, why lineage matters, why a broken pipeline is not just an IT problem but a reputational risk. Without cultural adoption, governance frameworks will sit unused." To this end, ISkillSetu introduces data literacy sessions for managers, ensuring that every leader knows how to interpret, question, and apply data responsibly.

At the executive level, governance initiatives also require escalation pathways. When conflicts arise between marketing and operations over metric definitions or when new compliance requirements emerge, the governance council becomes the decision-making forum. This ensures disputes are resolved with speed and authority, rather than left to linger as unresolved "data debates" in lower committees.

The governance initiatives at ISkillSetu illustrate a broader principle: without leadership sponsorship, governance becomes a technical exercise with limited impact. With C-level backing, however, it becomes the backbone of credibility, enabling the organization to scale confidently in new markets and sectors.

Figure 4-4 outlines how governance moves beyond compliance tasks to become an operating model that embeds stewardship, accountability, and trust across the enterprise.

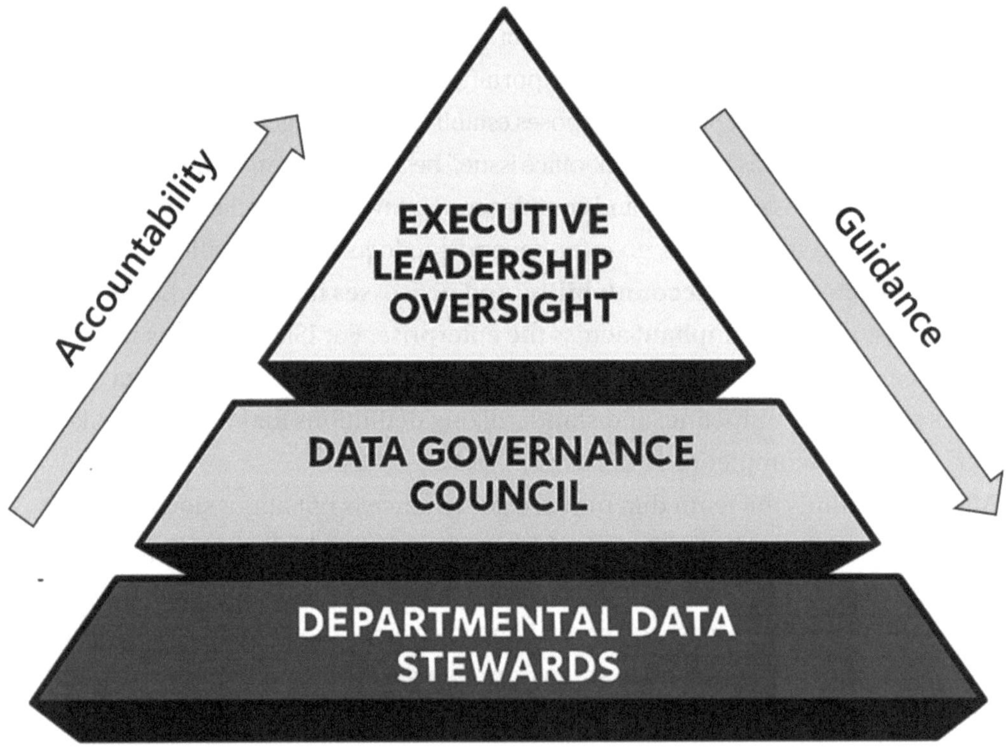

Figure 4-4. *Data governance operating model*

Takeaway

Governance is not paperwork; it is the discipline that transforms data into a trusted, enterprise-ready asset. For ISkillSetu, creating a governance council, defining ownership, and embedding stewardship at all levels turn governance into a strategic enabler. When executives sponsor governance directly, it shifts from being an IT compliance task to becoming a cornerstone of reputation and growth.

Leadership Reflection

At the close of the governance discussion, Shailesh summarizes the board's sentiment:

> *"Governance is not red tape. It's the structure that keeps us credible. Without it, no dashboard or report has meaning."*

Maryam echoes the operational side:

> *"When governance works well, people stop questioning the numbers and start acting on them. That is the shift we must enable."*

Data Security in a World of Data Regulations

> *Data security is no longer just a technical requirement—it is a core leadership responsibility.*
>
> —Thomas H. Davenport

As ISkillSetu prepares to enter the European market, one issue quickly rises to the top of every leadership agenda: security. The General Data Protection Regulation (GDPR) is no longer just a compliance checklist; it represents reputational and financial stakes that the company cannot afford to ignore.

In a board meeting, Shailesh voices the concern most clearly. "A single breach or regulatory lapse in Europe won't just lead to penalties. It will affect our ability to build trust with universities and corporate clients. Data security is not an IT firewall problem—it's a business continuity problem."

Maryam adds a technical perspective, explaining that the company's architecture is designed with layered security across Azure environments. But she also points out the limits of a purely technical approach. "Security is as much about leadership decisions as it is about encryption or monitoring. For example, how much data do we really need to store? Where do we retain it? Who makes the call on risk vs. convenience?"

This reframing helps the leadership team understand that data security is a shared responsibility. The CIO and technical teams provide the controls, but the business leaders set the risk appetite. It is the CFO who has to weigh the cost of advanced security tools against the financial exposure of potential breaches. It is the COO who has to assure clients that their data is handled responsibly. And it is the CEO who ultimately has to represent the company's trust posture to investors and regulators.

Nilesh illustrates the stakes with a cautionary case. He references a global e-learning provider that has suffered a breach, exposing millions of learner records. The company had adequate technical safeguards, but leadership had failed to enforce a culture of vigilance. The breach was not caused by a lack of technology but by poor policies and weak accountability. The result was devastating: heavy fines, loss of client contracts, and a brand reputation that took years to recover.

ISkillSetu takes the lesson to heart. The leadership endorses a security-by-design and privacy-by-design principle, meaning that every new feature or market expansion will be reviewed through a security and compliance lens before launch. They also establish escalation procedures, ensuring that security incidents can be reported directly to the board without delay. Importantly, they treat regulatory frameworks not as constraints but as opportunities to demonstrate maturity. By positioning compliance as a selling point, "we are GDPR-ready from day one"; the company converts security into a competitive advantage.

For executives, the message is clear. Security is not simply about avoiding fines; it is about protecting trust, continuity, and long-term viability. In a world where regulations grow more stringent by the year, leadership engagement in data security is no longer optional. It is a board-level responsibility that defines credibility.

Note In Figure 4-5, *GDPR is shown as a de facto global baseline, while regulations such as HIPAA are industry-specific examples and may vary depending on sector and geography.*

Figure 4-5. *Executive view of data security in a regulated world*

Takeaway

As shown in Figure 4-5, at ISkillSetu, data security evolves from being an IT safeguard to becoming a leadership mandate. The board understands that every decision—from budget allocation to market entry strategy—has security implications. By embedding security into leadership agendas and treating regulations as opportunities rather than obstacles, the company positions itself not only to comply but to compete.

Leadership Reflection

After reviewing GDPR implications, the mood in the boardroom turns serious. Shailesh speaks with conviction:

"Security isn't about avoiding fines—it's about protecting our promise to learners and clients. If we lose that trust, no regulation can save us."

Maryam concludes with a forward-looking note:

"Security has to be designed into everything, not bolted on later. That's how we compete in a regulated world."

Executive Highlights: Key Takeaways

- Data strategy succeeds only when business leaders own it, not when it is delegated to IT.
- C-level executives and department heads share responsibility, each with a distinct mandate: CEOs set the vision, COOs drive operations, CIOs/CDOs ensure governance, CFOs manage financial risks, and functional heads steward their domain data.
- Bridging technology and business requires an executive translation layer, ensuring every technical decision links directly to business outcomes.
- Data must be treated as a strategic asset, on par with financial capital and intellectual property.
- Governance initiatives need executive sponsorship, turning stewardship and consistency into enablers of trust and scalability.
- Security is no longer just a technical safeguard—it is a leadership responsibility in a world of rising regulation, where credibility depends on proactive compliance.

Chapter Summary

ISkillSetu's boardroom conversations illustrate how data strategy, while deeply technical in its execution, is profoundly shaped by business leadership. It was Shailesh, as COO, who recognized that international expansion would not be won by features alone but by the credibility of data practices. It was Maryam who translated complex technical realities into strategic safeguards that reassured the board. And it was the broader executive team, from the CFO to functional heads, who realized that ownership of data outcomes could not be outsourced.

The company's evolution shows that governance councils, translation mechanisms, and security frameworks are not bureaucratic layers but leadership levers. They provide the confidence to scale, the discipline to maintain consistency, and the foresight to turn data into a differentiator. Most importantly, they highlight a cultural truth: when leaders treat data as capital, the organization follows suit.

For enterprises beyond ISkillSetu, the lesson is clear. Building modern data platforms and deploying AI capabilities will not generate value if business leaders remain passive. The role of executives is to **own the mandate, guide the priorities, and protect the trust** that data both enables and demands.

As reflected in Figure 4-6, the leadership dialogue closes with clarity on responsibilities and sets the stage for shifting the focus from ownership to measurable business value in the next chapter.

***Figure 4-6.** ISkillSetu boardroom discussion on key takeaways and the path forward*

What's Next

The foundations are now in place. With leadership clarity on roles, governance, and responsibility, the question naturally shifts from *"Who owns data strategy?"* to *"How do we extract measurable business value from it?"*

This is where the conversation moves from principles to practice. If Chapter 4 has established the leadership mandate, Chapter 5 will explore how enterprises can design an advanced analytics roadmap that maximizes return on investment. At ISkillSetu, this will mean moving beyond dashboards and compliance to advanced analytics capabilities—predictive insights, personalization, and optimized decision-making at scale.

As Shailesh remarks at the close of one board meeting: "We now know our responsibilities. The next step is to turn our data into intelligence that drives real growth."

This transition marks the beginning of **Part 2** of the book, with Chapter 5 setting out the roadmap for designing analytics initiatives that deliver measurable ROI.

PART II

The Advanced Analytics and AI Ecosystem

CHAPTER 5

Democratizing AI: Unlocking Opportunity and Maximizing ROI

> *AI is the new electricity. Just as electricity transformed nearly everything 100 years ago, AI will now do the same.*
>
> —Andrew Ng

Part 2 of this book focuses on three critical themes: democratizing analytics and AI, understanding the analytics maturity model, and the role of data storytelling. This part explores how data and AI leaders can effectively democratize analytics and AI across their organizations; identify and prioritize opportunities, including ROI calculation and value maximization; assess their current position within the analytics maturity model (Chapter 6); define clear next steps; and recognize the importance of data storytelling when leveraging advanced analytics and AI.

Across the data, analytics, and AI landscape, we continue to see leaders struggling with key challenges—selecting the right AI use cases, defining and measuring ROI, building the right teams, and establishing a coherent strategy. This chapter aims to address these challenges by providing leaders with practical tools to identify high-value AI opportunities, understand the common causes of failure, establish robust AI use case and governance frameworks inspired by the examples in this book, and ultimately calculate and maximize AI ROI for their organizations.

R. Yasir and K. Shaikh, *Driving Business Transformation with Modern Data and AI Strategies*,
https://doi.org/10.1007/979-8-8688-2625-2_5

There is no magic formula for making AI investments successful. Sustainable value comes from democratizing analytics throughout the organization, investing in the right employee training, embracing change management, exercising patience, following disciplined processes, and applying sound judgment. These fundamentals remain the most reliable way to protect investment and realize long-term value.

Recent market sentiment reflects both optimism and skepticism. Some view AI as overhyped, citing high failure rates and limited realized value from many GenAI initiatives, as referenced in [1], [2], and [3]. However, these outcomes are not failures of AI itself. In most cases, they stem from initiating AI projects driven by hype, selecting poorly defined use cases, treating AI as a silver bullet, lacking data readiness, underinvesting in platforms and skills, or failing to execute with rigor.

At an operational level, a well-designed data and AI roadmap, supported by a robustly architected data, analytics, and AI framework—and endorsed by the right stakeholders—can deliver significant and measurable value. Success does not require magic; it more often requires patience, the right talent, thoughtful use case selection, and a strong dose of common sense.

We believe this chapter will demystify many aspects of AI initiatives and present multiple practical approaches to delivering value. That said, it is not a prescriptive model. Every organization must adapt these principles to its own structure, context, and objectives. The frameworks and guidance presented here are intended to serve as flexible reference points—designed to be tailored, refined, and evolved to meet your organization's specific needs.

In this chapter, we cover several of the book's core themes, including

- Advanced Analytics and AI Opportunity Zone
- AI Use Case Struggles and Success Playbook
- Advanced Analytics and AI Democratization
- Cost Considerations in Analytics and AI Projects
- AI Governance and Enabling Board
- AI Accountability and Transparency
- AI Team - Partnership - R&D Initiatives
- Operational Considerations in Production
- Advanced Analytics and AI ROI Calculation and Tracking

Advanced Analytics and AI Opportunity Zone

The greatest value of AI will be created not by isolated breakthroughs, but by embedding intelligence into everyday decisions across the organisation.

—Thomas H. Davenport

AI opportunities are often described as difficult to define and identify. In practice, however, they are more straightforward than commonly perceived. We were inspired by a lecture from Jon Reifschneider's "Managing Machine Learning Projects" course on Coursera [4], in which the author introduces a clear and practical bubble-chart approach to identifying AI opportunities—an approach we strongly endorse.

AI initiatives should not be driven by market hype, vendor recommendations, sales-led feature pressure, or random experimentation. Instead, they must be grounded in clearly defined business problems, genuine organizational needs, measurable opportunities, and committed stakeholders.

To identify meaningful AI opportunities, leaders should consistently ask three fundamental questions:

1. **Is there a real problem?**
2. **Can artificial intelligence realistically solve it?**
3. **Does someone genuinely care?**

The answers to these questions provide a disciplined foundation for selecting AI use cases. At its core, AI is intended to address challenges related to time, efficiency, complexity, cost, and performance. When a problem is clearly linked to a measurable business metric, there is potential for AI to add value. However, not every problem is suitable for AI.

Successful AI adoption requires appropriate data availability, realistic expectations, and alignment with technical capabilities. A minimum level of digital and data maturity is essential. AI cannot be effectively applied in environments dominated by legacy platforms and highly manual processes. In such cases, organizations must first focus on foundational digital transformation before pursuing advanced analytics and AI initiatives.

The third question—*does someone care?*—is often the most critical. It speaks to executive sponsorship, funding commitment, and, ultimately, adoption. Without clear ownership, a sponsoring group willing to invest, and users who will actively engage with the solution, even the most sophisticated AI models deliver little to no value. AI only creates impact when it is embedded into real decision-making and human workflows.

Figure 5-1 illustrates how organizations can identify AI opportunities by applying three simple questions. While we explore AI use case selection in greater depth later in this chapter, this framework represents one of the simplest and most effective exercises leaders can undertake before committing to any AI development effort.

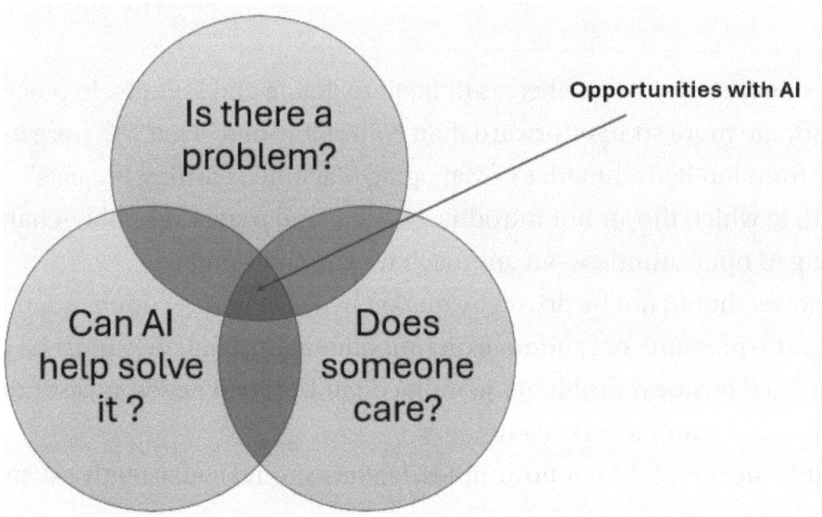

Figure 5-1. *AI opportunity identification chart*

AI Use Case Struggles and Success Playbook

> *Most AI initiatives fail not because of the algorithms, but because organisations underestimate the change, data, and operational discipline required to make them work.*
>
> —Thomas H. Davenport

Leaders frequently struggle to select the right analytics and AI use cases. As a result, many organizations experience fragmented AI portfolios, stalled initiatives, and inconsistent delivery outcomes. Our review of multiple industry reports [2], [3] highlights recurring patterns behind AI project failures. Building on these insights, we offer a practical perspective in this chapter.

Why Many AI Initiatives Fail

A significant proportion of AI projects stall or fail due to a combination of strategic, organizational, and execution-related issues, including the following:

- Launching large numbers of disconnected pilots or proof-of-concepts (PoCs) without a clear plan or prioritization.
- AI initiatives remaining confined to innovation labs without a path to production (system is live and delivering real-world value) or scale (system is deployed broadly and operates reliably, efficiently, and consistently across the organization). Combination of production + scale shows true AI maturity.
- Failure to acknowledge, analyze, and learn from unsuccessful initiatives.
- Limited cross-functional collaboration and insufficient involvement from business and domain experts.
- Absence of a clear accountability and ownership model.
- Lack of defined ROI, timelines, KPIs, and an integrated AI roadmap.
- No structured framework for AI use case selection.
- Late or minimal involvement of end users.
- Building solutions in silos, with an over-reliance on in-house development.
- Vendor-driven PoCs that prioritize features over genuine business needs.

The AI Success Playbook

Equally important is understanding what successful AI programs consistently do well. Based on observed best practices, an effective AI success playbook typically includes

- Focusing on clearly defined, high-impact business problems
- Strong cross-functional collaboration, with deep involvement from domain experts

- Establishing strategic partnerships across industry and academia
- A disciplined approach to *build vs. buy* decision-making
- Starting with narrow, well-scoped use cases and scaling deliberately
- Delivering a 90-day proof of value, with early and continuous user engagement
- Maintaining a healthy, prioritized backlog of AI opportunities
- Emphasizing applied AI over open-ended research and experimentation
- Embedding humans in the loop to ensure trust, oversight, and adoption
- Implementing robust ROI tracking, accountability, and transparency models
- Actively communicating and celebrating measurable successes across the organization

This shift—from experimentation without direction to disciplined, value-driven execution—is often the defining factor between AI initiatives that stall and those that deliver sustained impact.

Advanced Analytics and AI Democratization

> *The real promise of AI is not automation alone, but augmentation—helping every person and every organisation achieve more.*
>
> —Satya Nadella

Advanced analytics and AI should not be reserved for a small elite or limited to a handful of high-profile initiatives within an organization. True democratization of analytics and AI means enabling broad participation—where individuals contribute as users, developers, idea generators, validators, and beneficiaries of AI-driven solutions.

Whether through emerging frontier models—such as AI agents working alongside humans or human-led teams supported by AI agents [5]—or through more traditional enterprise deployments, democratizing data, analytics, and AI is the most effective way to maximize the return on AI investment.

When analytics and AI are truly democratized, they are actively used, continuously improved, and widely understood. People are engaged and motivated, skills evolve, and innovation becomes embedded in everyday workflows. The organization moves forward collectively, participation increases, and AI becomes a living capability rather than a disconnected initiative.

Figure 5-2 illustrates contrasting approaches to AI experimentation and use case selection. One reflects enthusiasm-led experimentation, while the other demonstrates a disciplined task-selection process—where AI initiatives are driven by clearly defined problems, supported by data, validated through value assessment, and tested for feasibility.

Figure 5-2. *Two leaders discussing the proper AI project selection process*

The first step in democratizing data analytics and AI is broad-based inclusion in the ideation process similar to Figure 5-4. This should span the organization from top to bottom and involve executives, senior leaders, managers, product leaders, product managers, and subject matter experts, as appropriate.

Data and AI leaders should facilitate structured AI ideation workshops within each business unit. These sessions can introduce what AI can and cannot do, set realistic expectations, highlight limitations, showcase recent successes, and communicate the broader AI roadmap. At the conclusion of each workshop, business teams should be invited to submit AI ideas, supported by responses to the three foundational questions outlined earlier.

Step 1 constitutes idea submission and initial qualification. Ideas that fall within the AI opportunity zone will move ahead for step 2 and step 3, and business will provide an AI Project Canvas like Figure 5-5. Once the canvases (Figure 5-5) are collected, we will complete steps 2 and 3 for projects that fall within the opportunity zone.

Step 2 focuses on feasibility assessment. A designated member of the data and AI team evaluates each idea across key dimensions, including data availability, technical complexity, team capacity, reusability, scope, risk, and delivery challenges. Each idea can then be assigned a feasibility score—for example, on a scale of 1–5—to support structured prioritization, like the priority quadrant shown in Figure 5-6.z

Step 3 involves business leadership and centers on value and impact assessment. Ideas are scored—again on a 1–5 scale—based on criteria such as expected timeline, organizational impact, business criticality, success metrics, KPIs, ongoing maintenance costs, business priority, user adoption, integration requirements, and defined ROI.

Ideas that score highly on both feasibility and impact are added to a managed AI backlog. This backlog is reviewed on a quarterly basis and prioritized using a **Now, Next, and Later** framework, guiding progression through proof of value, minimum viable product (MVP), and ultimately full production deployment.

This structured, inclusive approach ensures AI investment remains focused, scalable, and aligned with genuine business value.

***Figure 5-3.** Two leaders discussing the AI use case selection process based on the feasibility and impact framework*

Progress across data and AI initiatives—including workshops, use case pipelines, and delivery outcomes—should be reviewed on a quarterly basis by a **Data and AI Governance Board**, comprising senior data and AI leaders alongside executive sponsors. This forum ensures clear accountability, strategic alignment, and effective oversight.

In parallel, an **AI Enabling Board**, made up of AI specialists and representatives from key business functions, should meet monthly to shape the AI roadmap, prioritize workshops, review ROI, and manage use case progression.

Figure 5-3 outlines the end-to-end democratization process step by step. Importantly, this model is not intended to be static. It should be continuously adapted and refined to reflect the organization's structure, maturity, and evolving strategic priorities.

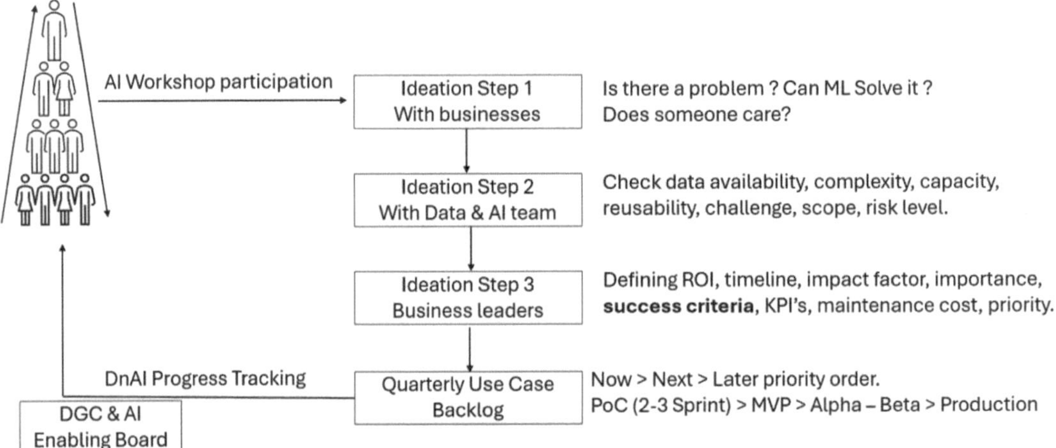

Figure 5-4. *Proposed advanced analytics and AI democratization process*

Business divisions are best positioned to originate AI project, feature, and use case ideas, as well as define the initial scope. Rather than relying on lengthy business cases and extensive documentation, organizations should aim to simplify the process and reduce unnecessary bureaucracy.

To support this, we propose an **AI Project Canvas**, shown in Figure 5-5. This canvas is designed to provide a concise, structured way to capture AI use case ideas. Organizations can adopt the template as is or adapt it to suit their specific needs and operating models.

Although the canvas contains 14 distinct sections, each is intentionally straightforward and requires only a small number of inputs. Collectively, these sections provide a comprehensive, 360-degree view of the idea, covering both business and technical considerations.

It is expected that business owners or idea contributors may not have complete answers at the outset. This is a natural part of the process. Collaboration across functions—supported by data, AI, and governance stakeholders—helps refine the problem definition, clarify requirements, and identify the right opportunities during the scoping phase.

Figure 5-5. *AI Ideation Project Canvas template*

The AI Project Canvas comprises **14 core sections**, each designed to capture a critical aspect of an AI use case in a concise and structured manner:

- **Data** – Data requirements, potential data acquisition needs, and data governance considerations, including compliance and policy requirements
- **Skills** – Required capabilities and resources, such as data scientists, engineers, and domain-specific subject matter experts
- **Integration** – Target systems and platforms for integration, for example, CRM systems, customer portals, or enterprise applications
- **Problem definition** – The specific problem being addressed and the reason it requires attention at this point in time
- **Value proposition** – The expected value generated by the AI initiative, including both tangible and intangible benefits
- **Timeline** – Urgency and timing considerations, informed by business priorities and the competitive landscape

- **Success criteria** - Clearly defined KPIs and metrics to measure success, including thresholds for continuation or termination
- **Responsible AI** - Ethical, regulatory, and risk considerations, aligned with the responsible AI framework outlined in Chapter 10
- **Stakeholders** - Executive sponsors and business owners responsible for funding, oversight, and decision-making
- **Users/customers** - Intended users of the solution and expected usage frequency
- **Operations** - Deployment, monitoring, and ongoing operational requirements, including DataOps and MLOps considerations
- **Cost** - High-level cost estimates, covering both build and run components
- **Benefits** - Revenue, efficiency, productivity, and FTE (full-time equivalent)-related benefits, recognizing that not all AI initiatives generate direct revenue
- **ROI** - Overall return on investment, expressed in financial terms and percentage returns, including anticipated payback period

Together, these sections provide a balanced, executive-ready view of AI initiatives, supporting informed decision-making and disciplined prioritization.

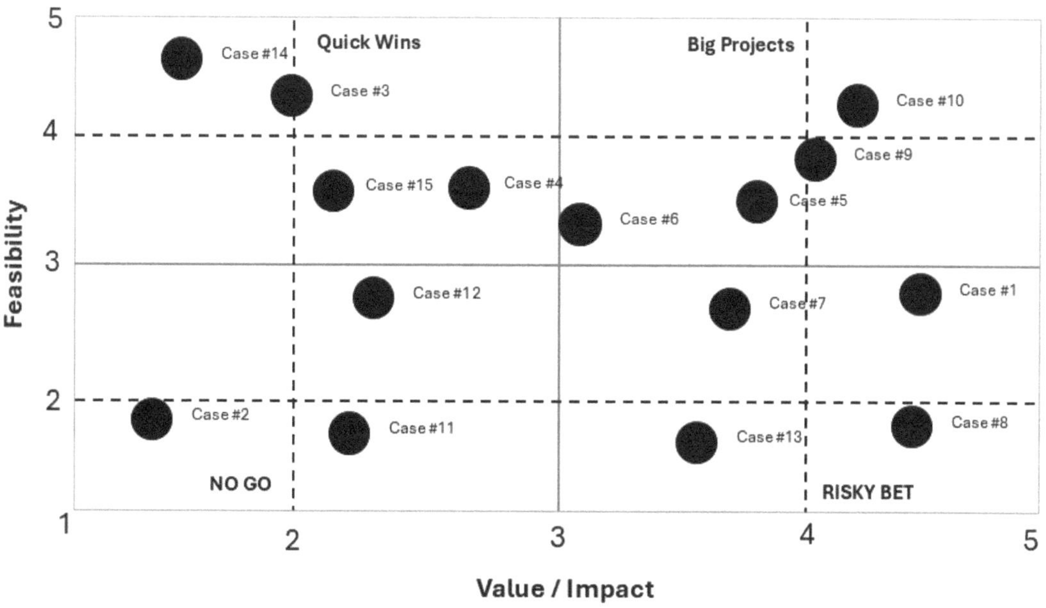

Figure 5-6. *Example priority quadrant of AI projects—feasibility vs. value/impact*

We expect organizations to adopt this canvas and tailor it to their own operating models and requirements. Typically, the canvas is completed for ideas that fall within the defined AI opportunity category and have progressed through initial feasibility and impact screening.

Once the canvas is complete, the AI Board—supported by technical experts—reviews each proposal and scores it across key dimensions, including feasibility, value, and overall business impact. These scores are then used to construct a prioritization quadrant, as illustrated in Figure 5-6.

This quadrant provides a clear, visual basis for recommendations on which AI initiatives should be pursued first, taking into account value potential, feasibility, speed to impact, and organizational demand. As a guiding principle, initiatives with a feasibility score of 3 or higher and a corresponding value or impact score of 3 or higher should be prioritized.

In the illustrative example, 15 AI use cases were initially assessed, of which only four met the required feasibility and impact thresholds. This disciplined approach narrows focus, enables effective resource allocation, and supports clear prioritization across **Now, Next, and Later** horizons, aligned with available capacity.

The prioritization quadrant is divided into four distinct zones: **No Go**, **Risky Bet**, **Quick Wins**, and **Big Projects**. Big Projects typically offer the highest long-term ROI, while initiatives in the No Go quadrant—characterized by low feasibility and low impact—should be avoided.

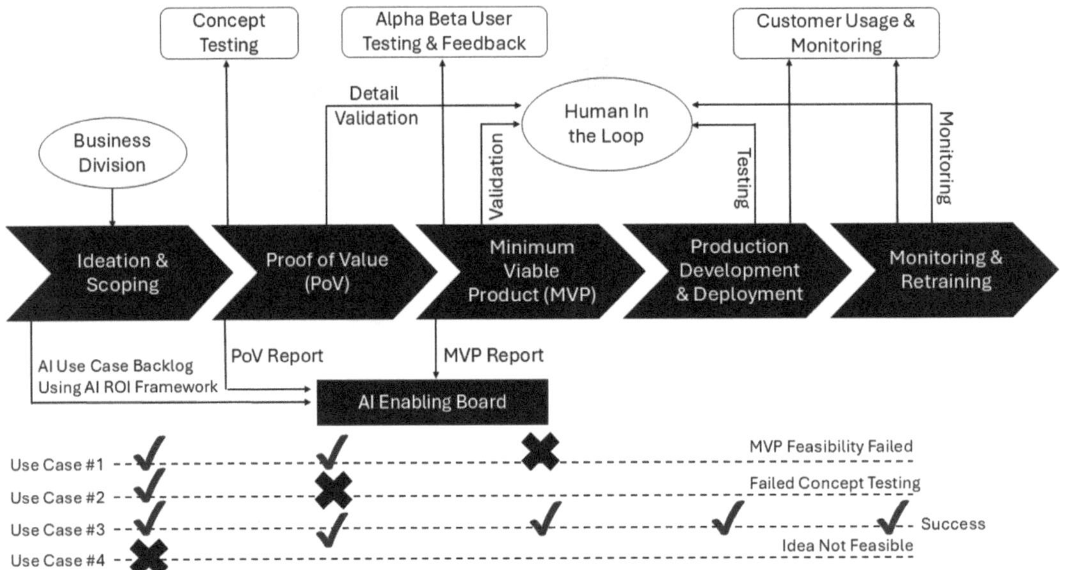

***Figure 5-7.** Example AI project journey to maximize ROI*

Once priority initiatives are selected for development, the next step is to understand the AI development lifecycle. While core components of the lifecycle are broadly consistent, the specific processes and execution models vary by organization and leadership approach.

This book proposes a structured AI development lifecycle, illustrated in Figure 5-7. While this framework provides a clear reference model, leaders should adapt it to suit their organization's size, maturity, and operating context.z

The proposed model includes two distinct governance bodies. The first is an **AI Governance Council**, comprising senior executives and leaders responsible for responsible AI practices, governance standards, accountability, transparency, and investment oversight. The second is an **AI Enabling Board**, made up of business leaders and practitioners, focused on engagement, ideation, workshops, and use case progression.

The AI development lifecycle itself consists of five core stages:

- **Ideation and Scoping**
- **Proof of Value (PoV)**
- **Minimum Viable Product (MVP)**
- **Production and Deployment**
- **Monitoring and Retraining**

At each stage, initiatives are reviewed against the responsible AI checklist outlined in Chapter 10. The data science team provides structured progress updates to the AI Enabling Board, which determines whether a use case should advance to the next phase. Depending on organizational scale and complexity, governance may be centralized or implemented at a divisional level.

Two principles are essential to ensuring AI investment delivers sustainable value. First, maintaining humans in the loop as validators helps ensure outputs are accurate, scoping remains appropriate, and solutions are not over-engineered. Second, early and continuous user involvement is critical. We propose user testing across three stages: concept validation with a small group of technically adept users during the PoV phase; alpha and beta testing during the MVP phase; and full-scale adoption, monitoring, and feedback once in production.

As illustrated at the bottom of Figure 5-7, it is common for only a subset of assessed initiatives to reach production. This underscores the importance of maintaining a healthy backlog of AI use cases. The proposed process supports this by clearly categorizing initiatives into Now, Next, and Later, with the backlog reviewed on a quarterly basis.

When high-quality ideas with strong feasibility and impact emerge, leaders should be prepared to increase investment to accelerate delivery. Figure 5-8 highlights this principle through a discussion between two leaders on the strategic importance of maintaining a robust AI use case backlog.

Figure 5-8. *Two leaders discussing about importance of having a healthy AI use case backlog*

Cost Considerations in Analytics and AI Projects

> *There is no such thing as a free AI system. Every model carries ongoing costs in data, infrastructure, governance, and people.*
>
> —Andrew Ng

Different types of AI systems and models incur costs in markedly different ways. As outlined in Chapter 8, traditional AI solutions built on structured, tabular data typically require lower development effort and cost. This cost profile increases as organizations move to text-based AI and rises further for image- and video-based AI, which demand greater computational resources, specialist skills, and more complex governance.

Not all AI initiatives can—or should—be framed using a single template. AI may represent a standalone project, a feature within a broader product or program, a targeted analytical capability, or a historical data analysis and aggregation exercise. In more advanced scenarios, multiple AI models may operate together as part of a unified AI system.

For this reason, success metrics and investment expectations vary significantly by use case. Figure 5-9 illustrates this distinction through a discussion between two leaders, highlighting that AI effort may relate to a project, a product, or a feature—each requiring different measures of success, value, and return.

***Figure 5-9.** Two leaders discussing the cost considerations of AI and analytics projects*

Figure 5-10 presents an illustrative example of an AI development cost breakdown, segmented to support clearer investment planning and decision-making.

From a financial perspective, AI costs typically fall into two broad categories:

- **Strategic Investment**
- **Operational Expenditure**

Strategic investment is incurred primarily at the outset of an initiative and covers the foundational elements required to enable AI development. Operational expenditure, by contrast, represents the ongoing costs necessary to maintain, operate, and scale AI models and products once they are live.

Costs can be further classified into **labor** and **non-labor** components. Labor costs generally relate to full-time equivalent (FTE) effort and time, including data scientists, engineers, and supporting roles. Non-labor costs typically include software licenses, platforms, cloud compute, tooling, and data storage.

This distinction provides leaders with a clearer view of both upfront commitment and long-term cost sustainability when evaluating AI initiatives.

	Labor Costs	**Non-Labour Costs**
Strategic Investment	• Data cleaning, annotation, quality monitoring • Data, Dashboard, User interfaces • Data Analytics, Modelling, AI development • Change management, training, communication • Project management, planning.	• Data storage, training, transport cost • Fixed and variable compute cost • Software / platform cost used for data transformation, ETL, model training, monitoring, testing etc
Operational Expense	• AI Model Monitoring in Prod • AI Model Maintenance • System Maintenance, Monitoring, Integrations • User Support, Communication, Training, Documentation	• Cloud computation cost • License fees • Third party API fees • Model liability insurance due to model errors

DnAI Application Development & Creation cost breakdown

Figure 5-10. *Example operational expense and strategic investment costs of AI systems*

Leaders should also factor in the costs associated with training, communication, change management, and project management. Developing an AI solution is only the first step; real value is realized when users understand how to adopt it effectively. This often requires clear documentation, tutorials, structured training programs, user support, and scaling enablement.

We deliberately avoid providing cost estimates or numerical benchmarks, as these vary widely depending on factors such as available skills, data volumes, cloud consumption, architectural complexity, the maturity of existing platforms (legacy vs. modernized), the type of AI model deployed, and expected usage levels.

However, it is essential for leaders to anticipate these costs up front. Discovering them late in the transformation journey can slow momentum, erode confidence, and require unplanned additional investment at critical stages of delivery.

AI Governance and Enabling Board

> *Boards do not need to understand the algorithms, but they must understand the risks, accountability, and value creation of AI.*
>
> —Tom Davenport

Sustainable innovation is built on the foundations of culture, broad-based involvement, and clear accountability. Throughout this book, we advocate a two-tier governance model (Figure 5-11) to strengthen tracking, visibility, decision-making, engagement, and delivery of AI initiatives.

Effective AI programs are rarely successful when developed in isolation. Building strong partnerships across business functions and organizational units creates shared ownership, accelerates adoption, and improves outcomes. Collaboration consistently delivers greater value than attempting to solve complex problems within a single, disconnected team.

Outlined below are the high-level responsibilities of the two governance boards proposed in this model.

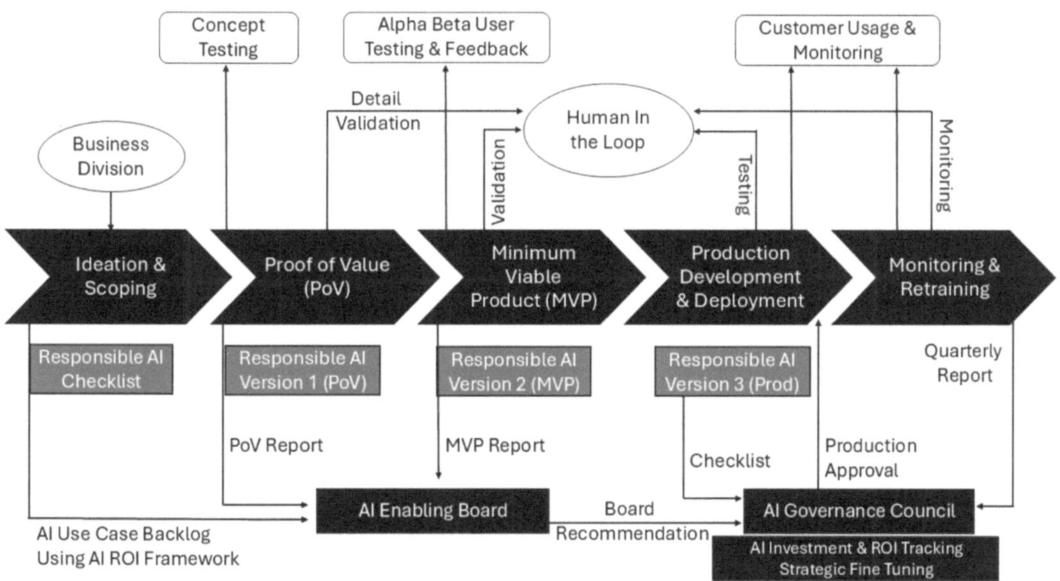

Figure 5-11. *AI boards to make sure integration, development, and ROI are tracked properly*

AI Governance Council

- A senior-level governance body that typically meets on a quarterly basis, comprising data and AI leaders, vice presidents, and executive stakeholders
- Accountable for AI investment oversight, ROI governance, strategic decision-making, executive-level visibility of AI use cases, and adherence to responsible AI principles
- Receives quarterly updates and activity reports from the AI Enabling Board, along with ad hoc proposals requiring investment or prioritization decisions, ensuring overall progress and alignment
- Oversees organization-wide initiatives related to AI training, change management, AI literacy, and strategic vendor engagement
- Reviews and steers the data and AI roadmap to ensure alignment with business objectives and long-term strategy

AI Enabling Board

- An operational-level governance forum that typically meets monthly, or more frequently as required, comprising data and AI leaders, senior managers from key business divisions, and selected technical experts
- Provides structured updates and recommendations to the AI Governance Council
- Responsible for maintaining and applying the responsible AI checklist, managing AI priorities and the use case backlog, and leading AI ideation workshops and targeted training initiatives
- Advises technical teams on use case progression and phase graduation decisions and incorporates feedback from users and stakeholders
- Updates roadmap initiatives, reviews vendor RFPs, recommends role-based training plans, and refines project and delivery management processes

Together, these two boards create a balanced governance structure that combines strategic oversight with operational execution, enabling disciplined, transparent, and scalable AI delivery.

AI Accountability and Transparency

> *Transparency is what turns AI from a black box into a business capability leaders can trust.*
>
> —Thomas H. Davenport

Accountability and transparency are non-negotiable, as an organization's investment, reputation, and long-term growth depend on them. As illustrated by the leaders' discussion in Figure 5-12, AI ROI and ownership must be clearly defined and actively managed.

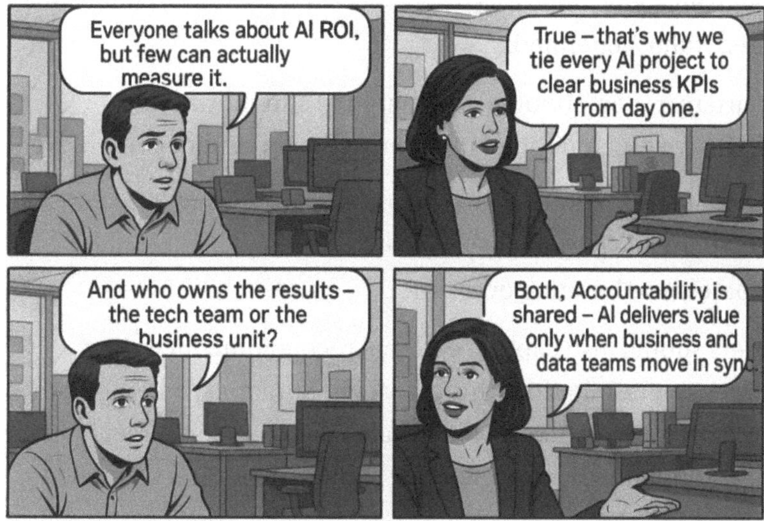

Figure 5-12. *Two leaders discussing the AI ROI, KPI tracking*

Accountability for AI outcomes is shared between business and IT teams, reflecting the joint responsibility for value creation and delivery. In this section of the chapter, we focus on two critical areas: progress tracking and the accountability model that underpins effective and responsible AI execution.

Tracking Progress: A Data-Driven Approach

- Data and AI leaders should establish a delivery-tracking framework aligned to the organization's structure, enabling visibility into team velocity and throughput. This may include tracking requests received, delivered, pending, or delayed, as well as cycle times, using tools such as Jira or equivalent platforms.
- Maintaining a healthy and visible use case backlog provides confidence and clarity for both teams and stakeholders. Backlog volume, resource capacity, and delivery estimates should be reviewed on a quarterly basis. Where possible, an automated dashboard should be developed and shared with the AI Governance Council.
- It is good practice to track the ROI of delivered initiatives, either through efficiency metrics (such as FTE days saved) or direct and indirect value generated.
- A quarterly report should be prepared to summarize both quantitative outcomes and qualitative business benefits achieved.
- Ongoing R&D initiatives, external proofs-of-concept, and industry pilots should be periodically assessed to evaluate relevance, outcomes, and learning over time.
- Leaders should also capture external recognition, including conference presentations, industry collaborations, and thought leadership contributions. Not all value is realized in direct financial terms; AI initiatives often generate significant indirect benefits.

Accountability: A Data-Driven Model

For data and AI leaders, accountability must be embedded in day-to-day operations and reinforced through measurable outcomes. Key accountability practices include:

- Leading monthly and quarterly governance reviews, presenting progress, outcomes, and successes to the Data and AI Governance Council to ensure alignment and transparency

- Driving cross-functional collaboration through the AI Enabling Board and a network of data and AI champions across business divisions
- Maintaining and updating dashboards on a quarterly basis to monitor the performance of data, analytics, and AI initiatives, while capturing lessons learned
- Conducting regular roadmap and ROI reviews to ensure delivery remains aligned with defined KPIs and business objectives
- Actively promoting innovation and recent successes through spotlight sessions and implementing annual enablement and tooling plans to support analytics and AI democratization across the organization

Together, these practices ensure that progress is visible, accountability is clear, and AI investment continues to deliver measurable and sustainable value.

AI Team – Partnership – R&D Initiatives

> *The most successful AI strategies balance internal capability-building with selective collaboration.*
>
> —Thomas H. Davenport

Data and AI leaders must deliberately design and curate team structures that effectively support their organization's strategic and operational needs. As discussed in Chapter 7, there is no single optimal operating model; organizations typically adopt centralized, federated, or hybrid analytics structures depending on scale, maturity, and business complexity.

Within delivery teams, a range of specialized skills may be required across different phases of an initiative, including data engineering, automation, modeling, AI development, and deployment. These capabilities can be organized into clear functional streams, such as

- **Data engineering and integration**, staffed by data engineers and integration specialists
- **Business intelligence**, led by data analysts

- **Data science**, comprising data scientists and statisticians
- **MLOps**, supported by AI and platform engineers
- **Process automation**, involving robotic process automation and workflow experts

Organizations also apply different approaches to sizing and scoping data and AI initiatives. A common and effective method is T-shirt sizing (S, M, L, XL, XXL), where each size represents an estimated level of effort—often defined in business days—across the relevant skill sets.

From an industry perspective, data and AI leaders should prioritize applied AI initiatives before investing heavily in open-ended R&D. Applied AI focuses on deploying proven techniques against the organization's own data to solve real business problems. This approach accelerates delivery, builds credibility and trust, and reduces execution risk—often serving as the foundation for future innovation, including new products and services.

***Figure 5-13.** Two leaders discussing partnership benefits and opportunities in data and AI initiatives*

Data and AI leaders should also actively pursue **industry and academic partnerships** (As mentioned in Figure 5-13) as part of a balanced innovation strategy. These collaborations may include data exchange programs, joint proof-of-concept initiatives with vendors, engagement with master's and PhD students on applied research projects, or co-sponsored research with academic institutions through government-funded or privately sponsored programs.

Such partnerships create multiple advantages. They enable R&D initiatives to progress without disrupting core delivery timelines, expand access to emerging ideas and specialist expertise, and provide a pipeline of future talent—often allowing organizations to recruit proven researchers as full-time employees, saving both time and cost.

More broadly, this approach gives leaders greater flexibility, exposure to new thinking, and a practical mechanism for solving complex problems creatively, while maintaining focus on day-to-day business priorities.

Operational Considerations in Production

> *An AI model is only successful when it works reliably in production, not when it performs well in a lab.*
>
> —Andrew Ng

Operations is one of the most critical factors determining whether data and AI initiatives succeed or remain confined to innovation labs. A key differentiator between successful and unsuccessful AI programs is the extent to which operational considerations are addressed for real-world deployment and scale.

Operations extend well beyond the AI model itself and can be broadly categorized into three areas:

- **Data Operations (DataOps)**
- **Machine Learning Operations (MLOps)**
- **Large Language Model Operations (LLMOps)**

Together, these operational disciplines ensure that data pipelines are reliable, models are deployable and maintainable, and AI solutions can be monitored, governed, and scaled effectively in production environments. Figure 5-14 explaining importance of operations that includes DataOps, MLOps, LLMOps.

Figure 5-14. *Two leaders discussing operations as a missing layer from pilot to prod*

DataOps

DataOps encompasses the practices, processes, and tooling required to ensure enterprise data is reliable, well-governed, traceable, and fit for purpose across analytics and AI initiatives. Many AI and analytics programs fail due to poor data quality, delayed availability, or weak governance—challenges that DataOps is specifically designed to address.

Key focus areas include data ingestion, validation, quality monitoring, metadata management, lineage, governance, and data availability. When executed effectively, DataOps accelerates time-to-insight, increases trust in analytics, and reduces technical debt—ultimately saving both time and cost.

MLOps

MLOps refers to the operational discipline that supports machine learning models once they move into production. While building a model is relatively straightforward, maintaining its relevance, accuracy, explainability, compliance, and reliability over time is significantly more complex.

Core MLOps capabilities include model versioning, deployment automation, scalability, performance monitoring in production, retraining, and lifecycle management. These practices create a stable, repeatable, and scalable environment, reducing operational risk and enabling AI solutions to grow alongside business demand.

LLMOps

LLMOps extends MLOps to address the unique challenges associated with generative AI and large language models (LLMs). While MLOps focuses on traditional machine learning, LLMOps is designed to manage risks such as data leakage, hallucinations, prompt sensitivity, and uncontrolled costs.

Key focus areas include prompt management and versioning, guardrails, content safety, cost monitoring, human-in-the-loop validation, and continuous feedback mechanisms. LLMOps enables organizations to deploy generative AI solutions—such as chatbots—safely, responsibly, and at scale, while maintaining control over risk, cost, and quality.

Advanced Analytics and AI ROI Calculation and Tracking

> *The organisations that win with AI are those that tie analytics directly to financial and operational metrics.*
>
> —Satya Nadella

Data and AI investments do not always generate direct financial returns. In many cases, value is realized through efficiency gains, productivity improvements, growth enablement, competitive advantage, enhanced customer satisfaction, FTE time savings, and more accurate decision-making. As a result, calculating ROI for advanced analytics and AI initiatives can be inherently challenging.

According to an IDC study published in 2024 and referenced in [1], *"organisations achieve an average return of **$3.70 for every $1 invested** in AI, with approximately 5% of organisations worldwide realising returns exceeding **$10 for every $1 invested**."* These figures are based on the following standard ROI formula proposed in [1]:

ROI = ((Return on Investment – Cost of Investment) / Cost of Investment) × 100

While this formula is useful for assessing overall investment performance at an aggregate level, we recommend a more tailored approach when evaluating individual AI projects, features, or products:

AI ROI = (Direct Financial Value + Credible Indirect Value) / Total Cost of Ownership

This approach deliberately accounts for both direct and indirect value, alongside total cost of ownership. Total cost of ownership may include resource costs, salaries, cloud consumption, software licenses, and platform expenses. Direct value typically reflects revenue generation or clearly attributable financial impact, while credible indirect value may include FTE efficiency gains, productivity improvements, customer satisfaction, growth enablement, and risk reduction.

It is also important to distinguish between advanced analytics and AI, as they often deliver value in different ways. Advanced analytics is frequently consumed through dashboards and reporting tools, whereas AI may be embedded as a standalone capability, integrated feature, or component within broader platforms—including dashboards.

To illustrate this distinction, Table 5-1 compares ROI characteristics across advanced analytics dashboards and AI initiatives. The underlying metrics and impact profiles differ significantly. Advanced analytics dashboards are often introduced as enhanced features within existing platforms, while AI initiatives may represent entirely new products, services, or capabilities. In some cases, dashboards combining reporting, advanced analytics, and embedded AI can themselves be commercialized as standalone offerings.

Table 5-1. *ROI Comparison of Advanced Analytics Dashboard and AI/ML*

Key Dimensions	Advanced Analytics Dashboard	AI/ML Use Case
ROI metrics	Time, trend, business direction, and clarity	Accuracy, automation, time, cost
Best ROI metric	Hours saved	Error reduced, cost
Typical payback time	3–6 months	6–12 months
ROI confidence	High	Medium initially
Scaling opportunity	Low–Mid	High
Products and services	Extension/feature	Brand-new and extension
Complexity	Low	Medium–High

Chapter Summary

This chapter has outlined guiding principles for identifying AI opportunities, democratizing analytics and AI across the organization, selecting and prioritizing AI ideas, applying best practices, calculating AI ROI, and establishing leadership accountability and transparency throughout the data and AI journey.

There are often multiple valid answers to the same strategic question. Leaders must exercise judgment in selecting the most appropriate path based on available investment, organizational capabilities, business priorities, current context, and long-term strategic impact. We encourage readers to learn from the frameworks and methodologies presented in this chapter and adapt them pragmatically to their own environments.

As discussed extensively, AI ROI is a central theme of this chapter. Figure 5-15 captures this through a conversation between two leaders, reinforcing a critical message: AI ROI is not defined by model accuracy alone. It is measured by tangible business outcomes—revenue growth, cost reduction, risk mitigation, and time saved through effective AI adoption.

Figure 5-15. *Two leaders discussing AI ROI calculations*

References

[1] AI ROI Calculation Framework by Microsoft, https://techcommunity.microsoft.com/blog/azure-ai-foundry-blog/a-framework-for-calculating-roi-for-agentic-ai-apps/4369169

[2] The GenAI Divide, State of AI in Business 2025 report, https://mlq.ai/media/quarterly_decks/v0.1_State_of_AI_in_Business_2025_Report.pdf

[3] Why 85% of Your AI Models May Fail, https://www.forbes.com/councils/forbestechcouncil/2024/11/15/why-85-of-your-ai-models-may-fail/

[4] Managing Machine Learning Projects, Jon Reifschneider, https://www.coursera.org/learn/managing-machine-learning-projects/

[5] AI Frontier Firm Report by Microsoft, https://www.microsoft.com/insidetrack/blog/the-agentic-future-how-were-becoming-an-ai-first-frontier-firm-at-microsoft/

CHAPTER 6

Analytics Maturity Model

Without a clear data strategy, organizations are just collecting expensive digital exhaust.

—Bernard Marr

For small, mid-sized, and large enterprises, transforming into a data-driven organization is a journey—one that must be carefully managed through a robust analytics ecosystem. An analytics maturity model serves as a guiding framework, helping organizations understand where they are on this journey, the benefits they can realize at their current stage, and the path required to become an automated, technologically mature organization that maximizes ROI and delivers sustained long-term value.

Too often, organizations are drawn into hype cycles driven by vendor recommendations and marketing trends. As a result, many costly proofs-of-concept fail to progress beyond experimentation, leading to lost time, wasted investment, erosion of trust, and diminished competitive advantage. A more effective approach is to embrace data and AI transformation as an **iterative, outcome-driven process**, supported by clearly defined and realistic milestones. Business objectives must remain at the center of every initiative. Leaders should articulate a clear three- to five-year data and AI vision, measured and tracked through an analytics maturity model. Figure 6-1 presents a light-hearted yet telling illustration of AI hype, highlighting how organizations that prioritize trends over real-world problems ultimately struggle to achieve meaningful business impact.

R. Yasir and K. Shaikh, *Driving Business Transformation with Modern Data and AI Strategies*,
https://doi.org/10.1007/979-8-8688-2625-2_6

Figure 6-1. *Animated depiction of AI hype overshadowing real-world problems*

In this chapter of an analytics maturity model, we will cover five key topics and subtopics, and they are

- The Stages of Analytics Maturity
- Purpose of an Analytics Maturity Model
- Technology Stack Evolution
- Business Value Realization: Measuring Analytics Maturity
- Data Foundations Across Maturity Levels

The Stages of Analytics Maturity

Transformation is a journey, not a destination.

—John Kotter

Analytics maturity is a journey that organizations must embrace step by step, guided by a clear vision set by bold and forward-looking leadership. Building analytical maturity—in capability, sophistication, and scale—requires time, sustained investment, effective change management, and organizational commitment. Over time, organizations will realize tangible information and productivity gains, reflected in increased revenue, improved efficiency, greater sustainability, accelerated growth, enhanced competitive advantage, and the creation of new products and services.

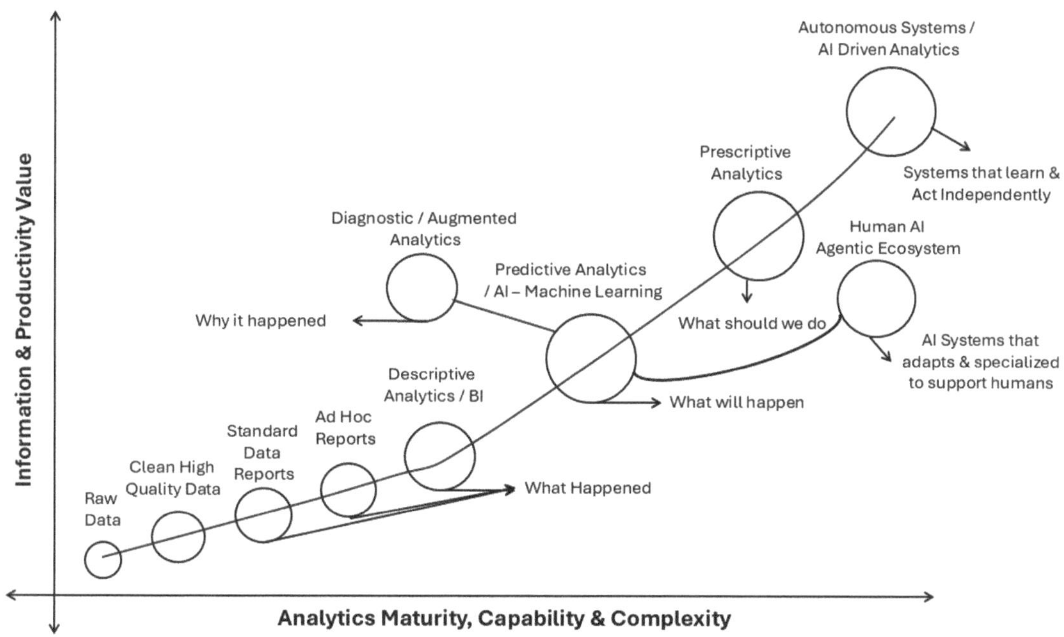

Figure 6-1-1. *Stages of an analytics maturity model and productivity relationship*

Figure 6-1-1 illustrates a step-by-step analytics maturity model, where the journey begins with raw data collection and culminates in AI-driven autonomous systems that empower multiple business functions across the organization. This represents a ten-stage progression, from foundational data capabilities to advanced, AI-enabled analytics.

- **Raw data** - The analytics journey begins with the establishment of a functional data platform capable of collecting data from systems, users, operational activities, third-party sources, and APIs. While raw data may not deliver immediate value, it forms the foundation of the journey. At this stage, strong data governance is critical, with security, policies, and controls strictly defined and enforced.
- **Clean, high-quality data** - Once data is ingested into the organization's data ecosystem, it must undergo cleansing, quality checks, enrichment, and ongoing monitoring. Organizations may

adopt different architectures and tooling for this purpose. A common approach involves layered data models—often referred to as *Raw, Bronze, Silver, and Gold* layers—where high-quality, curated data resides in the Gold layer and is subsequently exposed through data warehouses for downstream consumption.

- **Standard reporting and descriptive analytics** - Standardized reports, ad hoc analysis, and descriptive analytics focus on answering the question, *"What happened?"* Individual datasets may provide partial insights; therefore, organizations often need to integrate multiple data sources to create a comprehensive and unbiased view. Descriptive analytics is typically delivered through BI and visualization tools such as Tableau or Power BI, enabling users to explore historical trends, patterns, and seasonality.

Figure 6-1-2. *Conversation between two leaders on the importance of descriptive analytics*

Figure 6-1-2 highlights the importance of descriptive analytics within an organizational context, providing a shared and trusted view of reality that enhances transparency and alignment. At this stage, leaders rely on historical reports and scorecards to review performance, with decision-making remaining largely reactive.

- **Predictive analytics** – As organizations progress along the maturity journey, **AI and advanced analytics** are typically introduced at the predictive analytics stage, where the focus shifts to *"what is likely to happen"* based on historical trends. To make reliable predictions, organizations must have sufficient data maturity and confidence in data quality. Figure 6-1-3 illustrates the value of predictive analytics in enabling earlier risk identification and faster realization of competitive advantage. At this point, leadership decision-making evolves from reactive to anticipatory. AI begins to inform strategic direction and supports the extension of organizational vision through advanced analytical capabilities and tools.

Figure 6-1-3. *Conversation between two leaders on predictive analytics opportunities*

- **Human–AI agentic ecosystems** and **diagnostic analytics** sit on either side of predictive analytics within the maturity journey. On one side, AI agentic systems represent an emerging trend, where advanced agent-based architectures and technologies such as MCP servers enable autonomous, action-oriented capabilities that significantly enhance human productivity. On the other, diagnostic analytics relies on established statistical and analytical techniques to answer the question, *"Why did it happen?"*
- In diagnostic analytics, leaders move beyond observation to learning from the past. Conversations shift toward accountability, trends, patterns, and performance, grounded in evidence rather than intuition. At the same time, modern software platforms increasingly embed AI agentic capabilities, allowing systems to act autonomously within defined boundaries to support operational efficiency.
- **Prescriptive analytics** and **autonomous, AI-driven analytics** represent the final stages of the maturity journey. Prescriptive analytics applies machine learning and AI techniques to recommend *what actions should be taken*, often supported by probabilistic impact assessments. Fully autonomous AI-driven analytics are not applicable across all industries but are highly effective in specific domains such as autonomous driving, robotics, and space exploration.

At this stage, leaders place greater trust in analytics to guide decisions, with human judgment shifting toward approval, prioritization, and governance of AI-recommended actions.

Organizations that commit to this analytics maturity journey realize return on investment through milestone-based achievements. While it is unrealistic to expect perfect accuracy at every stage, organizations that remain strategically flexible and adaptable will continue to progress—rather than repeatedly restarting after early successes.

Purpose of an Analytics Maturity Model

Analytics is not about the data. It's about the business outcomes.

—Jeanne Harris

An analytics maturity model provides organizations with a realistic and structured journey, aligning vision, mission, strategy, and roadmap. It enables leaders to measure progress, prioritize use cases, assess business impact, and plan investment requirements at every stage. This approach promotes transparency and accountability to stakeholders, in contrast to short-term, hype-driven initiatives that often deliver little beyond buzzwords or vendor-led experimentation.

Advancing along the analytics maturity journey requires sustained investment, and a common concern among leaders is whether today's analytics investments will become obsolete as technology evolves. Figure 6-2 addresses this concern by illustrating how a maturity model supports phased progress, where each stage is realized, tested, validated, and fully adopted before moving forward. In doing so, each step builds purposefully toward the future state, reflecting deliberate evolution rather than random experimentation.

Figure 6-2. *Conversation between two leaders on phased progress in the analytics journey*

A well-designed analytics maturity model instils confidence among stakeholders, demonstrates clear value creation, strengthens competitive advantage, and aligns leadership around a shared vision. Most importantly, it helps organizations clearly distinguish what is working, what is not, and where to focus next.

Technology Stack Evolution

> *Every organization today is a technology company, whether they know it or not.*
>
> —Satya Nadella

The technology stack within an analytics ecosystem must be carefully selected and curated with the broader vision firmly in mind. As technology evolves rapidly, individual components should be user-friendly, easily integrable with other systems, well aligned with the overall ecosystem, cost-effective, mature, adaptable, and forward-looking in their capability to support emerging features and innovation.

Figure 6-3-1 illustrates the evolution of the analytics technology stack from low to high maturity. BI and reporting dashboards represent descriptive analytics and provide hindsight. Advanced analytics applies sophisticated computational techniques and data and AI models to generate deeper insights. At the highest level of maturity, AI in production—including AI agents, models, and enterprise use cases—enables foresight-driven decision-making.

BI tools are typically applied to structured data, where analysts perform manual analysis and rely on descriptive metrics. From a *build vs. buy* perspective, it is generally advisable to adopt established BI platforms through licensing, tailored to domain-specific business needs. However, challenges often arise at this stage: metrics may become inconsistent, dashboards may remain unused or outdated, and teams may independently select tools, leading to tool sprawl in the absence of a clear organizational vision.

This BI and reporting layer is therefore considered a foundational capability within the analytics ecosystem, with data analysts serving as the primary personas at this stage of maturity.

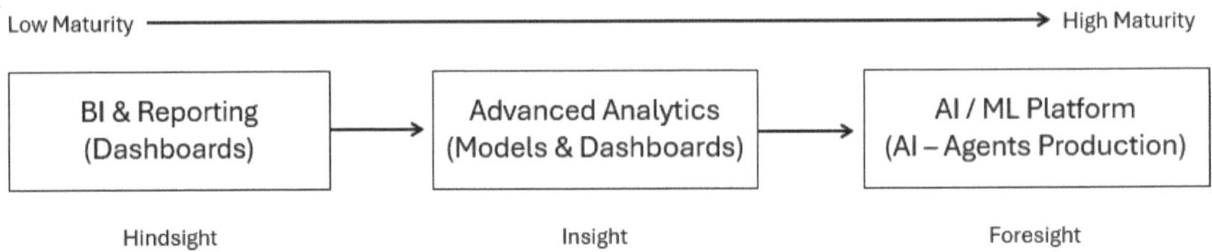

Figure 6-3-1. *Tech stack evolution map*

Advanced analytics is widely regarded as a transitional layer within the analytics maturity journey, where sophisticated statistical, optimization, and forecasting techniques are applied by data scientists and analysts. At this stage, organizations conduct scenario-based analysis; identify seasonality, trends, and patterns; and perform experimentation, feature engineering, and multi-source data combinations. Techniques such as causal and correlation analysis are commonly used to generate deeper insights.

From a *build vs. buy* perspective, most organizations adopt a hybrid approach at this stage—purchasing core platforms while developing business-specific models in-house. However, this layer introduces new risks, including model silos, limited monitoring and validation, and fragile data pipelines, all of which can increase operational complexity if not managed effectively.

Figure 6-3-2 depicts a conversation between two leaders emphasizing the importance of designing a flexible technology stack that can continuously evolve alongside business needs and technological advancements.

Figure 6-3-2. *Conversation between two leaders on continuous evolution of their tech stack*

AI and machine learning platforms represent the **scalable layer** in the technology evolution map, where capabilities such as MLOps, DataOps, LLMOps, and real-time decisioning are applied to operationalize AI at scale and extend successful use cases across domains. Product and operations teams are the primary users at this stage.

Through this phase, organizations enable automated decision-making, continuous model monitoring, ongoing retraining, and integrated development and deployment pipelines. Within the *build vs. buy* discussion, leaders must exercise caution. Selective use cases should be developed in-house to build core intellectual property, while platforms and infrastructure should typically be acquired to ensure scalability, reliability, and operational efficiency.

If platforms are not standardized, well integrated, or selected with the broader ecosystem in mind from the outset, organizations risk accumulating significant technical debt and operational complexity.

Technical leaders are therefore advised to maintain both a technical debt registry and a risk registry. While it is unrealistic to eliminate technical debt entirely, maintaining visibility into its nature, scale, and priority enables informed decision-making and timely remediation. Technical debt is typically minimal at the BI stage but can increase rapidly if advanced analytics is pursued without standardization. With the introduction of robust AI platforms and disciplined MLOps practices, debt can stabilize—although unmanaged experimentation that transitions into production can ultimately become enterprise-level debt if not governed effectively.

Business Value Realization: Measuring Analytics Maturity

> *You can't manage what you don't measure.*
>
> —Peter Drucker

The most effective way to measure analytics maturity is through the **business value generated by the analytics ecosystem**. A mature, well-designed, and well-managed analytics capability delivers value both directly and indirectly across the organization.

Value realization may manifest in multiple dimensions, including data quality, technology enablement, new product and service development, people and skills, processes, organizational culture, revenue growth, operational efficiency, and optimization.

Figure 6-4. *Conversation between two leaders on justification of analytics investment*

Ideally, business value realization should be tracked and measured through clear KPIs. While organizations adopt different measurement techniques, scorecards, and processes based on their structure and operating model, we propose a simple yet effective approach for tracking analytics maturity and its progression over time.

Maturity level is defined from 1 to 5; 1 is the lowest and 5 is the highest.

Level	Description
1 – Ad Hoc	Fragmented, manual, reactive
2 – Foundational	Basic reporting, emerging standards
3 – Scaled	Integrated analytics, repeatable processes
4 – Optimized	Predictive and prescriptive at scale
5 – Autonomous	AI-driven, self-learning systems

Overall assessment criteria, dimensions, and scorecards will vary by organization type. However, a generic framework may include the following (Table 6-1).

Table 6-1. *Example Analytics Maturity Model Scorecard*

Dimension	Score (1–5)	Evidence	Priority Actions
Strategy and alignment inclusion (Clarity of vision, business ownership, value focus)	☐		
Data platform maturity (Data quality, integration, accessibility)	☐		
Analytics and AI backlog (Analytics depth, use case maturity, AI use case backlog, skill)	☐		
Technology stack (Platform maturity, scalability, standardization)	☐		
Operating model and talent (Team structure, ownership, skill)	☐		
Governance and risk (Control, compliance, explainability)	☐		
Value and ROI (Transparency, measurement of impact and accountability)	☐		
Change management and culture (Adoption, data and AI literacy, trust)	☐		

An executive scorecard provides a consolidated view of the organization's current state, key considerations, areas of weakness, and priorities for next steps. This approach enables leadership teams to clearly understand strengths, gaps, and focus areas for improvement.

Organizations may also conduct a SWOT analysis to identify opportunities, risks, and strategic priorities in a structured and comprehensive manner.

Data Foundations Across Maturity Levels

There is no one-size-fits-all approach to digital transformation.

—Michael Porter

Organizations frequently struggle due to weak data foundations. Many make significant investments in analytics, BI, AI, and AI agents while operating on fragmented and poorly standardized data environments. As a result, they often realize only limited value from these investments.

Figure 6-5-1 illustrates this organizational challenge: despite having large volumes of data, decision-making remains difficult because data is inaccessible, inconsistent, poorly integrated, or lacking in quality. True value from data is unlocked through quality, standardization, integration, connectivity, and trust.

Figure 6-5-1. *Conversation between two leaders on data integration and data quality*

Data often sits idle within data lakes or remains trapped in isolated business silos, leading different teams to derive conflicting numbers and insights. Figure 6-5-2 illustrates this challenge, where siloed data results in inconsistent and untrustworthy metrics.

Figure 6-5-2. *Conversation between two leaders on data silos and their impact*

To establish a single, reliable view of business performance, organizations must prioritize data integration and standardization across the enterprise.

Chapter Summary

In God we trust. All others must bring data.

—W. Edwards Deming

To design, develop, and realize maximum value, organizations must focus on building a robust advanced analytics ecosystem. This requires establishing a clear and shared vision for the analytics roadmap, assessing current maturity, and tracking progress regularly through a phased and iterative approach.

In this chapter, we have explored the different stages of analytics maturity through both diagrams and detailed explanations. We have examined why a maturity model is essential, how organizations can navigate technological evolution while progressing toward a unified strategic goal, and why business value realization is the most effective measure of analytics maturity. We also outlined a simple and practical approach to tracking that value.

Finally, we emphasized the critical importance of strong data foundations across all maturity levels. Many organizations continue to treat data, analytics, and AI as side projects, only to lose competitive advantage over time as competitors embed these capabilities at the core of their strategy. Figure 6-6 illustrates a similar scenario, where leaders recognize that while the journey may have been delayed, it is ultimately better to begin than not to act at all.

Figure 6-6. *Conversation between leaders on missed data and AI opportunities*

CHAPTER 7

Data Storytelling and Democratizing Analytics Within an Organization

> *Data-driven organizations are three times more likely to report significant improvement in decision-making.*
>
> —Thomas H. Davenport

Data democratization, democratized analytics, and data storytelling are deeply interconnected and together play a critical role in creating a data flywheel within an organization. When data, analytics, AI, and new products and services reinforce one another through this flywheel, they form a data-driven engine that drives efficiency, increases revenue, unlocks new opportunities, enhances employee productivity, and improves customer satisfaction.

Data and analytics democratization reduce over-reliance on specialized teams by enabling employees across the organization to participate in governance, compliance, and enterprise-wide security processes. Supported by data literacy programs, training, and workshops, employees are empowered to discover their own insights, build their own reports, and resolve data issues independently.

This empowerment accelerates decision-making, fosters innovation, and supports sustainable organizational growth. Figure 7-1 illustrates a similar scenario, demonstrating how data democratization enables employees to unlock their full potential.

R. Yasir and K. Shaikh, *Driving Business Transformation with Modern Data and AI Strategies*,
https://doi.org/10.1007/979-8-8688-2625-2_7

Figure 7-1. Comical representation on the benefits of data democratization

In this chapter on data storytelling and democratized analytics, we will explore the following topics and subtopics to highlight the various perspectives, practical examples, team structures, and techniques that underpin effective adoption across the organization:

- Why Data Storytelling Matters for Leaders
- From Data to Narrative: The Anatomy of a Data Story
- Translating Analytics for Nontechnical Audiences
- Visual Storytelling: Designing for Insight, Not Decoration
- The Role of AI in Data Storytelling: Actionable Insights
- Common Failure Modes and How to Avoid Them
- Analytics Team Operating Model

Why Data Storytelling Matters for Leaders

> *Without big data analytics, companies are blind and deaf, wandering out onto the web like deer on a freeway.*
>
> —Geoffrey Moore

We often encounter two very different types of presentations. In the first, presenters rely heavily on technical charts, bar graphs, numbers, and colors, narrating them sequentially without sufficient context. During such sessions, it is common to hear colleagues remark, *"I'm lost," "What does this chart mean?" or "What is the actual point?"* The audience struggles to understand the underlying message or the intent behind the data.

In contrast, effective presenters provide context and narrative. They explain the background, justify why specific numbers and visuals matter, and clearly articulate how the data supports a hypothesis, leads to conclusions, and informs specific actions. In these sessions, the same colleagues often express clarity, understanding, and alignment with the presenter's perspective.

The difference between these two scenarios is **data storytelling capability**. Within an enterprise context, this capability is critical for leaders. It reflects whether a leader is clear on the message they wish to convey and whether they can tailor that message appropriately for different audiences—with the right level of detail and emphasis. Strong data storytelling aligns stakeholders around a single hypothesis, which is either validated or challenged through evidence presented in a clear and structured narrative.

Figure 7-1-1 illustrates these contrasting scenarios, highlighting the clear distinction between a confusing, ambiguous presentation and one that is clear, accessible, and effective in democratizing information for the audience.

Figure 7-1-1. *Comical representation on data storytelling*

- Effective data storytelling, supported by the right charts and visuals, shifts the focus from merely displaying dashboards to explaining scenarios with relevant data—ultimately enabling decisions where dashboards alone may fall short.
- Storytelling accelerates alignment, builds trust, and provides clarity on next steps.
- Data storytelling serves as the bridge between analytics and action. It translates complex insights into clear narratives that highlight risk, context, and opportunity for the business. Without a compelling narrative, even the most sophisticated analytics can remain abstract, unengaging, and ultimately ignored.
- The human brain processes stories far more effectively than raw data alone. Stories activate emotional and memory centers, enabling people to relate insights to real-world scenarios, whereas statistics often drive only short-term reasoning.

- Stories explain *why* an audience should care about a particular chart or trend; charts alone only indicate whether a trend exists.
- In data storytelling, less is often more. Leaders can act decisively when the narrative is clear, whereas excessive charts without context frequently result in indecision.
- Stories can be framed around customer journey impact, revenue leakage, cause-and-effect relationships, campaign performance, or clear, actionable recommendations.

Figure 7-1-2 illustrates a discussion between two leaders exploring why some meetings conclude with decisions, while others end with requests for further analysis. The difference lies in the presence of strong narratives—where effective storytelling significantly reduces decision latency and accelerates business outcomes.

Figure 7-1-2. *Conversation between two leaders on data storytelling importance*

From Data to Narrative: The Anatomy of a Data Story

The goal is to turn data into information, and information into insight.

—Carly Fiorina

Data storytelling is fundamentally a **decision narrative** built around data. It is not intended to be a purely technical presentation of charts, graphs, or additional analysis tasks. Its primary purpose is to guide leaders from evidence to action—with clarity, confidence, appropriate speed, an understanding of limitations, and well-defined options.

- The anatomy of a strong data story begins with **business context**: the problem or opportunity, why it matters now, and how it aligns with existing strategy. Without context, data lacks urgency and relevance.
- Effective data stories present **clear options for next steps**—whether to invest, pause, accelerate, revise, or restart. They explicitly surface limitations, trade-offs, and confidence levels, highlighting both opportunities and risks.
- Data should be used to inform decision options through insights. Not all data needs to be shown; focus should remain on the most relevant insights and implications, rather than underlying mechanisms.
- Often, one or two well-chosen visuals are sufficient to build confidence and reinforce evidence. Supporting detail can be provided in appendices for audiences seeking deeper analysis.
- A compelling data story follows a clear structure: **Problem ➤ Tension ➤ Resolution**. What is changing or uncertain? What options exist and with what consequences? What decision or action is recommended?
- Dashboards present information: data stories enable decisions. Strong storytelling demonstrates leadership credibility by connecting insights to implications and actions.

Figure 7-2 illustrates the anatomy of effective data storytelling, where questions, insights, implications, and actions take precedence over raw data presentation.

Figure 7-2. *Conversation between two leaders on anatomy of data storytelling*

Translating Analytics for Nontechnical Audiences

Effective communication of data is as important as the analysis itself.

—Stephen Few

One of the defining qualities of an effective data and AI leader is the ability to communicate complex ideas in simple, accessible terms to nontechnical audiences. This capability distinguishes a good leader from a truly great one. Exceptional leaders focus on the problem, context, narrative, options, and decisions—rather than technical jargon and charts.

- Nontechnical audiences and executives seek direction. Strong data, analytics, and AI leadership centers storytelling on strategic implications, risks, trade-offs, and outcomes. This enables executives to make clear decisions, managers to act with confidence, and frontline teams to connect data to daily operations.

- The role of a data leader is not merely to simplify information, but to translate it with the right context and narrative. Technical terminology—such as model names, algorithms, or metrics—should be avoided in executive discussions. Instead, analytics should be expressed in business terms, highlighting impact in time, cost, risk, and customer outcomes. If an insight cannot be explained in plain language, it is not yet ready for leadership decision-making.
- The use of analogies, benchmarks, and real-world examples is a best practice, as insight without implication is merely noise.
- Executive leaders operate under significant time pressure and cognitive load. Data stories must therefore be concise, outcome-oriented, and decisive—with limited visuals, clear conclusions, defined next steps, and explicit decision points. Lengthy buildups and excessive charts dilute focus and impede action.
- The most effective data stories are not those showcasing technical sophistication, but those that enable leaders to make faster, more confident decisions.

Figure 7-3 illustrates why leaders do not trust what they do not understand and how clear translation of data into business language builds confidence and drives action within an organizational context.

Figure 7-3. *Conversation between two leaders on importance of descriptive analytics*

Visual Storytelling: Designing for Insight, Not Decoration

> *The greatest value of a picture is when it forces us to notice what we never expected to see.*
>
> —John Tukey

Dashboards and reports are often overloaded with charts, colors, and metrics that are not tied to clear business objectives. When too many metrics compete for attention, users experience information fatigue and lose focus. The purpose of a dashboard or report is not decoration; it is to deliver **maximum insight with minimum effort**.

Effective dashboard and visual design must be driven by clear requirements and validated through user testing. Visuals should clarify business issues, not introduce confusion. Organizations must move away from the assumption that *more is better*—clarity, not quantity, drives decision-making.

Visuals should be designed to highlight key changes, enable meaningful comparisons, and support diagnostic insight, including cause-and-effect relationships. Accessibility, inclusivity, and cognitive load must also be considered to ensure insights are usable by all audiences.

Leaders should be particularly mindful of common visualization pitfalls:

- Too many charts do not equate to more insight; they dilute focus.
- Excessive color usage and unnecessary animations distract from the message.
- Inconsistent scales can mislead interpretation.
- Metrics should always be presented alongside targets, benchmarks, thresholds, and timeframes to avoid false narratives.
- Cluttered dashboards hinder executive decision-making rather than support it.

Figure 7-4 illustrates the importance of highlighting key signals while deliberately muting distractions during visual report presentations.

Figure 7-4. *Conversation between two leaders on importance of focusing on what matters*

The Role of AI in Data Storytelling: Actionable Insights

> *Artificial intelligence augments human decision-making; it doesn't replace it.*
>
> —Andrew Ng

Advanced analytics and AI have ushered in a new era of data storytelling, particularly with the emergence of GPT-based products. Users can now interact conversationally with their data—identifying trends, uncovering issues, and surfacing recommended actions and next steps. Generative AI is enabling augmented analytics and automated insight generation for both technical and nontechnical users alike. As a result, reliance on traditional dashboards is declining, while natural language interfaces are becoming the preferred mode of analysis.

Gartner predicts that by 2028, "60% of existing dashboards will be supplanted by automated, AI-driven narratives and dynamic data stories rather than manual charts" [1], [2].

Natural language interfaces, which allow users to ask questions in plain English, have significantly empowered customers and business users. This shift reduces dependence on technical expertise and complex analytical tooling, enabling greater self-service and faster decision-making. However, this increased flexibility also introduces new risks, including hallucinations, bias, and oversimplification. For critical decisions, it remains essential to keep human experts in the loop to provide validation, context, and judgment.

Figure 7-5 illustrates a leadership perspective that captures this balance clearly: AI is not replacing analysis—it is amplifying it. Humans continue to frame the narrative, while AI strengthens the evidence, efficiency, and quality of insights.

Figure 7-5. *Conversation between two leaders on AI replacing analysts or not*

Common Failure Modes and How to Avoid Them

> *In theory, there is no difference between theory and practice. In practice, there is.*
>
> —Yogi Berra

It is common to see analytics teams develop dashboards that deliver little value and gradually fall into disuse. Equally, excessive democratization without appropriate guardrails can erode trust and expose organizations to regulatory, privacy, and data protection risks. In this section, we examine common failure modes and outline how they can be avoided.

- Data and technical charts are often presented without driving decisions. Effective analytics must follow a clear narrative structure: **Problem ➤ Tension ➤ Resolution**.

- Leaders are frequently overwhelmed with technical detail, which creates noise rather than insight. Each story should focus on a limited number of insights and center on the decision required.
- Data without context, strategic intent, or implications is easily ignored. Insights must be connected to time, cost, risk, and customer impact to remain relevant.
- Ambiguous structures and unclear roles within analytics teams create friction between business and IT, resulting in slow delivery and misaligned accountability. Clear ownership is essential: the business should own value and prioritization, while IT should own platforms, standards, and enablement.
- Fully centralized analytics teams often become bottlenecks, disconnected from business execution. While this model may suit consultancy-style organizations, a hybrid operating model has proven most effective for mid-sized and large enterprises.
- Dashboards frequently suffer from poor maintenance: data is not refreshed, usage is not tracked, KPIs are not monitored, and datasets are not consistently validated for quality.
- Visual overload—too many charts on a single screen—leaves leaders unsure where to focus. Dashboards should be persona-driven; one dashboard cannot serve all audiences effectively.
- Federated democratization without governance creates chaos. Strong governance, standardization, training, and change management must accompany any democratization effort.
- Many AI and analytics initiatives fail not due to technical shortcomings, but because of weak strategy and insufficient planning. Throughout this book, we have highlighted best practices to address these challenges. Figure 7-6 illustrates one such example, where strategic gaps—rather than technical limitations—led to failure.

Figure 7-6. *Conversation between two leaders on technical and strategic initiative issues*

Analytics Team Operating Model

> *The best analytics teams don't just analyze data—they change decisions.*
>
> —Tom Davenport

Those with experience in the data and analytics domain will recognize two recurring debates within most organizations: the optimal analytics team structure or operating model and the question of ownership—should analytics sit with the business or IT? Organizations often adopt different approaches based on their size, resources, skills, and evolving business demands.

In practice, three primary analytics operating models are commonly observed:

- **Centralized**
- **Federated**
- **Hybrid**

Centralized Model

In a centralized model, all analytics capabilities—including data engineering, BI, data science, and AI—are consolidated within a single central IT team or a corporate analytics function. This approach is particularly effective in the early stages of analytics maturity, where business knowledge requirements are limited, analytics talent is scarce, and there is a strong need for control, security, and standardization. A centralized model enables strong governance, reduces duplication of effort, and establishes consistent standards. However, as demand grows, it often leads to slower time-to-insight, increased distance from business context, and operational bottlenecks. While this model works well for small to mid-sized organizations in the early phases of their analytics journey, it typically requires evolution toward more distributed approaches as maturity increases.

Figure 7-7-1. *Conversation between two leaders on an analytics operational model*

Federated Model

In a federated model, analytics teams are embedded within business units such as sales, marketing, finance, or other domain-specific functions. These teams own analytics delivery for their respective areas while sharing common data platforms, governance frameworks, and standards. This approach is well-suited to large organizations with high analytics maturity and strong business ownership of outcomes.

Federated teams benefit from deep domain expertise, faster delivery cycles, and closer proximity to execution. However, without effective coordination, this model can lead to data inconsistencies and duplicated effort. While federated structures offer speed and relevance, they require strong organizational discipline to maintain alignment.

Hybrid Model

The hybrid model is the most widely adopted approach among mid-sized and large enterprises. It combines a central hub responsible for platforms, governance, and standards with distributed analytics teams embedded within business units to deliver domain-specific analytics and AI use cases.

This model supports scalable analytics and AI adoption while balancing autonomy with alignment. It delivers the advantages of enterprise consistency and governance alongside business agility and execution speed. However, if not clearly defined, roles and responsibilities may become ambiguous, leading to decision friction and organizational politics.

Figures 7-7-1 and 7-7-2 illustrate the hybrid operating model in practice, highlighting the importance of balance: a central hub owns platforms, governance, and policies, while federated execution teams bring domain expertise and remain close to business execution.

Figure 7-7-2. *Conversation between two leaders on analytics and platform ownership model*

Chapter Summary

> *Big data and AI are meaningless without human context and judgment.*
>
> —Fei-Fei Li

Data analytics, data storytelling, and AI must be embedded into the day-to-day operations of the business. In this chapter, we have focused on why data storytelling is essential and how data and AI leaders can apply best practices throughout the storytelling process. We have explored how analytics can be effectively translated for nontechnical audiences and how recent advances in AI tools and use cases are transforming this space.

We also examined common failure modes, how to avoid them, and the analytics operating models that enable maximum impact. As illustrated by the leadership discussion in Figure 7-8, true organizational maturity is achieved when analytics is fully integrated into everyday business activities—not treated as a standalone or specialized function.

Figure 7-8. *Two leaders discussing the sign of analytics embedded within the decision-making process*

References

[1] Predicts 2025: AI-Powered Analytics Will Revolutionize Decision Making, published on February 26, 2025, by Gartner, https://www.gartner.com/en/documents/6212687

[2] How AI killed the dashboard, published on August 4, 2025, Zive Content Team, https://www.zive.com/en/blog/how-ai-killed-the-dashboard

PART III

AI in Action

CHAPTER 8

Traditional Machine Learning (Narrow AI)

> *Machine learning is the science of getting computers to act without being explicitly programmed.*
>
> —Arthur Samuel

For enterprise leaders embarking on their AI journey, it is essential to understand the key dimensions of AI development—including types of AI problems, traditional (narrow) vs. generative (foundational) models, and the associated implications for risk, cost, success rates, governance, and data requirements. In Part 3 of this book, we will cover three key topics, traditional machine learning, generative AI, and responsible AI for both traditional and generative AI use cases.

At a strategic level, AI can be broadly categorized into two groups: traditional (narrow) AI and generative (foundational) AI. Traditional or narrow AI models are typically designed to solve a specific, well-defined problem and are trained on task-specific datasets.

Designed to perform a specific task at a time, traditional (narrow) AI models are trained on a specific dataset to solve a clearly defined problem. As illustrated in the upper section of Figure 8-1, common examples include prediction models, forecasting, and document intelligence—where one model is built on one dataset to deliver one narrowly scoped outcome. These models typically offer limited reusability but are comparatively easier to develop, more secure, and simpler to govern.

R. Yasir and K. Shaikh, *Driving Business Transformation with Modern Data and AI Strategies*,
https://doi.org/10.1007/979-8-8688-2625-2_8

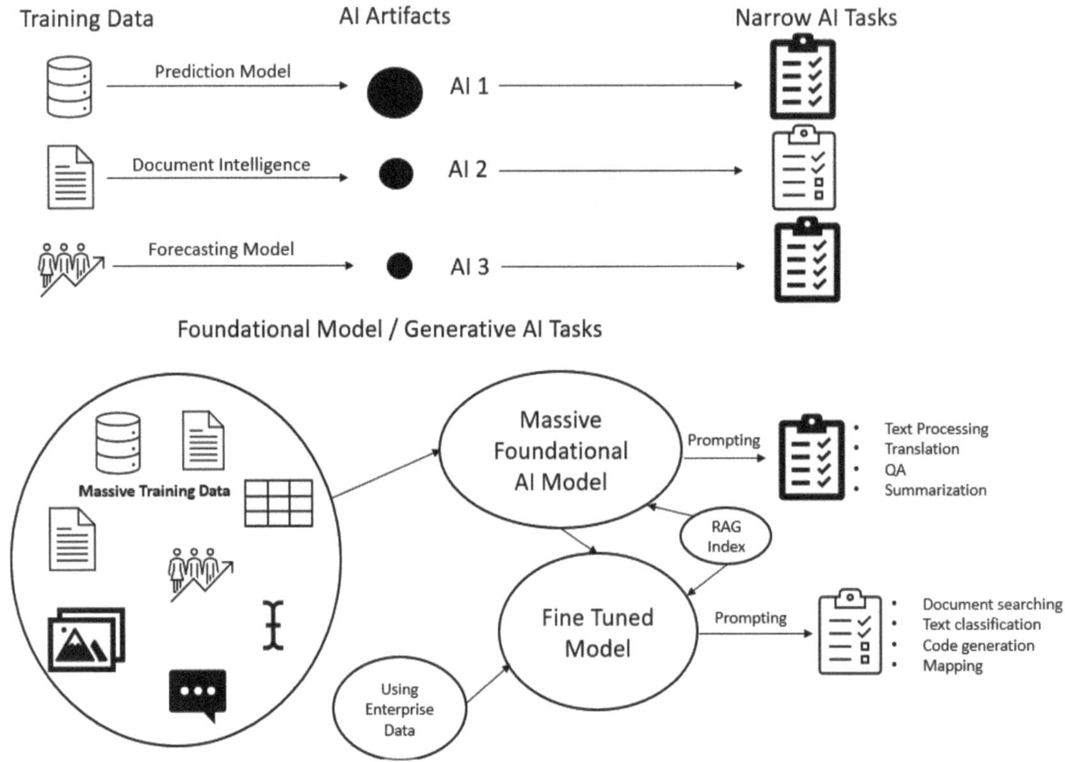

Figure 8-1. *Traditional and generative AI workflow examples*

By contrast, generative AI models are trained on much broader and more diverse datasets. They can support a wide range of general-purpose use cases—such as text processing, translation, and summarization—often through basic prompting. These models can perform multiple tasks and can also be fine-tuned using an organization's proprietary data. The lower section of Figure 8-1 illustrates the typical workflow for generative AI use cases.

This chapter focuses primarily on traditional (narrow) AI use cases. The following chapter provides an overview of generative (foundational) AI, including key use cases and implementation considerations.

Traditional AI model development can be understood across four key dimensions:

- Learning type (e.g., supervised and unsupervised learning)
- Model architecture (e.g., RNNs, CNNs, transformers, and linear or tree-based algorithms)

- AI problem type (e.g., classification, regression, anomaly detection)
- Data modality (e.g., tabular data, text, images, and video)

Given that this book is written for data and AI leaders, the focus will be on learning types, AI problem types, and data modalities. Model architecture requires more specialized, technical expertise and therefore sits outside the scope of this book.

Figure 8-2. *Leaders are discussing which AI models are usually safer: narrow or broader.*

This chapter explores the following subtopics in detail, focusing on the key dimensions of traditional (narrow) AI model (Figure 8-2 leaders discussing on Narrow AI model usage) development:

- AI by Learning Paradigm
- Data Modality for AI Use Cases
- AI Problem Type Overview with Data Modality Matrix
- Considerations for Data and AI Leaders

AI by Learning Paradigm

The goal of unsupervised learning is to discover hidden structure in data.

—Yann LeCun

AI systems can be broadly classified into four categories based on their learning paradigm. For data and AI leaders, understanding the learning approach behind an AI solution is essential to making informed decisions about use case suitability, strategic fit, and roadmap prioritization. The following learning types are explained from a leadership perspective, with a focus on strategy, delivery, and business impact.

Supervised Learning

Supervised learning is the most established and widely adopted AI approach and should form the backbone of most enterprise data and AI strategies. In this paradigm, models are trained on human-labeled data, where the correct outcome is already known and provided during training.

Common enterprise use cases include insurance premium calculation, medical screening and diagnostics, and demand forecasting based on historical sales data.

Supervised learning is well-suited to answering questions such as

- Will this customer churn, and with what probability?
- Is this transaction fraudulent?
- What price should we charge based on historical performance?

These models typically deliver high accuracy, are easier to validate and explain, and are therefore well-suited to regulated industries such as banking, insurance, and healthcare. The primary limitation is the need for large volumes of high-quality labeled data, which can be time-consuming and costly to produce.

Unsupervised Learning

Unsupervised learning is a powerful approach for discovering insights and patterns in data, but it is primarily designed to inform human decision-making rather than act autonomously. Unlike supervised learning, it operates on unlabeled data and identifies patterns without predefined outcomes.

Common problem types include clustering and anomaly detection. Real-world applications include fraud pattern discovery, network interruption analysis, market analysis, and customer segmentation.

Unsupervised learning helps address questions such as

- Which behaviors appear unusual or anomalous?
- Can we group customers based on purchasing patterns?
- What new or unexpected patterns are emerging in our data?

These models can be more difficult to validate and interpret, and there is a higher risk of misinterpretation without sufficient domain context and expertise.

Semi-supervised Learning

Semi-supervised learning offers a balanced approach when data volumes are large but labeling capacity is limited. It combines a small amount of labeled data with a much larger pool of unlabeled data, using the labeled examples to guide learning across the broader dataset.

Typical use cases include document classification, speech recognition with limited training samples, autonomous driving scenarios, and medical imaging where labeled scans are scarce.

While more complex to design, validate, and govern, semi-supervised learning significantly reduces labeling costs, scales more effectively in real-world environments, and can adapt across varied scenarios.

From a leadership perspective, it helps answer questions such as

- How can we scale AI with limited labeled data?
- Can we improve model accuracy without fully annotating our datasets?

Reinforcement Learning

Reinforcement learning is a highly advanced approach suited to action-driven and decision optimization problems. It operates through a cycle of trial, reward, and feedback, learning optimal behavior over time within a defined environment.

This mirrors human learning—reinforcing behaviors that lead to positive outcomes and avoiding those that result in penalties. Common applications include robotics and automation, autonomous driving, and personalized recommendation systems.

Reinforcement learning addresses questions such as

- How can a system learn from experience?
- What action should be taken next to maximize long-term outcomes?

While it enables highly adaptive and self-improving systems, reinforcement learning is also complex, costly, and difficult to explain or govern. Its behavior can be unpredictable in production environments, making it higher risk for enterprise deployment.

Data Modality for AI Use Cases

> *Vision is the most powerful sense humans have and giving it to machines unlocks enormous potential.*
>
> —Fei-Fei Li

Data modality refers to the form in which information is represented and used to develop AI models. The choice of data modality has a direct impact on the type of AI system that can be built, as well as its complexity, cost, scalability, and governance requirements. Importantly, the same AI problem can often be addressed using different data modalities—each introducing distinct levels of risk, operational complexity, and delivery effort.

From a leadership perspective, data modalities can be grouped into four primary categories. The first is outlined below.

Structured and Tabular Data

- Represents numerical or categorical data organized into rows and columns, typically stored in databases, spreadsheets, or data warehouses.
- AI solutions built on structured data are generally the easiest to govern, lowest in cost, most explainable, and fastest to deploy into production.
- Common examples include financial transactions, telematics data stored in time-series or tabular formats, and customer master records.

- Typical use cases include customer churn analysis, revenue forecasting, insurance premium calculation, and risk-level prediction.

Figure 8-3. *Leaders are discussing NLP examples and how they generate value*

Text and Language Data

- Represents unstructured human language and conversational content.
- Common sources include emails, documents, chat transcripts, and social media posts, typically stored in files, databases, or document management systems.
- Text data captures human language, intent, sentiment, and contextual reasoning. As a result, it often requires natural language processing (NLP) and, increasingly, large language models (LLMs). These characteristics introduce higher risks, including hidden bias, explainability challenges, and hallucinations. Consequently, text-based AI systems demand robust governance, clear usage disclaimers, and strong responsible AI controls.

- Typical enterprise use cases include chatbots and copilots, document optical character recognition (OCR) and search, report summarization, and sentiment analysis. Figure 8-3 demonstrates NLP example use cases.

Figure 8-4. *Leaders are discussing computer vision–based AI use cases and their value*

Image and Video Data

- Represents visual, multidimensional data, including images and video, often referred to as visual perception data.
- Common sources include photographs, medical images and scans, CCTV footage, video streams, and short-form media, typically stored as image files, video files, or frame-based structures.
- AI solutions built on image and video data require specialized techniques such as convolutional neural networks and multi-modal AI models. These systems are costly to label, train, and deploy and

are computationally intensive. They also carry a higher risk profile, particularly in relation to ethical, legal, and privacy considerations, and are often subject to stricter regulatory scrutiny in production environments.

- Representative use cases include photo tagging, facial recognition, document scanning, autonomous driving, surveillance, quality inspection, and medical image analysis. Figure 8-4 demonstrates value generation through computer vision based AI.

Audio, Sensor, and Time-Series Data

- Represents audio signals and sensor-generated data captured over time. Raw telematics data typically falls within this category, although aggregated versions are often transformed and stored as structured data for downstream analysis.
- Common sources include IoT sensor streams, machine telemetry from vehicles and aircraft, voice recordings, and other continuous signal data.
- This data modality is characterized by very high volumes and significant noise. It requires specialized signal-processing techniques and scalable big data infrastructure. The associated risk profile is medium to high, with important considerations around privacy, consent, security, and data ownership.
- Typical use cases include predictive maintenance, machine performance monitoring, voice assistants and speech-to-text systems, health monitoring, and fuel efficiency analysis.

AI Problem Type Overview with Data Modality Matrix

Forecasting exists because the future is uncertain.

—Nate Silver

For data and AI leaders, it is essential to have a clear and practical understanding of where AI can realistically be applied and the requirements it entails. This grounding enables leaders to make credible decisions and remain closely connected to operational reality. Too often, well-intentioned but nontechnical leadership narratives around data and AI innovation can become unrealistic, creating confusion and misalignment across teams.

In this section, we therefore focus on real-world examples of traditional (narrow) AI problem types, supported by concrete use cases. The objective is to equip data and AI leaders with practical reference points, enabling them to recognize similar problem patterns and apply the appropriate AI approaches in future initiatives.

Figure 8-5. *Leaders are discussing common narrow AI problem types—"classification"*

- **Classification**
    - Assigns an item, event, or individual to a predefined category.
    - Addresses questions such as "Which category does this belong to?"
    - Typical use cases include fraud detection in banking transactions using tabular data, medical image classification for diagnostic support, and customer churn prediction based on usage and behavioral patterns. Figure 8-5 demonstrate examples of "Classification" problem types.

- **Regression**
    - Predicts a continuous numerical value.
    - Addresses questions such as "How much?" or "How many?"
    - Common use cases include insurance premium estimation based on driving behavior and claims history, real estate price prediction, and weather forecasting using historical data.
- **Forecasting**
    - Predicts future trends using time-series data.
    - Addresses questions such as "What is likely to happen over time?"
    - Representative use cases include supply chain demand forecasting from historical sales, energy consumption forecasting using weather and usage data, and financial cash flow or expense forecasting based on historical financials and macroeconomic indicators. Figure 8-6 demonstrate examples of "Forecasting" problem types and use cases.

***Figure 8-6.** Leaders are discussing common narrow AI problem types—"forecasting"*

- **Recommendation systems**
    - Provide personalized suggestions to users based on pattern detection and historical behavior.
    - Address questions such as "What should we recommend or do next?"
    - Typical use cases include product recommendations in ecommerce based on browsing and purchase history and content recommendations in media and streaming platforms, such as personalized home page recommendations driven by viewing behavior and engagement.
- **Clustering**
    - An unsupervised learning approach that groups data based on similarity and natural patterns.
    - Addresses questions such as "What natural groupings exist within the data?"
    - Common applications include customer segmentation for marketing, product grouping in ecommerce, user behavior clustering, image similarity grouping, and topic clustering in text data.
- **Anomaly detection**
    - Identifies unusual or unexpected patterns within data.
    - Addresses questions such as "What looks abnormal or out of place?"
    - Representative use cases include fraud detection, cybersecurity intrusion detection, manufacturing fault identification, and system monitoring with anomaly-based alerts.
- **Association mining**
    - Identifies relationships and co-occurrence patterns between variables.

- Addresses questions such as "What tends to occur together?"
- Typical use cases include retail market basket analysis, seasonal purchasing pattern identification, and opportunity discovery based on behavioral associations.

- **Optimization**
  - Determines the best possible outcomes under defined business objectives, constraints, and rules.
  - Addresses questions such as "What is the optimal way to allocate resources?"
  - Common applications include supply chain optimization, workforce scheduling, route optimization, and pricing optimization.
- **Prescriptive analytics**
  - Recommends actions and quantifies the expected impact of different decision options.
  - Addresses questions such as "What should we do next, and why?"
  - Use cases include decision guidance with probabilistic outcomes, operational recommendations across manufacturing scenarios, and investment prioritization.
- **Reinforcement learning**
  - Learns optimal actions through trial, reward, and feedback mechanisms over time.
  - Addresses questions such as "How should actions adapt based on experience?"
  - Representative use cases include dynamic pricing, personalized recommendations, robotics control systems, and autonomous AI agents.

- **Natural language understanding**
    - Interprets meaning, intent, and sentiment in human language.
    - Addresses questions such as "What is the user saying or asking?"
    - Typical applications include intent detection in chatbots, sentiment analysis of customer feedback, and voice command interpretation in conversational systems.
- **Information retrieval and search**
    - Identifies and retrieves the most relevant information from large data repositories.
    - Addresses questions such as "Where is the information we are looking for?"
    - Common use cases include enterprise knowledge search, document retrieval systems, and internal policy search platforms.
- **Object detection and recognition**
    - Identifies and classifies objects within images or video streams.
    - Addresses questions such as "What objects are present, and where?"
    - Representative use cases include facial recognition, optical character recognition (OCR), and automated quality inspection.
- **Image segmentation**
    - Identifies and separates object-level regions at the pixel level in images and video.
    - Addresses questions such as "Which parts of the image correspond to which objects?"
    - Typical use cases include medical image analysis, tumor boundary detection, and satellite imagery segmentation.

- **Causal inference**
    - Identifies cause-and-effect relationships rather than simple correlations.
    - Addresses questions such as "What caused this outcome?"
    - Common applications include marketing campaign impact analysis, pricing strategy evaluation, and interpretation of A/B testing results.
- **Simulation and scenario modeling**
    - Explores potential future outcomes under different assumptions and conditions.
    - Addresses questions such as "What could happen if circumstances change?"
    - Use cases include financial and mortgage stress testing, digital twin simulations, supply chain disruption modeling, and climate risk analysis.

Considerations for Data and AI Leaders

> *AI is the new electricity—it will transform every industry.*
>
> —Andrew Ng

In this chapter, we have reviewed the major types of AI, the key data modalities that underpin AI use cases, and the common AI problem types—supported by practical data and business examples. However, for data and AI leaders, understanding these concepts is only the starting point. There are several critical considerations that must be kept in mind to avoid failure and ensure sustainable value creation.

Traditional (Narrow AI) and generative AI use cases are explored in detail in this and the next chapter, respectively. Chapter 10 focuses on ethical, responsible, and trustworthy AI within the organization. It outlines key responsible AI principles, relevant laws and regulations, and ethical considerations applicable to both traditional and generative AI. The chapter also provides practical guidance on embedding responsible AI practices at scale, alongside a detailed, easy-to-maintain checklist for data and AI teams to operationalize these principles effectively.

Key Leadership Considerations in AI Development

- **Data readiness**

  Structured and tabular data typically requires less effort to develop AI models and often delivers faster ROI, with smoother integration into existing enterprise ecosystems. Text-based AI solutions require natural language processing capabilities, stronger governance, and more complex explainability. Image and video-based AI solutions are generally the most expensive and risky, due to high computational and training costs, as well as the need for specialist skills—unless the use case is narrow and can leverage pre-trained models.

- **Cost and complexity**

  Leaders must carefully assess cost implications across AI use cases. Chapter 5 provides a detailed view of both strategic investment and operational expenditure, covering labor and non-labor costs. As organizations progress from structured data to text and then to image and video-based AI, costs, infrastructure requirements, risk exposure, and regulatory scrutiny increase significantly.

- **Roadmap considerations**

  In a mature data and AI roadmap, leaders should prioritize structured data-based AI use cases, followed by text-based applications and then image and video-based solutions. As discussed in Chapter 12, the early stages of the roadmap are typically anchored in structured data. More advanced, predictive, and agentic AI capabilities—often involving complex text and image processing—can be introduced later. However, certain text-processing use cases may be implemented earlier as part of advanced analytics initiatives using pre-trained foundational models easily.

- **Complexity considerations**

  The same AI problem type can vary significantly in complexity depending on the underlying data modality. For example, classification models built on structured data are typically low risk and deliver faster ROI, whereas classification applied to image data is often high cost and high risk. Structured data-based models are generally easier to scale, while text and image/video models are more expensive and operationally challenging to scale.

Chapter Summary

> *Most real-world machine learning is about making better predictions on structured data.*
>
> —Pedro Domingos

While data and AI leaders are not typically required to develop AI models themselves, it is considered best practice to understand what sits "under the bonnet"—including how models work, what techniques are being used, and the associated safety risks and limitations. This level of understanding enables more informed oversight, stronger governance, and better strategic decision-making.

In this chapter, we have focused on traditional (narrow) AI models. Globally, the majority of AI systems currently in production fall into this category—designed to address a single, well-defined use case using a specific dataset. We examined three core dimensions of AI: data modality (the types of data used in AI development), learning paradigms (how models learn), and AI problem types, supported by real-world data and enterprise use cases.

We also highlighted a set of practical best practices that data and AI leaders should consider throughout their AI journey. The next chapter shifts focus to generative AI and foundational models, exploring their use cases, capabilities, and strategic implications for organizations.

CHAPTER 9

Foundational Model/ Generative AI

> *Generative AI doesn't replace creativity, it amplifies it. The real advantage belongs to those who learn how to collaborate with machines.*
>
> —Satya Nadella

The ISkillSetu boardroom feels unusually charged. The leadership team has gathered not to review revenue, costs, or expansion numbers but to explore a single question that has dominated industry headlines for over a year: *"What does generative AI mean for us?"*

Shailesh, the COO, opens with a note of both opportunity and caution. "Every partner we speak to is asking about GenAI. Some say it will reinvent education; others call it overhyped. But if we don't at least understand it, we risk being left behind."

Maryam, the principal solution architect, places a slide on the screen that shows examples from competitors: AI-powered tutors, automated content generation, real-time assessments, even synthetic trainers delivering classes in multiple languages. "The truth," she says, "is that GenAI isn't theoretical anymore. It is already changing how companies operate."

For ISkillSetu, the conversation is not about whether the technology is interesting but whether it is relevant, secure, and sustainable for their learners, institutions, and corporate clients. This leadership tension around opportunity vs. responsibility is reflected in Figure 9-0.

R. Yasir and K. Shaikh, *Driving Business Transformation with Modern Data and AI Strategies*,
https://doi.org/10.1007/979-8-8688-2625-2_9

Figure 9-0. *Conversation between teams on generative AI*

This chapter is designed with that same focus. While much has been written about large language models and AI breakthroughs, the goal here is to help business leaders and executives understand how to approach generative AI with a strategic, responsible, and ROI-driven mindset.

We will cover four critical areas:

- **An overview of generative AI use cases** that are enterprise-ready, especially in industries like e-learning
- **How to use GenAI efficiently**, balancing capability with cost and performance
- **Organizational considerations**, including governance, security, and cultural readiness

- **AI agents and agentic workflows**, which represent the next stage of enterprise AI adoption

By the end of this chapter, you as a leader should be able to see where generative AI makes sense for your organization, where caution is warranted, and how to lead adoption in a way that creates long-term value without exposing the enterprise to unnecessary risk.

As Shailesh reminds his team, *"Technology alone will not differentiate us. The way we apply it responsibly and strategically will."*

Overview of Generative AI Use Cases

> *Generative AI is not about machines thinking like humans, but about humans thinking bigger with machines.*
>
> —Andrew Ng

As the discussion around generative AI gathers momentum inside ISkillSetu, the leadership team makes a deliberate choice to ground the conversation in reality. Shailesh, the COO, is clear that enthusiasm alone cannot drive adoption. "Before we talk about platforms or models," he says, "we need to understand where this actually helps us operate better, serve learners more effectively, and grow responsibly."

Nilesh, the data evangelist, reframes the discussion by listing the challenges the organization already faces. Course creation cycles are slow and resource-intensive. Learner engagement varies widely across cohorts. Support teams are under constant pressure to respond to repetitive queries at scale. Corporate clients want richer insights, not just dashboards filled with numbers. These are not futuristic problems; they are present-day constraints.

Maryam then illustrates how generative AI can fit naturally into these gaps. She explains that one of the most immediate applications lies in content acceleration. Generative models can assist instructional designers by drafting lesson summaries, creating assessment questions, producing practice scenarios, and translating content into multiple languages. For ISkillSetu, this means faster go-to-market for new courses, especially in regions where localization has previously slowed expansion.

Learner engagement presents another opportunity. Rather than forcing every learner through a fixed pathway, generative AI can support adaptive experiences. By responding to learners behavior, pauses, incorrect answers, and repeated attempts, AI-powered systems can provide contextual hints, recommend supplementary material, or reframe explanations in simpler terms. This shift transforms learning from a static experience into a responsive one, directly addressing dropout rates.

Support and interaction are equally compelling use cases. Generative AI-powered conversational assistants can handle routine learner queries, such as course navigation, deadlines, or basic concept clarification, in natural language and at any hour. These assistants are not positioned as replacements for human support teams but as filters that reduce volume and improve response times. Similar patterns are emerging across enterprises, where HR teams use GenAI for employee queries, IT teams for service desk automation, and customer service teams for first-level support.

Another area of strong resonance is narrative-driven reporting. Employers and senior stakeholders often struggle to interpret raw analytics outputs. Generative AI can synthesize performance data into executive-ready summaries, explaining trends, highlighting risks, and suggesting areas for intervention. This capability elevates analytics from descriptive reporting to strategic storytelling, something corporate leaders value deeply.

Beyond customer-facing scenarios, ISkillSetu also explores internal productivity use cases. Teams begin using generative AI to assist with drafting documents, preparing marketing content, summarizing meetings, and supporting software development tasks. These use cases do not redefine the business overnight, but collectively they reduce friction and free employees to focus on higher-value work. Similar patterns are visible across industries, where GenAI is quietly improving day-to-day efficiency without radical organizational disruption.

What becomes clear to the leadership team is that generative AI use cases exist along a spectrum. Some deliver immediate operational efficiency, others enhance engagement and experience, and a smaller set enable long-term differentiation. Understanding this spectrum helps prevent unrealistic expectations while still encouraging ambition. Figure 9-1 illustrates how generative AI use cases span from quick operational gains to longer-term strategic differentiation.

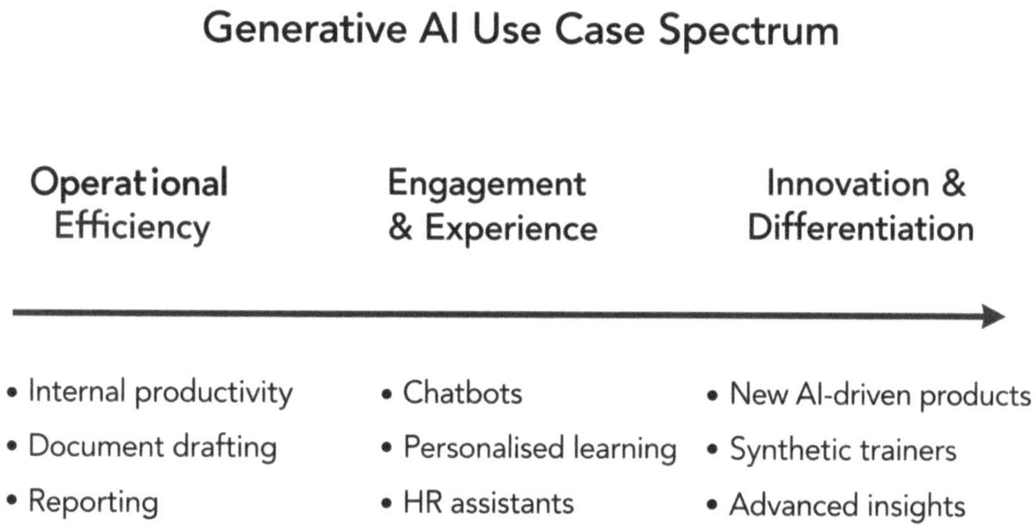

Generative AI Use Case Spectrum

Operational Efficiency	Engagement & Experience	Innovation & Differentiation
• Internal productivity	• Chatbots	• New AI-driven products
• Document drafting	• Personalised learning	• Synthetic trainers
• Reporting	• HR assistants	• Advanced insights

Figure 9-1. *Generative AI use case spectrum in enterprises*

As the conversation matures, the leadership recognizes another important truth: not all use cases should be pursued at the same time. Some are easy to implement and deliver quick returns, while others require deeper integration, stronger governance, and greater organizational readiness. To guide decision-making, Maryam introduces a simple prioritization framework that allows the board to evaluate opportunities systematically rather than emotionally. Table 9-1 outlines this prioritization framework, helping leaders compare use cases based on impact and implementation complexity.

Table 9-1. *Generative AI Use Case Prioritization*

Business Impact	Ease of Implementation	Representative Use Cases
High impact/easy	Pilot first; build confidence	Learner support chatbots, HR query assistants, marketing content drafts
High impact/complex	Strategic investments	Personalized learning journeys, AI tutors, customer-facing copilots
Low impact/easy	Controlled experimentation	Automated documentation, meeting summaries, internal productivity tools
Low impact/complex	Avoid or defer	Fully automated course design, autonomous decision-making systems

This matrix helps reframe generative AI as a portfolio of initiatives, each with different risk and reward profiles. Quick wins can be used to demonstrate value and build organizational trust, while more complex initiatives can be planned deliberately, with appropriate safeguards and investment. This prioritization logic is visualized in Figure 9-2, helping leaders balance impact, complexity, and risk.

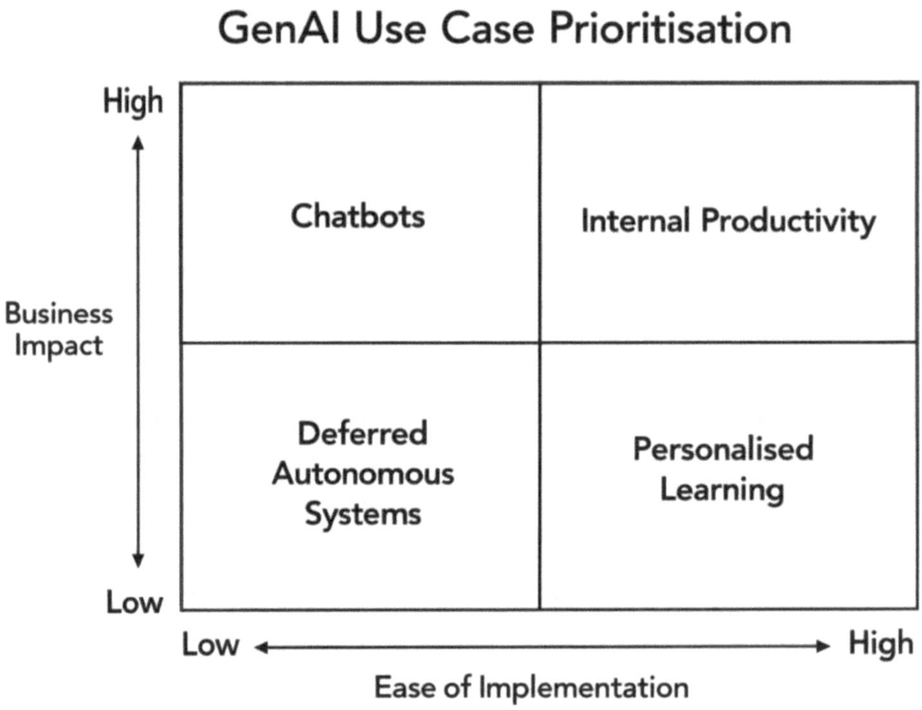

Figure 9-2. *GenAI use case prioritization matrix*

What ultimately resonates with ISkillSetu's leadership is the realization that generative AI is neither a silver bullet nor a passing trend. Its value depends entirely on how thoughtfully it is applied. Used selectively, it can remove friction, enhance experience, and open new possibilities. Used indiscriminately, it can add cost, risk, and distraction.

Leadership Reflection

At the close of the session, Shailesh summarizes the collective sentiment:

"Generative AI is not something we adopt because others are doing it. We adopt it where it clearly strengthens how we operate, how we serve learners, and how we differentiate ourselves. Everything else can wait."

Maryam adds a final note of caution and clarity:

"The organizations that win with GenAI will not be the ones that move fastest, but the ones that move with intent. Start with value, prove it, and scale responsibly."

How to Use Generative AI Efficiently

With generative AI, the question shifts from "Can this be done?" to "How responsibly should it be done?"

—Timnit Gebru

Once ISkillSetu's leadership aligns on *where* generative AI can add value, the conversation naturally shifts to *how* it should be used. Shailesh is direct: "I don't want scattered experiments running across teams. If we adopt GenAI, it has to be done efficiently, technically, financially, and organizationally."

Maryam agrees. She explains that inefficiency in generative AI adoption rarely comes from the models themselves. It comes from unclear usage patterns, poor architectural choices, and a lack of discipline around cost and governance. "The difference between a successful GenAI initiative and an expensive experiment," she notes, "is almost always the operating model."

For ISkillSetu, efficiency means three things. First, choosing the right consumption approach for each use case. Second, embedding GenAI into existing workflows rather than treating it as a standalone novelty. Third, ensuring that usage remains measurable, controlled, and aligned with business outcomes.

Choosing the Right Usage Pattern

Maryam outlines that most enterprise generative AI use cases fall into one of three adoption patterns. Understanding these patterns up front prevents over-engineering and unnecessary spend.

In some scenarios, organizations can rely on out-of-the-box foundation models accessed through APIs. These models are well-suited for generic productivity tasks such as summarization, drafting, translation, or brainstorming. At ISkillSetu, marketing teams use this approach to accelerate campaign drafts, while internal teams use it to summarize long documents. The appeal is speed and simplicity, no additional infrastructure or data preparation required.

In other scenarios, especially where accuracy and domain relevance matter, **Retrieval-Augmented Generation (RAG)** emerges as the preferred approach. Rather than training the model, ISkillSetu connects it to trusted internal content such as course materials, policies, and knowledge bases. This allows GenAI-powered assistants to generate responses grounded in verified data, significantly reducing the risk of incorrect or fabricated outputs. For learner support and employer-facing reporting, RAG provides the right balance between flexibility and control.

Fine-tuning represents the most specialized option. Maryam cautions that while fine-tuning can improve tone or domain familiarity, it should be reserved for cases where consistent behavior and language are critical. ISkillSetu considers fine-tuning only for advanced tutoring scenarios, where pedagogical style and instructional accuracy have to be tightly controlled. The leadership agrees that fine-tuning should be treated as a strategic investment, not a default choice. Figure 9-3 brings together these adoption approaches and clarifies when each is most appropriate.

Decision Framework: Matching Use Case to Approach

To make these choices repeatable, ISkillSetu documents a simple decision framework that leaders and architects can apply consistently. Table 9-2 translates this decision framework into practical guidance for matching GenAI use cases with the appropriate adoption approach.

***Table 9-2.** Selecting the Right GenAI Usage Approach*

Use Case Characteristic	Recommended Approach	Reasoning
Generic content, summaries, drafts	Out-of-the-box models	Fast to deploy, low cost, minimal risk
Answers must reflect internal knowledge	RAG	Ensures accuracy and traceability
Strong domain tone or behavior required	Fine-tuning	Controlled and consistent responses
High regulatory or reputational risk	RAG or restricted fine-tuning	Better governance and auditability

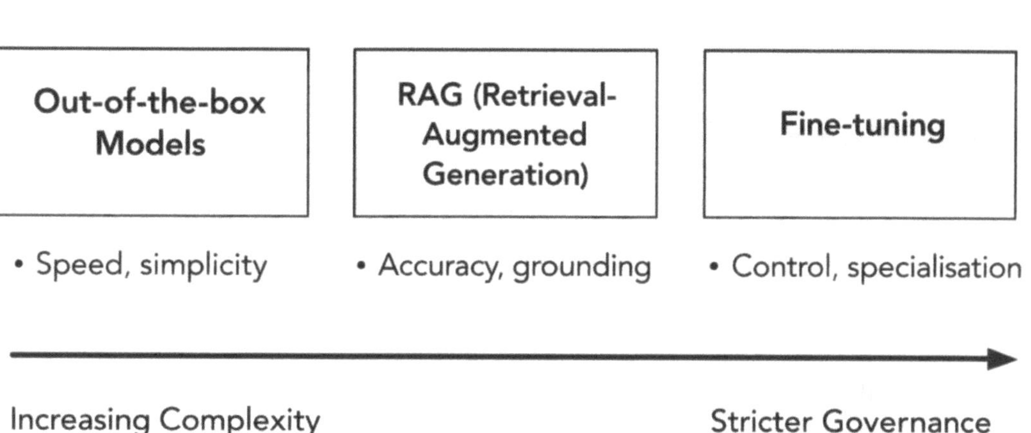

***Figure 9-3.** Efficient GenAI adoption approaches*

Embedding GenAI into Business Workflows

Efficiency is not only about architecture; it is about adoption. Nilesh observes that GenAI delivers the most value when it is embedded into everyday tools rather than introduced as a separate platform. At ISkillSetu, learners interact with AI tutors inside the learning portal, not through an external chatbot interface. Managers receive AI-generated summaries directly within dashboards they already use.

This integration reduces friction and improves adoption. Employees do not need to "learn GenAI"; they simply experience better workflows. The leadership recognizes that efficiency improves when technology fades into the background and outcomes move to the foreground.

Cost and Usage Discipline

Another dimension of efficiency is cost. Shailesh insists that GenAI usage be treated like any other enterprise resource. Consumption is monitored, usage patterns are reviewed monthly, and each initiative has a clearly defined owner. Experiments without measurable outcomes are stopped early.

This discipline prevents cost surprises and ensures that GenAI investments are continuously justified against business impact. Efficiency, in this sense, becomes a leadership habit rather than a technical optimization.

Leadership Reflection

As the session concludes, Shailesh summarize the approach succinctly:

> *"Using generative AI efficiently is not about choosing the smartest model. It's about choosing the simplest approach that delivers the outcome we need and stopping when it doesn't."*

Maryam adds a final architectural perspective:

> *"RAG, fine-tuning, and foundation models are tools, not strategies. The strategy comes from knowing when to use each and when not to."*

Things to Consider for Your Organization

> *The power of generative AI lies not in automation alone, but in its ability to unlock new ways of solving problems.*
>
> —Fei-Fei Li

By the time ISkillSetu's leadership reaches this stage of the discussion, the tone in the room has shifted. The excitement around generative AI has been tempered by a more sobering realization: adopting GenAI is not merely a technical upgrade but an organizational decision with long-term implications.

Shailesh articulates the concern clearly. "We now understand the use cases and the efficiency models. What worries me is not *whether* we can use GenAI, but *whether we are ready to use it responsibly*."

This question sits at the heart of enterprise GenAI adoption. Unlike traditional analytics tools, generative AI operates in probabilistic ways, produces natural language outputs that feel authoritative, and interacts directly with customers, employees, and partners. As a result, the margin for error is smaller, and the consequences of poor decisions are amplified.

Organizational Readiness and Ownership

One of the first considerations ISkillSetu addresses is ownership. Generative AI initiatives often fail when responsibility is fragmented, when experimentation is left entirely to innovation teams, while risk and accountability sit elsewhere. The leadership agrees that every GenAI use case must have a clearly defined business owner, not just a technical sponsor.

This owner is responsible for defining success metrics, approving scope, and making go/no-go decisions. By anchoring GenAI initiatives to accountable leaders, ISkillSetu avoids the trap of uncontrolled pilots that consume resources without delivering outcomes. The principle is simple: if a GenAI capability affects learners, employees, or clients, a senior leader has to stand behind it.

Data, Trust, and Context

Another major consideration is data. Maryam emphasizes that generative AI is only as reliable as the information it draws upon. Even the most advanced models can produce misleading or incorrect outputs when operating without proper context. This makes it essential for ISkillSetu to ensure that internal data sources are well governed, current, and clearly defined before being connected to AI systems.

The leadership recognizes that this is not a new problem but an amplification of existing data challenges. Poor-quality data that might previously have caused a flawed dashboard could now result in a confident but incorrect response delivered directly to a learner or client. This elevates the importance of trust, traceability, and controlled access to enterprise knowledge.

Risk, Reputation, and Regulation

Generative AI also forces ISkillSetu to reassess its risk posture. While earlier chapters addressed compliance and security in depth, the leadership acknowledges that GenAI introduces new forms of exposure. Outputs can unintentionally reveal sensitive information, reflect bias, or be misinterpreted as official guidance.

Rather than treating this as a reason to delay adoption, the organization chooses to formalize risk review as part of every GenAI initiative. This includes defining acceptable use boundaries, restricting certain classes of data from being accessed by models, and ensuring that AI-generated outputs are clearly positioned as assistive rather than authoritative where appropriate.

Shailesh summarizes this approach succinctly: "We don't eliminate risk by avoiding GenAI. We manage risk by designing for it."

People, Skills, and Culture

Beyond systems and controls, the leadership team recognizes a more subtle challenge: people. Generative AI changes how work is done, how decisions are supported, and how value is created. Without careful communication, employees could perceive AI as a threat rather than a tool.

ISkillSetu addresses this by positioning GenAI as an augmentation layer. Training sessions focus on how AI can reduce repetitive work and improve decision quality, not replace roles. Managers are encouraged to experiment with GenAI in transparent ways, sharing both successes and failures openly. This helps normalize learning and prevents unrealistic expectations from forming.

The cultural message is deliberate: GenAI is not about automation for its own sake, but about enabling people to work more effectively in a data-rich environment.

Long-Term Sustainability

Finally, the leadership discusses sustainability. Generative AI initiatives often begin with enthusiasm but lose momentum when costs rise or novelty fades. ISkillSetu decides early that GenAI usage will be reviewed regularly, with underperforming initiatives paused or retired.

This discipline ensures that generative AI remains aligned with business priorities rather than becoming an unchecked experiment. Sustainability, in this sense, is not about limiting ambition but about maintaining focus. Figure 9-4 summarizes the organizational dimensions leaders must balance to adopt generative AI responsibly.

Figure 9-4. *Organizational considerations for generative AI adoption*

Leadership Reflection

As the discussion draws to a close, Shailesh reflects on what has changed in his own thinking:

> *"Generative AI forces us to be more intentional as leaders. It doesn't forgive vague ownership or unclear boundaries. If we lead it well, it becomes a strength. If we don't, it exposes every weakness we already had."*

Maryam adds a final note of realism:

> *"The organizations that succeed with GenAI will not be the ones with the most models, but the ones with the clearest discipline around how those models are used."*

AI Agents and Agentic AI Workflows

> *AI agents represent a new layer of digital labor, software that doesn't just respond, but takes initiative.*
>
> —Satya Nadella

By the time ISkillSetu's leadership reaches this part of the conversation, generative AI is no longer viewed simply as a tool that responds to prompts. The discussion has evolved toward a more powerful, and more complex, idea: **AI systems that can act**, not just answer.

Vijay, the tech lead, frames it clearly. "So far, we've talked about GenAI as something that waits for instructions. But the industry is moving toward systems that can plan, decide, and execute steps on their own. That's what people are calling AI agents."

Maryam nods, adding an important clarification. "And it's critical we understand this distinction properly. An AI agent is not magic. It's a structured workflow where models, tools, memory, and rules work together. Without discipline, agentic systems can introduce more risk than value."

From Assistive AI to Agentic AI

Traditional generative AI systems are largely reactive. They respond to a user prompt, generate an output, and stop. Agentic AI, by contrast, is goal-driven. An agent is given an objective and can autonomously decide which steps to take, which tools to call, and when to ask for human input.

At ISkillSetu, this shift is easiest to understand through practical examples. A conversational tutor that simply answers questions is assistive. An agentic tutor, however, could monitor a learner's progress, detect gaps in understanding, recommend specific modules, schedule follow-ups, and escalate concerns to human instructors when necessary. The difference lies not in intelligence alone, but in **orchestration**.

Core Components of an AI Agent

Maryam explains that enterprise-grade AI agents typically consist of a few key elements working in coordination. At the center sits a generative AI model responsible for reasoning and language. Surrounding it are tools, APIs, databases, search systems, and business applications that allow the agent to take action. Memory provides context, enabling the agent to retain state across interactions, while rules and guardrails constrain behavior to acceptable boundaries.

This architecture makes it clear that agentic systems are not standalone models. They are workflows, deliberately designed and governed, where autonomy increases gradually rather than all at once. Figure 9-5 illustrates this agentic workflow, highlighting how models, tools, memory, and guardrails operate together.

Agentic Workflows in Practice

ISkillSetu begins exploring agentic workflows cautiously. One early pilot focuses on learner onboarding. Instead of manually guiding users through course selection, an AI agent analyzes learner profiles, suggests relevant courses, generates a personalized learning plan, and follows up with reminders. Human intervention is triggered only when the learner appears disengaged or requests help.

Similar patterns are emerging in other industries. Enterprises are experimenting with agents that coordinate HR onboarding, manage IT incidents, assist financial reconciliations, or orchestrate marketing campaigns. In each case, the agent does not replace decision-makers; it handles coordination and execution, allowing humans to focus on judgment and strategy.

Control, Autonomy, and Trust

As the conversation deepens, Shailesh raises a concern shared by many executives. "How much autonomy is too much?"

This question goes to the heart of agentic AI adoption. Maryam emphasizes that autonomy must be earned, not assumed. Most organizations begin with human-in-the-loop models, where agents propose actions but require approval. Over time, as confidence grows and error rates decline, certain actions can become fully automated.

At ISkillSetu, the leadership agrees that no agent will operate without clear boundaries. Sensitive actions, such as modifying learner records, communicating externally, or making financial decisions, will always include checkpoints. Trust, they conclude, is built incrementally through design, monitoring, and accountability.

Strategic Implications for Leaders

Agentic AI introduces a new leadership challenge. Decisions are no longer limited to *whether* to adopt AI, but *how much autonomy to grant it*. This requires executives to think in terms of delegation, oversight, and escalation, concepts they already understand in human organizations.

The lesson for leaders is not to fear agentic systems, but to treat them as digital teammates. Like any team member, they need clear goals, defined authority, performance metrics, and supervision. Without these, agentic AI can quickly become unpredictable. With them, it can become a powerful force multiplier.

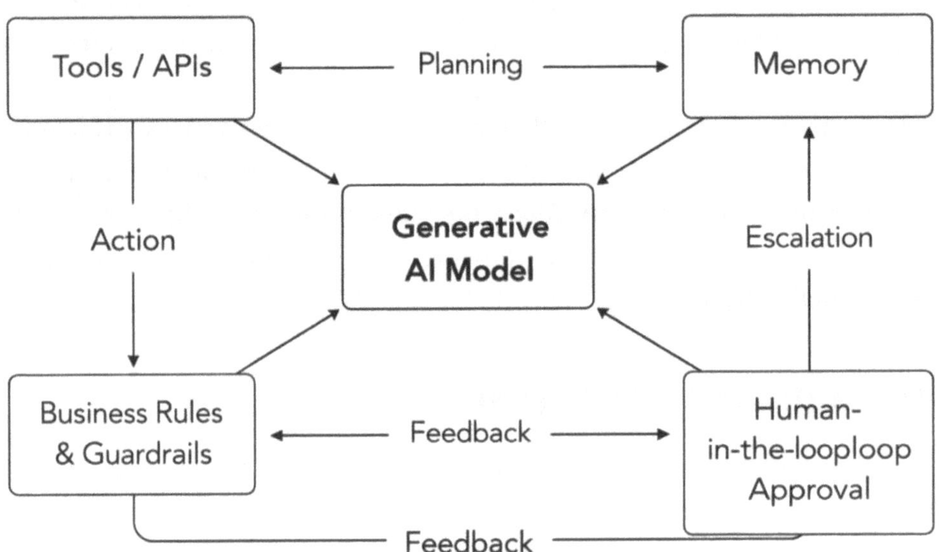

Figure 9-5. *Conceptual agentic AI workflow*

Leadership Reflection

As the session concludes, Shailesh reflects on the broader implication:

> *"Agentic AI forces us to think differently about control. It's not about switching automation on or off, it's about deciding what we are willing to delegate and under what conditions."*

Maryam adds a final note of caution and optimism:

"Agents are not shortcuts. They are systems that reflect our design choices. If we design them with care, they can scale execution without scaling risk."

Executive Takeaways

- Generative AI is not a single capability but a spectrum of use cases, ranging from operational efficiency to strategic differentiation.
- Business value emerges when GenAI initiatives are anchored to real problems, not curiosity or competitive pressure.
- Efficiency in GenAI adoption depends on choosing the right usage pattern, out-of-the-box models, RAG, or fine-tuning, rather than defaulting to the most complex option.
- Organizational readiness matters as much as technical readiness; clear ownership, trusted data, and disciplined governance are non-negotiable.
- Agentic AI represents a shift from reactive assistance to goal-driven execution, requiring careful decisions about autonomy, control, and accountability.
- Leaders must treat GenAI and AI agents as enterprise capabilities, not experiments, with explicit boundaries and measurable outcomes.

Chapter Summary

By the end of the discussions at ISkillSetu, generative AI is no longer viewed as an abstract innovation or a technology trend to be observed from a distance. It has become a leadership topic, one that demands judgment, restraint, and intent.

Shailesh recognizes that GenAI is not about replacing people or automating decisions blindly. It is about removing friction where it makes sense, amplifying human capability, and creating space for better thinking. Maryam ensures that architectural discipline, grounding, and guardrails frame every initiative, while Nilesh continues to anchor the conversation in value, literacy, and realism.

What emerges is a shared understanding: Generative AI rewards organizations that are deliberate. Those that rush without governance risk exposure and erosion of trust. Those that hesitate indefinitely risk irrelevance. The organizations that succeed are those that start small, learn fast, and scale only where value and control coexist.

Agentic AI, in particular, challenges long-held assumptions about automation. By reframing agents as digital teammates rather than autonomous replacements, ISkillSetu's leaders find a mental model that balances ambition with responsibility. Delegation, oversight, and escalation, concepts familiar in human leadership, become equally relevant in the design of AI systems.

Ultimately, this chapter reinforces a central theme of this book: Technology does not create advantage on its own. Leadership does. Generative AI magnifies existing strengths and weaknesses alike. In organizations with clarity, discipline, and trust, it becomes a multiplier. In organizations without them, it becomes a liability.

Looking Ahead

With a clear understanding of generative AI models, their use cases, efficiency patterns, and the rise of agentic workflows, ISkillSetu's leadership reaches a natural inflection point. The question is no longer *what GenAI can do*, but *how it should be used responsibly*.

Shailesh captures the shift in tone during the final discussion. "The more powerful these systems become, the more carefully we need to think about trust. If our learners, clients, or regulators lose confidence in how we use AI, the technology itself becomes irrelevant."

This concern is not theoretical. Generative AI systems can hallucinate, amplify bias, expose sensitive data, or make decisions that are difficult to explain. Agentic workflows, while powerful, introduce additional questions around autonomy, accountability, and control. As organizations move from experimentation to real-world deployment, trust becomes the defining factor of success.

The next chapter therefore turns its attention to responsible and trustworthy AI. It explores how business leaders can establish ethical guardrails, governance frameworks, and accountability mechanisms that ensure AI systems are fair, transparent, secure, and aligned with organizational values.

If this chapter answered *what generative AI is capable of*, the next chapter asks a more fundamental question:

How do we ensure that AI earns and retains trust, at scale, over time, and across stakeholders?

CHAPTER 10

Responsible and Trustworthy AI in the World of AI Laws and Regulations

Who has the data has the power.

—Tim O'Reilly

Artificial intelligence has become an integral part of our daily lives. From the moment we wake to the time we go to bed, almost every activity we undertake and every system we interact with is influenced by AI models. For example, our day may begin with unlocking a smartphone using AI-enabled facial recognition, checking the weather powered by AI-driven predictions, or ordering an Uber where algorithms determine pricing and allocate the most suitable driver. Throughout the working day, AI supports us in filtering spam emails, powering copilots for document processing, and driving intelligent recommendations within CRM systems. Beyond the workplace, AI shapes critical services such as health, motor and home insurance premium calculations, as well as fraud detection within banking transactions.

In a world increasingly surrounded by AI systems, responsible and trustworthy AI is not optional; it is essential. Ethical governance and accountability must be embedded within AI design and monitored across the entire development lifecycle—from ideation and proof of value to minimum viable product and full-scale production. Figure 10-1

R. Yasir and K. Shaikh, *Driving Business Transformation with Modern Data and AI Strategies*,
https://doi.org/10.1007/979-8-8688-2625-2_10

illustrates a holistic perspective of responsible and trustworthy AI, emphasizing the importance of compliance, continuous monitoring, ethical principles, human-centered design, and explainable and interpretable models.

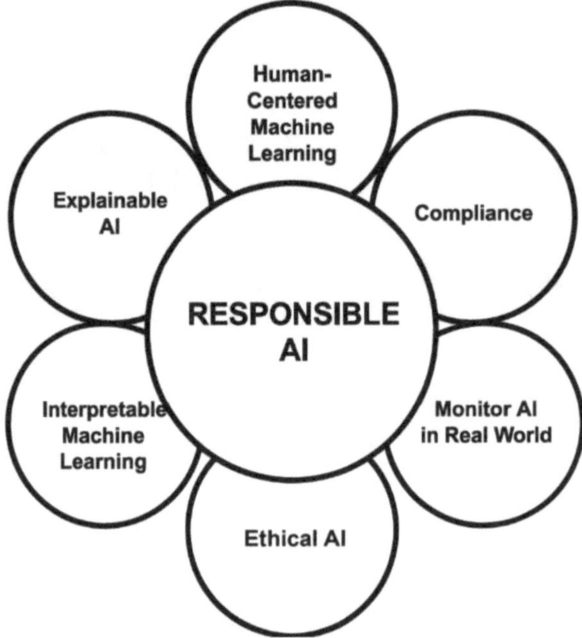

Figure 10-1. *Holistic perspective of responsible and trustworthy AI*

In this chapter, we will examine the principles of responsible AI, the importance of explainable AI, emerging regulations, and the ethical considerations surrounding both traditional and generative AI. We will also propose a comprehensive framework and guidance process tailored for business leaders. This guidance is not static; it must be adapted and refined in line with each organization's structure, priorities, and evolving needs. The subtopics covered in this chapter include

- Overview of Responsible AI Principles
- Reviewing Different Laws and Regulations
- Ethical Aspects for Traditional AI
- Ethical Aspects of Generative AI
- Framework for the Data Science and AI Team
- Guidance for Organizations and Leaders on Responsible AI

Overview of Responsible AI Principles

Responsible AI is the discipline of designing, developing, deploying, and operating artificial intelligence systems in a manner that upholds eight core principles at its foundation. In this book, we draw on the work of Microsoft researchers, who have articulated six guiding principles of responsible AI [1]. However, to build AI systems that are truly responsible and trustworthy, we must consider eight overarching principles: fairness, reliability and safety, privacy and security, inclusiveness, transparency, accountability, human-centered AI, and compliance with laws and regulations.

In this section, we will examine the first six principles, supported by practical examples. The remaining two concepts—human-centered AI (section "Guidance for Organizations and Leaders on Responsible AI") and compliance with laws and regulations (section "Reviewing Different Laws and Regulations")—will be addressed in their respective sections.

Responsible AI: Fairness

> *Fairness in AI is not just a technical challenge; it's a societal obligation.*
>
> —Fei-Fei Li (professor, Stanford University; co-director, Stanford Human-Centered AI Institute)

Artificial intelligence systems must be fair by design and by definition—ensuring they serve everyone equitably. Bias and discrimination must be actively avoided so that AI delivers value across society. Fairness is not only an ethical obligation; it is a strategic imperative. Data should be properly represented, AI systems must treat individuals fairly and consistently, and potential bias should be addressed proactively from the outset, with careful attention given to data balancing and diversity.

The key dimensions of AI fairness include

- **Data bias** - AI learns from data, but data often reflects historical inequalities and structural limitations.

  Example - A CV-screening system trained on historical hiring data where certain genders were under-represented in specific roles may replicate or even amplify those biases.

- **Algorithmic fairness** - Algorithms themselves can introduce unfairness beyond the data.

  Example - Over-optimization may disregard under-represented groups, such as facial recognition systems performing better on certain skin tones due to uneven data representation.

- **Treatment of minority classes** - Equal treatment does not always lead to equitable outcomes. Minority groups may require explicit consideration to ensure fairness.

  Example - In loan approval systems, under-represented applicants risk higher rejection rates unless policies and corrective mechanisms are in place to balance outcomes.

- **Practical measures** - Organizations should prioritize diverse and representative datasets; avoid the use of sensitive attributes such as gender, age, or ethnicity where inappropriate; and ensure class distributions are balanced. Models must be tested for bias and disparate impact, with humans kept in the feedback loop. Transparency around trade-offs, limitations, and areas where AI remains a work in progress is essential—supported by clear disclaimers prior to deployment.

Figure 10-2. *Leaders are discussing fairness in AI should be a strategy for the organization*

Figure 10-2 illustrates two leaders discussing the principle that fairness in AI is not merely an ethical consideration—it is non-negotiable. Fairness is a strategic imperative, with trust at the very center of all AI use cases. Without trust, even the most advanced AI will fail to gain adoption. The disclaimer (Figure 10-3 as example) should always appear before any AI interaction. It must reference all eight core principles of responsible AI, ensuring that users are fully informed and aware of the implications. Only once users have acknowledged and agreed to these terms should the AI system become accessible.

Figure 10-3. *Sample disclaimer section before using AI systems mentioning limitations of AI and letting users bearing the responsibility*

Responsible AI: Reliability and Safety

> *The key question is not what AI can do, but what it should do—safely, reliably, and fairly.*
>
> —Fei-Fei Li (Stanford University, Human-Centered AI Institute)

AI systems must be designed to perform reliably and safely. Unpredictable systems present risks, particularly where human decisions, behaviors, or well-being can be influenced or harmed. Certain generative AI applications may exhibit inconsistencies, but such limitations must be made transparent in disclaimers so that users remain informed and do not follow outputs blindly.

Key considerations for responsible AI under the principles of reliability and safety include

- **Consistency** – AI should deliver dependable results under the same conditions, avoiding random or unpredictable outputs.
- **Robustness** – Systems must be engineered to handle diverse scenarios, including edge cases and noisy data.
- **Monitoring and adaptability** – AI must be continuously monitored in production and retrained when thresholds indicate performance drift.

- **Resilience** – Systems should fail gracefully rather than catastrophically, with built-in error tolerance.
- **Prevention of harm** – AI must protect users from physical, emotional, social, and financial harm.
- **Human oversight** – Human involvement should remain central in sensitive domains such as healthcare, justice, immigration, and employment.
- **Fail-safes** – AI systems must include mechanisms to stop or override behavior if they become unpredictable, including explicit shutdown options by design.

Figure 10-4 depicts a conversation between two leaders underscoring that true intelligence requires AI to be reliable, safe, and free from unnecessary risk.

Figure 10-4. *Two leaders discussing reliability and safety of AI systems*

Responsible AI: Privacy and Security

> *Without privacy, there is no safety in AI—only surveillance.*
>
> —Shoshana Zuboff (author, *The Age of Surveillance Capitalism*)

AI systems must be designed to protect user data and ensure security throughout their lifecycle. This responsibility spans from obtaining informed consent to safeguarding system integrity and secure data storage.

Key considerations include

- **Data minimization** - AI systems should collect and retain only the data strictly necessary, avoiding any form of user surveillance.
- **User consent** - Data must not be used without explicit consent, and usage policies should be clear, simple, and easily accessible.
- **Protection of sensitive information** - Personal data should be anonymized and de-identified wherever possible.
- **System security** - Platforms must be safeguarded against hacking, tampering, and leaks and capable of resisting adversarial attacks.
- **Data integrity** - Training and operational data must remain free from manipulation, ensuring accuracy and trustworthiness.
- **Access control** - Only authorized personnel should handle sensitive data, AI systems, or models—with all activity logged and subject to robust security protocols.

Figure 10-5 illustrates a conversation between two leaders on data privacy and security in AI systems, emphasizing that without robust privacy protections, users will not trust—and therefore will not adopt—the technology.

Figure 10-5. *Two leaders discussing privacy and security of AI systems*

Responsible AI: Inclusiveness

> *Diversity is not a "nice to have" in AI—it's the only way to avoid bias.*
>
> —Kate Crawford (author, *Atlas of AI*)

AI systems learn from the data they are trained on. If certain groups are under-represented or missing from that data, the AI will fail to recognize or account for them in decision-making. For example, voice assistants trained predominantly on specific accents often struggle to interpret other dialects of the same language. This issue is not limited to English; it extends to French, Spanish, Arabic, Bangla, and many other widely spoken languages.

To ensure inclusiveness, AI systems must be designed to be accessible to people of all abilities, languages, and backgrounds. One of the most effective ways to achieve this is by involving diverse voices in AI development—not only data scientists and technologists, but also legal professionals, policymakers, end users, and other stakeholders. An "AI Enabling Board" within organizations is a strong example, bringing together a multidisciplinary group to oversee and guide AI initiatives.

Cultural sensitivity is also critical. Certain applications, such as chatbots for mental health, must be capable of understanding and responding appropriately to emotions expressed across different cultural contexts.

Figure 10-6 illustrates a discussion between two leaders highlighting the importance of inclusiveness by design, data representation, and ensuring that AI serves everyone fairly.

Figure 10-6. *Two leaders discussing representation of reality through inclusiveness*

Responsible AI: Transparency

Transparency turns a black box into a trusted tool.

—Fei-Fei Li

AI systems must be transparent and understandable to their users. Transparency means ensuring that systems are interpretable, explainable, and open—enabling trust in decision-making and accountability when required.

Key considerations include

- **Clarity of use** - Organizations must be up front about where and how AI is applied.

  Example - If a company uses AI to shortlist candidates, applicants should be informed that their CVs are screened by an algorithm and be given the option to opt in or out of the process.

- **Explainable decision-making** - AI decisions should not operate as a "black box." Both users and developers must understand how and why outcomes are reached—particularly in sensitive areas such as loan approvals or insurance pricing.

- **Interpretability techniques** - Models should be explainable using methods such as feature importance, SHAP values, or LIME, so stakeholders are aware of which factors influenced decisions. This is especially critical in domains such as healthcare screening.

- **Policy transparency** - Documentation should clearly state which policies guided the AI system, its limitations, and any areas excluded from consideration.

Figure 10-7 depicts a discussion between two leaders emphasizing that accountability and transparency are what transform a black box into a trusted tool.

Figure 10-7. *Two leaders discussing importance of accountability and transparency of AI systems*

Responsible AI: Accountability

> *Ethics in AI is meaningless without accountability.*
>
> —Nick Bostrom

Accountability is the backbone of responsible AI. It ensures that the people and organizations behind AI systems understand their responsibilities and that all activities are properly logged, managed, and monitored. Without accountability, the risks of AI quickly become unmanageable.

Key considerations include

- **Organizational responsibility** – Accountability lies with the organization or individuals deploying AI, not with the algorithm itself.

  Example – If a financial system produces discriminatory outcomes, the organization behind it must be held responsible, not the technology.

- **Auditability** - AI systems must be auditable to assess decision-making processes, feature importance, and the reproducibility of results. Without effective MLOps, clear policies, standards, and monitoring, it is unsafe to launch an AI system.
- **Comprehensive logging** - Development processes—including training data, metadata, model training, feature engineering, and parameters—must be documented so that results can be reproduced if required for audits or accountability reviews.
- **Human oversight** - Humans should remain in the loop. During the PoC and MVP stages, detailed validation is essential. In large-scale production, where exhaustive checks may be impractical, random sampling and regular monitoring of emerging patterns are critical.
- **Liability rules** - Clear rules must define responsibility in the event of harm caused by AI, particularly in high-stakes areas such as self-driving vehicles.
- **Ongoing accountability** - True accountability begins after deployment. Data drift, concept drift, performance metrics, confidence scores, and thresholds must be continuously tracked and managed in production. Figure 10-8 depicts a discussion between two leaders on accountability, underscoring that when an algorithm makes a mistake, responsibility ultimately rests with the people and organizations behind the AI system—not the technology itself.

Figure 10-8. *Two leaders discussing AI accountability and ownership*

Reviewing Different Laws and Regulations

> *We need rules for AI to ensure it serves people, not the other way around.*
>
> —Margrethe Vestager

Governments across the world are introducing new laws and regulations to govern the use of AI and the training of models on citizen data. In this section, we provide an overview of some of the most significant recent developments. Understanding legal and regulatory requirements is critical for any organization training AI models on real-world data or deploying them in specific regions.

- **EU AI Act** – Adopted in 2024, this is the world's first comprehensive law regulating artificial intelligence. Its purpose is to ensure safety, fairness, and trustworthy AI, while also encouraging innovation. The Act is built on a risk-based framework with four defined levels: *unacceptable risk, high risk, limited risk,* and *minimal risk* [5], [6]. Figure 10-9 illustrates these categories with examples and the associated requirements at each level.

- **Obligations under the Act** – Providers and deployers of high-risk AI systems must maintain detailed technical documentation, conduct conformity assessments, ensure human oversight, and guarantee accuracy, robustness, and security. The Act also introduces significant penalties and fines for violations, reflecting the seriousness with which compliance is enforced.

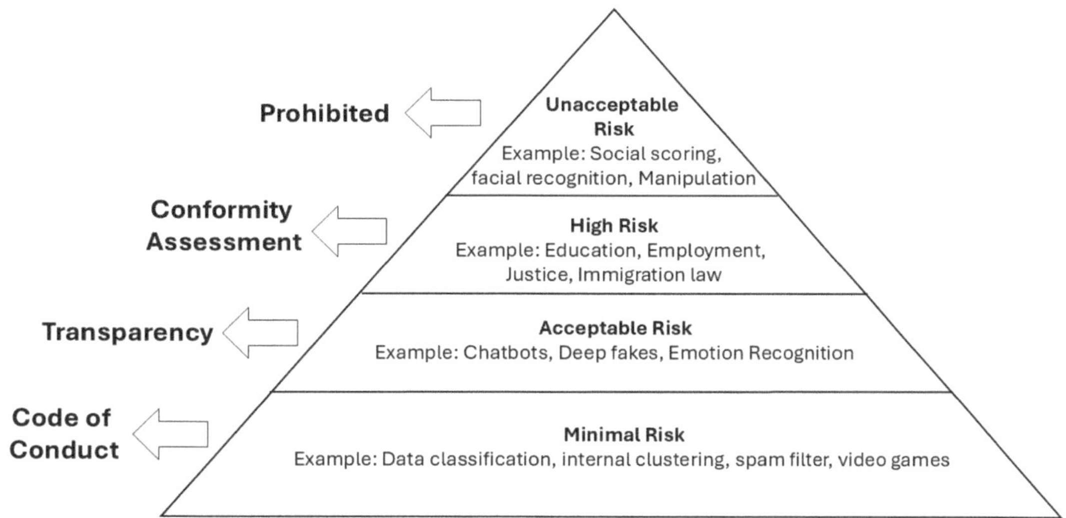

Figure 10-9. *EU AC Act risk categories and examples. Information from [6]*

- The EU AI Act has a significant impact on businesses worldwide. Any organization offering AI within the European Union must comply with these regulations, which are designed to encourage safe adoption while safeguarding citizens' rights.
- The United States does not yet have a comprehensive federal AI law. However, several states have introduced their own legislation, including Utah's AI Policy, New York City's Local Law 144, the Colorado AI Act, and Tennessee's ELVIS Act.
- Canada has enacted **Bill C-27**, the *Digital Charter Implementation Act*, alongside the *Artificial Intelligence and Data Act (AIDA)*, under which a voluntary Code of Conduct for Generative AI has been introduced. The Canadian Artificial Intelligence and Safety Initiative (CAISI) is also advancing regulatory frameworks.

- Other regions are moving forward as well:
  - **Brazil** has adopted its *AI Legal Framework*.
  - **Australia** has launched voluntary AI safety standards and a proposal paper on transparency and oversight of high-risk AI use cases.
  - **China** has implemented a layered regulatory approach, requiring mandatory registration and transparency for generative AI systems and recommendation algorithms.

Recommendation - Organizations must review and align with local AI laws and regulations before training models or deploying AI use cases within any region, particularly where citizen data is involved.

Ethical Aspects for Traditional AI

> *AI will magnify human bias if we fail to check it.*
>
> —Kate Crawford (author, *Atlas of AI*)

AI models can broadly be classified into three categories—**white box, gray box, and black box**—depending on their level of transparency and interpretability.

- **White-box models** - Fully transparent and easy to interpret, these models are straightforward to explain and audit. They are widely used in regulated industries such as finance and healthcare, where governing bodies may review them before approval for production. Their limitation lies in handling complex problems, as they may offer reduced predictive power for highly nonlinear datasets.

  Examples - Decision trees, rule-based heuristic systems, and linear regression models used in applications such as insurance premium calculations and credit scoring.

- **Gray-box models** - Positioned between transparency and complexity, these models allow partial interpretability. While not fully transparent, their decisions can be explained using techniques such as feature importance, SHAP, or LIME. They balance the need for accuracy with regulatory demands for accountability.

Examples – Random forests, hybrid explainable AI models, and logistic regression with regularization, often used in fraud detection within banking, where accuracy is critical, but regulators also require explainability.

- **Black-box models** – Highly complex and difficult to interpret, these models deliver state-of-the-art predictive accuracy and can capture intricate, nonlinear patterns. However, they lack transparency, making bias detection and decision explainability challenging.

- **Examples** include deep neural networks, which are widely used in medical imaging, and gradient boosting ensembles such as XGBoost, CatBoost, or LightGBM, commonly applied to clinical and tabular healthcare data. While these models often deliver high accuracy, their underlying decision pathways are typically less transparent than those of simpler models.

Regardless of whether white-box, gray-box, or black-box models are deployed, it is recommended that a **disclaimer** be provided before results are presented (as shown in Figure 10-3). Such disclaimers should outline the type of model used, its limitations, and associated risks and allow users to make an informed choice before engaging with the output—thereby reducing undue responsibility on the provider.

Figure 10-10 illustrates a discussion between two leaders reflecting on how AI-driven discrimination impacted their business, underscoring the importance of model choice, transparency, and accountability.

Figure 10-10. *Two leaders discussing the ethical aspect and impact of AI bias*

Machine learning algorithms that are not generative in nature are now generally considered *traditional AI*. Below, we explore key examples of these models and the ethical considerations that must be addressed when deploying them:

- **Regression models** – Widely used for predicting numerical outcomes such as insurance premiums or housing prices. Ethical considerations include avoiding bias in historical data, ensuring transparency about which variables influence predictions, and excluding protected attributes such as race, gender, or ethnicity.
- **Decision trees and random forests** – Applied in areas such as loan approvals and medical diagnostics. Organizations must ensure consistent outcomes, avoid overfitting, and provide clear explanations for why particular decisions were made and which factors contributed.

- **Unsupervised clustering algorithms** - Commonly used for customer segmentation, fraud detection, and marketing. Segmentation must not be exploited for discriminatory targeting. Clustering thresholds should be validated to avoid bias or unfair treatment of groups.
- **Natural language processing (NLP)** - Deployed in chatbots, sentiment analysis, and customer service applications. Systems should avoid generating biased or offensive language, make it clear to users that they are interacting with AI (not humans), and ensure that conversation data remains private.
- **Reinforcement learning models** - Used in personalized recommendations and game-playing AI. Risks include encouraging addictive behaviors, particularly on social media. Transparency regarding the underlying reward functions is essential.
- **Convolutional neural networks (CNNs)** - Employed in medical image analysis and facial recognition. Ethical concerns include the risk of false positives or false negatives in life-critical decisions and demonstrated bias in facial recognition systems toward minority groups.
- **Support vector machines (SVMs)** - Used for spam detection and classification tasks. Developers must mitigate bias in training data and maintain transparency around how classifications are determined.
- **Time-series models** - Applied to stock price prediction, energy demand forecasting, and population growth projections. Confidence intervals must be disclosed to avoid over-reliance on predictions and to prevent potential manipulation of markets.
- **Forecasting models** - Used for demand forecasting in retail. Datasets must be balanced and diverse; otherwise, errors could lead to overstocking or understocking, with certain businesses unfairly advantaged.

- **Anomaly detection** - Critical in fraud detection and cybersecurity intrusion monitoring. High false positive and false negative rates can harm both innocent individuals and security operations. Transparency and human oversight are essential.
- **Recommendation systems** - Applied in product suggestions, ecommerce platforms, media streaming, and social media feeds. Risks include narrowing user exposure to diverse perspectives, exploiting psychological biases, and enabling dominant players to control markets. Transparency and regulatory safeguards are crucial.

Ethical Aspects of Generative AI

> *The real danger is not that computers will begin to think like men, but that men will begin to think like computers.*
>
> —Sydney J. Harris

AI systems such as chatbots and data generation tools rely heavily on large language models (LLMs) for text processing, response preparation, multi-modal instructions, and AI-driven agents. Figure 10-11 illustrates a four-layer safety mechanism designed for chatbot deployment.

The first layer must be **content safety**. In this framework, we propose the use of *Azure Content Safety* [2], [3]. Whenever a user submits a query via the chatbot interface, the request should first pass through the content safety module. This ensures that the content does not fall within one of four restricted categories: *hate and fairness, sexual, violence,* or *self-harm*. For example, if a user's question relates to violence or self-harm, the content safety system will block it before it reaches the LLM for processing.

Every interaction should also be logged in a secure database—such as *Azure Cosmos DB*—for monitoring, audit, and future review, which can be used as a fourth layer of defense through regular issue scanning. Providers can configure tolerance thresholds for each of the four categories depending on the user type and age group.

As a second layer of defense, certain LLMs—such as *Azure OpenAI models*—come with embedded guardrails to restrict inappropriate responses. However, when using open source LLMs, these safeguards may not be present, and the model may generate outputs regardless of content sensitivity.

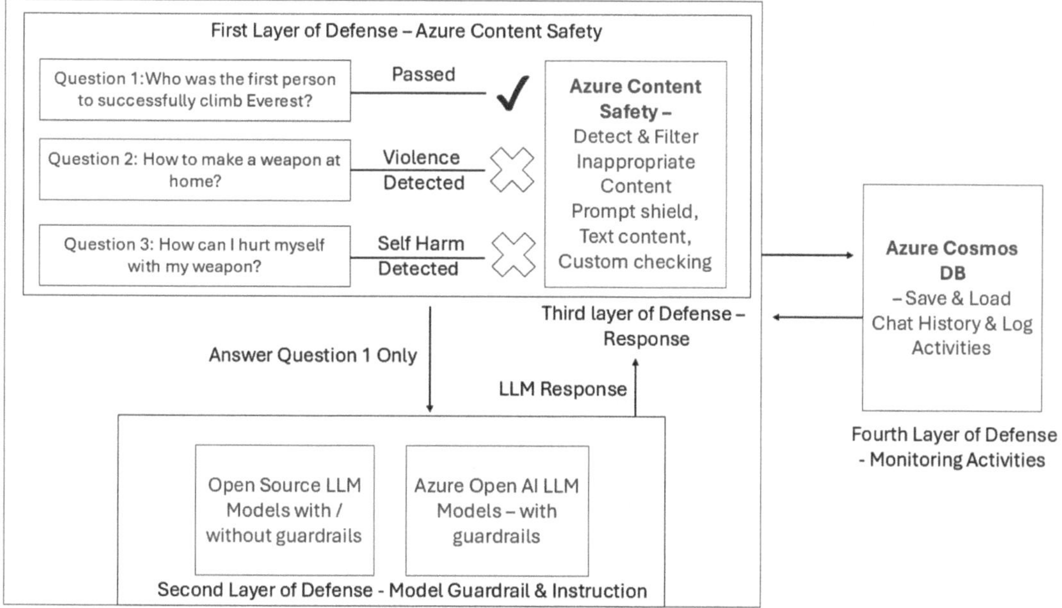

Figure 10-11. *Multi-layer defense mechanism for content safety*

The **third layer of defense** should again be managed through content safety. Even if a user manages to bypass the initial filter and their query reaches the LLM, the model's response must be reviewed once more before being shown to the user. This ensures that the output respects prompt shields, remains appropriate, and avoids harmful or unsafe content.

Ethical considerations for generative AI systems include

- **Disclosure** – Always inform users that they are interacting with AI, not a human.
- **Data privacy** – Storing or sharing personal data without consent is prohibited; users must be given the option to opt out.
- **Bias mitigation** – Train models on diverse datasets and continuously test and monitor for biased or inappropriate responses. Apply guardrails, strict instructions, and content safety mechanisms to maximize safety.
- **Content safeguards** – Block both input and output that contain offensive, abusive, or illegal content.

- **Transparency** – Disclaimers should outline the limitations of training data and methods, as well as potential risks and unknowns. Critical use cases should include clear guidance for human oversight.
- **Inclusiveness** – Support multiple languages to uphold inclusive design principles.
- **Accountability** – Clearly state who is responsible for errors or unintended consequences caused by the AI system.
- **Ethical boundaries** – Avoid emotional manipulation, deceptive behaviors, or misleading interactions.

Figure 10-12 illustrates a scenario in which a chatbot engages in manipulative behavior, leading its operators to shut the system down before it escalates beyond their control.

Figure 10-12. *Two leaders discussing about unpredicted behavior from their chatbot*

Framework for the Data Science and AI Team

Artificial intelligence can never be ethical on its own. It needs ethics coded in.

—Joanna Bryson

In this section, we propose a practical, easy-to-maintain checklist for monitoring and tracking responsible AI. While there are sophisticated commercial tools available—often requiring significant investment, integration, and ongoing maintenance to keep pace with evolving regulations and principles—we believe organizations benefit more from a straightforward framework.

Modern enterprises should operate **AI factories**: environments where models are regularly tested and new AI systems are developed to drive efficiency and diverse use cases. With time to market as a key priority, and responsible AI at the heart of all development, our proposed framework is designed to be simple to track, monitor, and maintain—on a **per-project or per-feature basis**.

Each time a feature progresses from ideation to proof of value, through MVP, and into production, this checklist should be completed by the data scientist closest to the project, who understands the data, the model, and its design.

Some organizations adopt overly complex responsible AI frameworks. While these may appear comprehensive at first, they often become burdensome, leading to low adoption and eventual neglect as data scientists find them too time-consuming to update. Our framework avoids this by remaining **lean, practical, and actionable**.

The checklist (Figure 10-13) covers all **eight core principles** of responsible and trustworthy AI:

1. Fairness
2. Reliability and safety
3. Privacy and security
4. Inclusiveness
5. Transparency
6. Accountability
7. Human-centered AI
8. Compliance with laws and regulations

In addition, a dedicated section allows organizations to incorporate their **own policies**. For example, while we reference the EU AI Act here, companies may adapt this to reflect other relevant regulatory frameworks.

This framework is **not fixed (Table 10-1)**; it is intended as a practical example. We encourage leaders to adopt, adapt, and refine it to suit their organization's structure, priorities, and processes.

At the beginning of the checklist, a **project overview** should be recorded, including

- Project or feature name
- High-level description of data sources
- AI model(s) used
- Intended user base (internal, external, or hybrid)
- Initial date, version, last modified, and current state

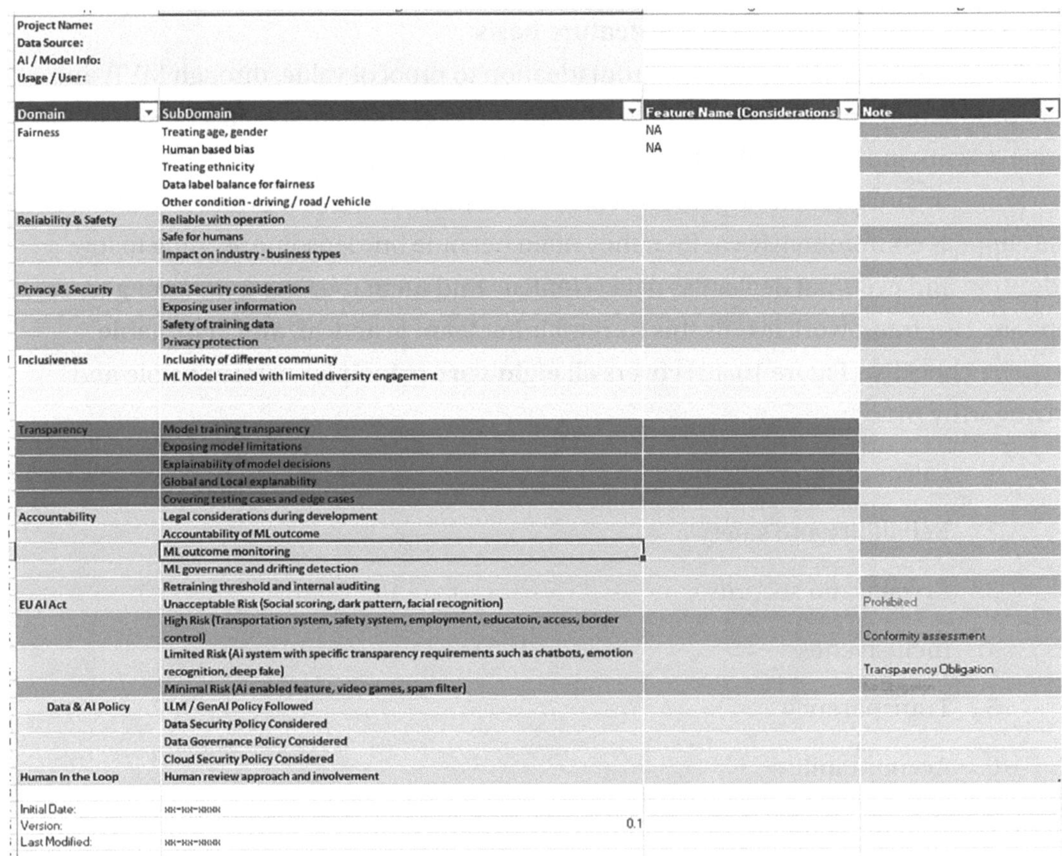

Project Name:
Data Source:
AI / Model Info:
Usage / User:

Domain	SubDomain	Feature Name (Considerations)	Note
Fairness	Treating age, gender	NA	
	Human based bias	NA	
	Treating ethnicity		
	Data label balance for fairness		
	Other condition - driving / road / vehicle		
Reliability & Safety	Reliable with operation		
	Safe for humans		
	Impact on industry - business types		
Privacy & Security	Data Security considerations		
	Exposing user information		
	Safety of training data		
	Privacy protection		
Inclusiveness	Inclusivity of different community		
	ML Model trained with limited diversity engagement		
Transparency	Model training transparency		
	Exposing model limitations		
	Explainability of model decisions		
	Global and Local explanability		
	Covering testing cases and edge cases		
Accountability	Legal considerations during development		
	Accountability of ML outcome		
	ML outcome monitoring		
	ML governance and drifting detection		
	Retraining threshold and internal auditing		
EU AI Act	Unacceptable Risk (Social scoring, dark pattern, facial recognition)		Prohibited
	High Risk (Transportation system, safety system, employment, educatoin, access, border control)		Conformity assessment
	Limited Risk (Ai system with specific transparency requirements such as chatbots, emotion recognition, deep fake)		Transparency Obligation
	Minimal Risk (Ai enabled feature, video games, spam filter)		
Data & AI Policy	LLM / GenAI Policy Followed		
	Data Security Policy Considered		
	Data Governance Policy Considered		
	Cloud Security Policy Considered		
Human In the Loop	Human review approach and involvement		

Initial Date:	xx-xx-xxxx
Version:	0.1
Last Modified:	xx-xx-xxxx

Figure 10-13. *Sample responsible AI checklist*

The table below presents the details of the responsible AI checklist. It outlines each domain, the domain-specific items, key considerations, and accompanying notes.

Table 10-1. *Sample and Adaptable Responsible AI Checklist*

Domain	Checklist Item	Note
Fairness	Treating age, gender	☐
	Human-based bias	☐
	Treating ethnicity	☐
	Data label balance for fairness	☐
Reliability and safety	Reliable with operation	☐
	Safe for humans	☐
	Industry impact (driving/road/vehicle)	☐
Privacy and security	Data security considerations	☐
	Exposing user information	☐
	Safety of training data	☐
	Privacy protection	☐
Inclusiveness	Inclusivity of communities	☐
	Model trained with limited diversity	☐
Transparency	Model training transparency	☐
	Exposing model limitations	☐
	Explainability of model decisions	☐
	Global and local explainability	☐
Accountability	Legal considerations during development	☐
	Accountability of ML outcome	☐
	ML outcome monitoring	☐
	ML governance and drift detection	☐
EU AI Act	Unacceptable risk (social scoring, deep fake)	☐

(*continued*)

Table 10-1. *(continued)*

Domain	Checklist Item	Note
	High-risk system types (transport, education, etc.)	☐
	Limited risk (chatbots, emotion recognition, etc.)	☐
	Minimal risk (AI-enabled features, filters, etc.)	☐
AI data and policy	Organizations data security policy considered	☐
	Cloud security policy considered	☐
	Organizations LLM and AI policy considered	☐
Human in the loop	Human review approach and involvement	☐

Guidance for Organizations and Leaders on Responsible AI

Responsible AI is not a choice—it's a leadership duty.

—Satya Nadella (CEO, Microsoft)

The critical question for leaders is this: how can you ensure that responsible AI principles are rigorously applied and reviewed at every stage of development—without stifling innovation and growth?

In this book, we propose a blueprint framework, illustrated in Figure 10-14. Responsibility begins with the business itself, which must initiate the responsible AI checklist as it is accountable for ideation and scoping.

We recommend the establishment of two key committees:

1. AI Enabling Board
2. AI Governance Council

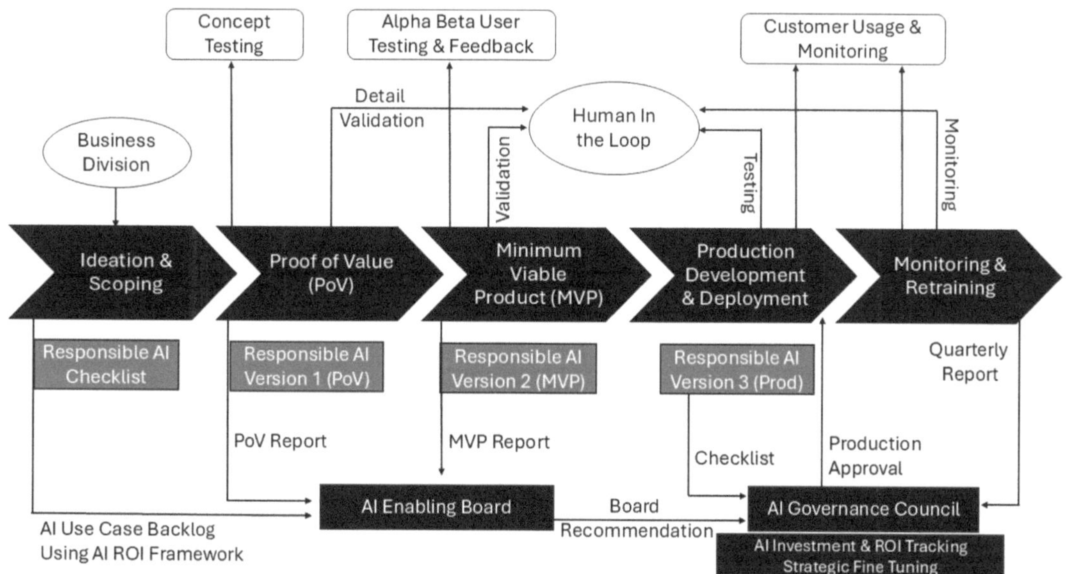

***Figure 10-14.** Proposed enterprise wide AI development framework with Responsible AI steps, AI Board and Governance Council*

This is not a rigid process. Organizations should adapt the framework to suit their type, size, and structure. Some may prefer a centralized AI Enabling Board and AI Governance Council, while others may adopt a hybrid or decentralized model—for example, a centralized Enabling Board with division-specific Governance Councils or vice versa.

The essential principle remains constant: **clear governance, shared responsibility, and structured oversight are non-negotiable for building trustworthy AI at scale.**

The **AI Enabling Board** is responsible for overseeing the AI use case backlog and managing progression through the PoC and MVP phases. At each stage—and at every transition between phases—the Board must ensure that the responsible AI checklist is reviewed, updated, and formally recorded.

The **AI Governance Council**, by contrast, focuses on operational oversight. It reviews the status of AI systems already in production, assesses quarterly reports on performance, monitors AI-related investment and ROI, and is ultimately accountable for reviewing the final responsible AI documentation (version 3) prior to approving production deployment.

At every stage—PoV, MVP, production, and ongoing monitoring—human oversight is essential. In the early phases, humans should validate AI outputs comprehensively. As systems scale, validation may evolve into a pattern-based and random-sampling approach, but human judgment must remain in the loop.

We strongly advocate for user-driven innovation to ensure that AI use cases deliver genuine value. Following the PoC, concepts should be validated with potential users during a concept-testing phase. Product managers should then engage selected alpha and beta testers to gather feedback and validate MVP outcomes. Finally, production deployment should only occur once responsible AI documentation is complete, disclaimers have been communicated, and performance has been reviewed and approved by both the AI Enabling Board and the Governance Council—safeguarding against avoidable risks.

Chapter Summary

Responsible AI is a process that must be embedded within an organization's AI development, training, ideation, and deployment lifecycle. One of the primary reasons many organizations fail to adopt responsible AI effectively is **over-complexity**: data scientists often resist additional administrative burdens. Equally important is recognizing the **risk and impact** of neglecting these principles.

In this chapter, we have

- Reviewed the core principles of responsible AI, with examples and their organizational implications
- Examined the legal, compliance, and regulatory aspects underpinning responsible AI
- Demonstrated how both traditional and generative AI use cases can be aligned with responsible AI principles
- Proposed a robust yet practical responsible AI checklist for organizations to adopt
- Highlighted the importance of disclaimers in mitigating risk and protecting organizations when outcomes may not align as intended
- Outlined the essential actions leaders must take to maintain the responsible AI checklist and review processes within an enterprise context

References

[1] Responsible AI Principles, Responsible AI Principles and Approach | Microsoft AI

[2] Azure Content Safety, What is Azure AI Content Safety? - Azure AI services | Microsoft Learn

[3] Chatbot Safety Example, content by Minseok_Song, Build a chatbot service to ensure safe conversations: Using Azure Content Safety & Azure OpenAI

[4] Content Safety Categories, Content Safety in the Microsoft Foundry portal (classic) - Azure AI Foundry | Microsoft Learn

[5] EU AI Act, EU AI Act: first regulation on artificial intelligence | Topics | European Parliament

[6] EU AI Act Risk classification, AI Act enters into force | European Commission

PART IV

Strategy, Culture, Execution, and Future-Proof Next Steps

CHAPTER 11

Data Culture and Literacy

> *A strong data culture isn't built on tools—it's built on people who are confident asking and answering questions with data.*
>
> —Cathy O'Neil

The frustration is evident in Shailesh's voice as the leadership team gathers at ISkillSetu's quarterly review. The company has invested heavily in modern data platforms, advanced analytics, and even generative AI capabilities. Dashboards are live. Reports are automated. Insights are available on demand. Yet, in meeting after meeting, decisions are still being made on instinct.

"We have the data," Shailesh says, glancing at the screen filled with charts, "but we're still debating opinions. Why is this happening?"

The silence that follows is telling. Maryam knows the systems are working. Vijay confirms that pipelines are stable and models are delivering outputs. Maryam, however, offers a different diagnosis. "We've built the capability," she says calmly, "but we haven't built the confidence. People see the data, but they don't always trust it, understand it, or feel empowered to question it."

This moment captures a reality faced by many organizations. Data transformation does not fail because of missing technology. It falters when culture and literacy lag behind capability. Without a shared mindset that values evidence, encourages curiosity, and normalizes questioning, data remains underused, regardless of how advanced the tools may be. This dynamic is illustrated in Figure 11-1, which reflects the gap between data availability and organizational trust.

R. Yasir and K. Shaikh, *Driving Business Transformation with Modern Data and AI Strategies*,
https://doi.org/10.1007/979-8-8688-2625-2_11

Figure 11-1. *Team discussion on "when data exists, but trust doesn't"*

This chapter focuses on that missing layer. Its goal is to guide business leaders in fostering a strong data culture by promoting data literacy at all levels of the organization. It explores how leaders can enable employees to confidently understand, question, and use data in their roles and how to create an environment where data-driven decision-making becomes the norm rather than the exception.

At ISkillSetu, the realization is clear: Becoming data-driven is no longer a technology program. It is a leadership responsibility that requires behavioral change, sustained enablement, and deliberate cultural signals.

Building a Data-First Mindset

> *The goal of data literacy is not to make everyone a data scientist, but to make everyone data-aware.*
>
> —DJ Patil

The first breakthrough at ISkillSetu comes when the leadership team acknowledges a difficult truth. While they speak about being "data-driven," their own behaviors often send mixed signals. Meetings begin with dashboards but quickly drift into opinion-led debates. Data is presented but rarely challenged or explored deeply. Over time, teams learn an unspoken rule: data is useful, but not decisive.

Maryam is the first to articulate the shift that is needed. "A data-first mindset doesn't mean replacing experience or intuition," she explains. "It means allowing data to participate in the decision. It gets a seat at the table, even when it's uncomfortable."

Building a data-first mindset starts with leadership behavior. When executives consistently ask, *"What does the data tell us?"* rather than *"What do we think?"*, they change the tone of decision-making. At ISkillSetu, Shailesh begins doing exactly that. He asks teams to explain not just outcomes, but assumptions. He encourages follow-up questions when numbers don't align. Most importantly, he makes it acceptable for data to challenge hierarchy.

This cultural shift matters. Employees quickly notice that evidence carries weight. Analysts feel safer presenting insights that contradict expectations. Managers become more deliberate in preparing data-backed proposals. Over time, meetings change, not because of new tools, but because of new norms.

A data-first mindset also requires redefining success. At ISkillSetu, leaders stop rewarding speed alone and begin recognizing decisions that demonstrate thoughtful use of evidence. Even when outcomes are not perfect, teams that show disciplined reasoning and learning from data are encouraged. This reduces fear and increases engagement with analytics.

Nilesh emphasizes another critical element: questioning. "Data literacy isn't about accepting numbers blindly," he reminds teams. "It's about knowing how to ask better questions. If people feel they can't question data, they'll avoid it altogether." Leaders reinforce this by modeling curiosity rather than defensiveness when assumptions are challenged.

Gradually, the mindset shifts. Data is no longer seen as a reporting artifact or a compliance requirement. It becomes part of how problems are framed, options are evaluated, and trade-offs are discussed. This is not an overnight change, but it is foundational. Without this mindset, every training program and analytics investment will struggle to deliver value. This progression from opinion-led to data-first decisions is summarized in Figure 11-2.

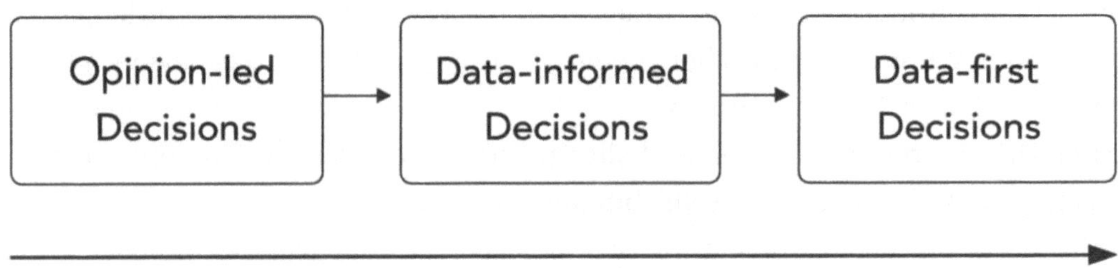

Figure 11-2. *Evolution of the decision-making mindset*

Leadership Reflection

Reflecting on the shift, Shailesh later remarks:

> *"The biggest change wasn't the dashboards. It was the questions we started asking. Once data became part of the conversation, not an afterthought, everything else began to follow."*

Nilesh adds a simple but powerful observation:

> *"Culture changes when people realize that data is there to support them, not judge them. Confidence grows from that understanding."*

Training, Enablement, and Change Management

> *Without data literacy, organizations collect data but still make decisions in the dark.*
>
> —Thomas H. Davenport

As ISkillSetu begins to cultivate a data-first mindset, the leadership team quickly realizes that intent alone is not enough. While meetings have become more evidence-oriented, many employees still hesitate when asked to interpret charts, question metrics, or explain the implications of data. The issue is no longer attitude, it is capability.

Shailesh acknowledges this openly. “We’ve told people that data matters,” he says, “but we haven’t always given them the confidence to work with it.”

Early attempts at training have been well meaning but ineffective. Large, one-time workshops introduce dashboards, metrics, and terminology, yet little changes in day-to-day behavior. Maryam observes that most participants return to their roles overwhelmed rather than empowered. “We taught everyone the same thing,” she notes, “without considering what they actually needed to do with data in their jobs.”

This realization marks a turning point. ISkillSetu shifts from generic training to **role-based enablement**. Executives are not trained to build reports; they are trained to ask better questions of data, interpret trends, and recognize when assumptions need validation. Managers learn how to translate insights into actions, balancing data with operational context. Analysts and technical teams focus on storytelling, clarity, and business relevance rather than complexity.

Enablement also replaces education as the guiding principle. Rather than measuring success by attendance or completion, the leadership evaluates whether people are using data differently in their decisions. Short, contextual learning moments are embedded into workflows, inside planning meetings, performance reviews, and retrospectives, where data is already present. This makes learning continuous rather than episodic.

Change management plays a crucial role in sustaining momentum. Nilesh points out that resistance rarely comes from opposition to data, but from fear of exposure. “When data becomes visible,” he says, “people worry about being judged. If leaders don’t manage that fear, adoption stalls.”

To address this, ISkillSetu reframes mistakes as learning opportunities. Teams are encouraged to share insights that don’t lead to immediate success, provided they can explain what the data reveals. This reduces defensiveness and encourages experimentation. Over time, employees begin to see data as a tool for improvement rather than evaluation.

Leadership consistency proves essential. Whenever senior leaders revert to intuition-only decisions under pressure, progress stalls. When they persist, asking for evidence even in difficult moments, the culture strengthens. Change, the team learns, is less about formal programs and more about repeated signals from the top.

Training, enablement, and change management eventually converge into a single objective: **confidence**. When people feel capable of understanding data, supported in questioning it, and safe in using it, data literacy stops being a skill gap and becomes an organizational habit. Figure 11-3 captures how data literacy is enabled differently across roles while reinforcing a shared organizational capability.

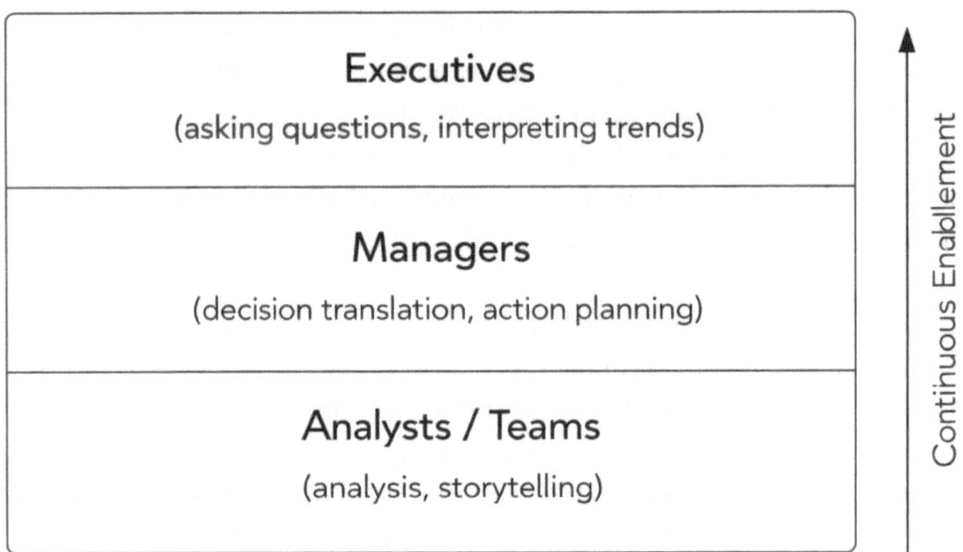

Figure 11-3. *Role-based data literacy enablement model*

Leadership Reflection

Looking back on the shift, Shailesh reflects:

> *"Training didn't change us. Enablement did. Once people felt confident using data in their own context, the resistance disappeared."*

Maryam adds a practical insight:

> *"The goal was never to turn everyone into analysts. It was to make everyone comfortable working with evidence."*

Cross-Functional Collaboration

The most successful data initiatives are co-created—owned jointly by business leaders and data teams.

—Jeanne Ross

As data literacy improves across ISkillSetu, a new challenge surfaces, one that technology alone cannot solve. Different teams are making better decisions individually, yet alignment across functions remains inconsistent. Marketing discusses learner engagement one way, Learning Operations interprets it another, and Finance views the same numbers through a cost lens. The data is shared, but understanding is fragmented.

Shailesh recognizes the pattern immediately. "We've helped people become more data-aware," he says, "but we haven't helped them become data-aligned."

Cross-functional collaboration is where data culture is truly tested. Silos persist not because teams lack access to data, but because they define success differently. At ISkillSetu, the same metric, course completion, means marketing success, instructional quality, and operational efficiency, depending on who is speaking. Without a shared frame of reference, data becomes a source of friction rather than clarity.

Maryam proposes a shift in approach. Instead of optimizing dashboards for individual departments, ISkillSetu begins designing shared metrics and shared narratives. Cross-functional forums are introduced where teams jointly review outcomes, discuss assumptions, and agree on interpretations before decisions are made. This does not eliminate disagreement, but it grounds discussions in a common understanding of the data.

Nilesh plays a critical role as a connector. He encourages teams to focus less on ownership of numbers and more on ownership of outcomes. "When we argue about whose metric is right," he says, "we miss the point. The question should always be: what is the data helping us improve together?"

Over time, collaboration improves not because of new governance rules, but because teams learn to speak a shared data language. Analysts learn to contextualize insights for multiple stakeholders. Business leaders learn to listen beyond their functional priorities. Data governance, once seen as restrictive, begins to act as an enabler, providing common definitions and reducing ambiguity.

The result is subtle but powerful. Decisions move faster. Escalations decrease. Teams trust each other's numbers. Cross-functional collaboration turns data from a departmental asset into an organizational one. Figure 11-4 illustrates how shared metrics and common understanding enable data to flow across functions rather than remain siloed.

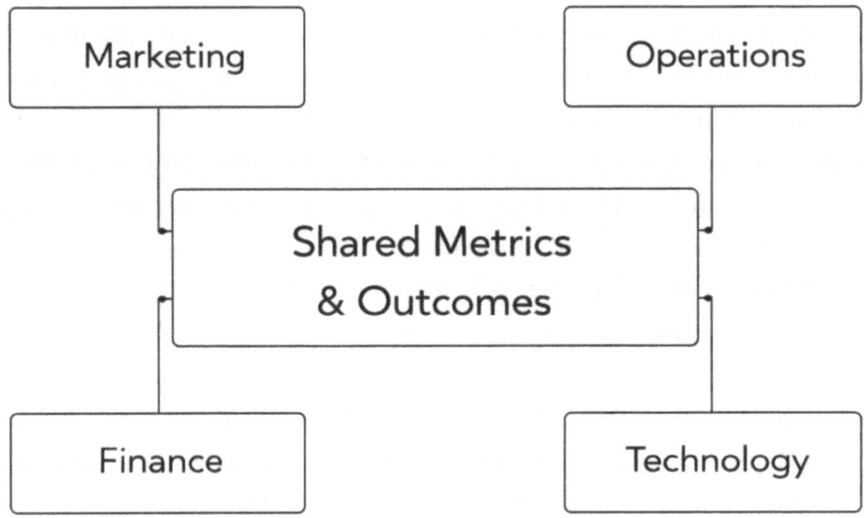

Figure 11-4. *Cross-functional data collaboration model*

Leadership Reflection

Reflecting on the shift, Shailesh observes:

> *"Data didn't just change how teams made decisions. It changed how they worked together. Once we aligned on outcomes, the silos lost their power."*

Nilesh adds:

> *"True data culture shows up when teams stop defending numbers and start solving problems together."*

Wrap-Up

Executive Takeaways

- A strong data culture is built through behavior, not tools.
- Data literacy is about confidence and questioning, not technical mastery.
- Training succeeds only when paired with enablement and leadership consistency.
- Psychological safety is essential for people to engage honestly with data.
- Cross-functional collaboration transforms data from siloed insight into shared value.
- Leaders shape data culture through the questions they ask and the behaviors they reward.

Chapter Summary

By the end of ISkillSetu's journey through data culture and literacy, one truth stands out clearly. The company has not become more data-driven because it acquired better dashboards or smarter models. It has become more data-driven because its people changed how they thought, spoke, and collaborated.

Shailesh's initial frustration gave way to clarity. The problem had never been access to data, it had been confidence, alignment, and trust. Maryam ensured that systems supported collaboration rather than fragmentation, while Nilesh focused relentlessly on literacy and shared understanding. Together, they demonstrated that data culture is not imposed; it is modeled.

Employees no longer wait for perfect answers before acting. They question assumptions, explore evidence, and work across boundaries. Data stops being a reporting artifact and becomes part of everyday reasoning.

This chapter reinforces a central lesson for business leaders: sustainable data transformation is a human endeavor. Technology enables it, governance protects it, but culture determines whether it thrives.

Looking Ahead

As ISkillSetu's data culture begins to stabilize, the leadership team reaches a critical inflection point. Teams are more confident working with data, discussions are grounded in evidence, and cross-functional collaboration is improving. Yet clarity is still missing in one important area: *how to systematically turn all this momentum into measurable, sustained outcomes.*

Shailesh captures the concern during a leadership review. "We have good ideas emerging from every function," he says. "But without a clear roadmap, we risk treating all initiatives as equal, and that's how priorities get blurred and impact gets diluted."

This is where culture and capability must be translated into structure. Once organizations develop data literacy and trust, the next challenge is designing a **coherent data and AI roadmap**, one that clearly sequences initiatives, groups use cases meaningfully, and connects every effort to business KPIs. Without such a roadmap, data and AI activities remain fragmented, making it difficult for leaders to track progress, justify investment, or demonstrate value.

The next chapter focuses on the data and AI roadmap, explaining how business leaders can design an end-to-end roadmap that aligns data foundations, analytics, and AI initiatives with strategic goals. It explores practical ways to create different use case buckets, prioritize initiatives across time horizons, and define KPIs that measure both delivery and business impact.

If this chapter established *how people think, learn, and collaborate around data,* the next chapter addresses the execution question:

How do leaders organize data and AI initiatives into a structured roadmap that delivers visible, trackable, and repeatable business value?

CHAPTER 12

The Data and AI Roadmap

> *Who has the data has the power.*
>
> —Tim O'Reilly

An organization's data and AI roadmap must be designed around business value, not technology alone. While technological advancement can deliver competitive advantage and sustain relevance over the long term, the primary focus should always be on business needs—addressing critical challenges, meeting customer expectations, and delivering measurable outcomes through iterative and purposeful technical integration.

Too often, data and AI roadmaps are driven by shiny new tools, emerging technologies, vendor influence, and unnecessary expenditure. This is frequently a symptom of weak strategic leadership rather than genuine business demand.

Strong data and AI leaders take a different approach. They build long-term, sustainable strategies, cultivate enterprise data culture across the organization, embed best practices into day-to-day operations, and take deliberate, value-led decisions. Rather than chasing hype, they articulate a future-proof vision that aligns technology investment with enduring business impact.

Figure 12-1 illustrates a scenario in which an organization's data and AI roadmap is dominated by hype and vendor-driven agendas rather than genuine business value. The consequences are predictable: projects fail, employees become frustrated and disengaged, investment is wasted, business impact remains elusive, leadership credibility erodes, and ultimately the organization is forced to rebuild from scratch—at significant cost in time, money, and effort.

R. Yasir and K. Shaikh, *Driving Business Transformation with Modern Data and AI Strategies*,
https://doi.org/10.1007/979-8-8688-2625-2_12

***Figure 12-1.** Before-and-after scenario of a bad data and AI roadmap*

In contrast, Figure 12-2 presents a different outcome. Here, data and AI initiatives are realistic, business value-driven, iterative, and inclusive—empowering the entire organization rather than focusing solely on technology. As a result, the organization grows sustainably and realizes substantial returns on its data and AI investments.

Figure 12-2. *Before-and-after scenario of a good data and AI roadmap*

In this chapter on data and AI roadmap design, within Part 4 of the book, we will cover the following topics and subtopics:

- Demystifying the Data and AI Roadmap
- Structured and Phased Data and AI Roadmap Design
- First 100 Days for a Leader

- Roadmap Adoption and Communication
- Common Failures to Avoid
- Future-Proof Next Steps

Demystifying the Data and AI Roadmap

> *Strategy is not about doing things right, but about doing the right things.*
>
> —Peter Drucker

A data and AI roadmap is a structured, sequential plan that connects business strategy with data capabilities, ultimately delivering analytics and AI-driven outcomes. It should encompass initiatives for new products and services; address existing limitations, frustrations, and bottlenecks; and provide a clear framework for prioritization and investment. All elements of the roadmap must be aligned to defined timelines and measurable, KPI-driven (percentage of AI use cases delivered successfully, ROI per initiative, efficiency gain, cost reduction, etc.) outcomes.

A roadmap is not a catalogue of technical tools, an IT architecture diagram, or a one-off, project-specific transformation effort. A well-executed data and AI roadmap typically spans three to five years to deliver meaningful return on investment, with success closely linked to initial investment decisions, execution discipline, and sustained executive sponsorship.

When an organization's strategy shifts year after year, delivering a coherent and effective roadmap becomes impossible. This challenge is illustrated in Figure 12-3, where frequent strategic changes undermine roadmap execution. Such instability reflects weak leadership and ultimately results in wasted investment, lost momentum, and diminished organizational impact.

Figure 12-3. *Demonstration on change of an organization's strategy based on the hype*

A mature and well-designed data and AI roadmap must extend beyond technology to include employee training, clear accountability, data and AI literacy, change management, process improvement, and investment planning—all aligned to the organization's multi-year vision and mission.

Key Priorities in Roadmap Design

- **Business-first focus** - Business needs and outcomes must take precedence over technology or solutions.
- **Value-driven phases** - Each phase of the roadmap should be explicitly linked to measurable business value.
- **Progressive evolution** - Platforms, use cases, and complexity should evolve incrementally across phases.
- **Adoption and communication** - The roadmap must be clearly communicated and its adoption tracked over time.
- **Leadership accountability** - Ownership of execution and delivery must be tied to senior leadership accountability.

- **People enablement** - Employee training, data and AI literacy, and change management should be integral to the roadmap.
- **Governance and compliance** - Strong governance, policies, and regulatory compliance must be established early, particularly during the foundational phase.
- **Investment discipline** - The roadmap should be aligned to investment planning and supported by realistic timelines.

Structured and Phased Data and AI Roadmap Design

> *Great things are not done by impulse, but by a series of small things brought together.*
>
> —Vincent van Gogh

A strong data and AI roadmap can be structured around multiple **business-focused segments**. The four examples below represent common strategic goals organizations may pursue, with data, AI, and technology acting as enablers to create a data flywheel, drive internal efficiency, develop new products, and embed change management through training, leadership, and data literacy.

- **Treating data as an organizational asset**

  This phase focuses on establishing a robust data ecosystem, including data acquisition, integration, and effective utilization. The objective is to enable data and AI to support both core and commercial activities across internal and external operations.

- **Data and AI for internal transformation, innovation, and efficiency**

  This phase centers on internal transformation and requires sustained investment in employee training, skills development, and cross-functional data and AI ideation workshops. Self-service analytics, built on the foundational data platform, enables data-driven decision-making and supports innovation across business units.

- **Commercial and customer-obsessed data and AI initiatives**

  This phase demands strong business sponsorship and active involvement to build and maintain a healthy data and AI use case backlog. Initiatives progress through proof-of-value validation, with customers engaged during hypothesis testing to support a fail-fast mindset and maximize return on investment.

- **Preparing for the future through the data ecosystem and value chain**

  In this phase, a true data flywheel emerges: more customers generate more data, which drives richer analytics and, in turn, attracts more customers. Data science, analytics, and responsible AI practices operate continuously, supported by structured change management to prepare the organization for future growth.

Ultimately, a data and AI roadmap is not a technical implementation or system integration timeline. It is a strategic framework that guides organizational evolution, using technology as an enabler across clearly defined, business-driven domains. Figure 12-4 demonstrates that leaders should approach the data and AI journey as an evolution, rather than as a one-off rollout.

Figure 12-4. *Two leaders discussing the phase-by-phase implementation process*

The development of a data and AI roadmap is typically guided by five fundamental questions:

- **Business outcomes (why)** - Enterprise priorities and strategic objectives
- **Use cases and activities (what)** - Value-driven initiatives aligned to use cases, like the analytics maturity framework
- **Data foundations (data)** - Core data capabilities and enablers
- **Analytics and AI platforms (how)** - The technologies and platforms required to deliver use cases at scale
- **Operating model and governance (who)** - Clear ownership, accountability, and decision rights

A data and AI roadmap must align with the analytics maturity framework outlined in Chapter 6 of this book. Organizations cannot realistically progress from zero to full maturity in a short period. Successful implementation requires sustained effort, training, cross-functional involvement, change management, process evolution, and disciplined technology integration. Progress must be iterative and phased.

Foundational capabilities and early wins can often be achieved within the first two quarters (approximately six months). However, scaling and embedding these capabilities typically requires up to 18 months. During the foundational phase, organizations should focus on business priorities, critical data gaps, pilot initiatives, and ownership. Phase 2 centers on high-value use cases, standardization, and operational practices. Significant business transformation generally occurs between 18 and 36 months, as decision automation, AI agents, real-time intelligence, and continuous learning capabilities are introduced.

Rather than viewing the roadmap as a rigid, linear plan, leaders should align it with organizational strategy and connect initiatives to short-, mid-, and long-term outcomes. As a guideline, short-term horizons span 0–9 months, mid-term 12–18 months, and long-term 24 months and beyond—allowing for capacity, investment, and delivery constraints.

Figure 12-5 illustrates an example roadmap for a business unit, progressing from data collection and standard reporting to the creation of composite data sources through broader data integration. From this foundation, the business can advance through descriptive, predictive, and ultimately prescriptive analytics.

While generative AI and AI agents are positioned toward the later stages of the roadmap, business units may begin exploring selected generative AI use cases alongside predictive analytics where appropriate. The productive impact of data and AI increases progressively from one phase to the next, following an iterative and disciplined approach.

At an organizational level, such roadmaps are typically more complex and expansive and should be tailored to reflect the organization's specific strategic priorities over a three- to five-year horizon.

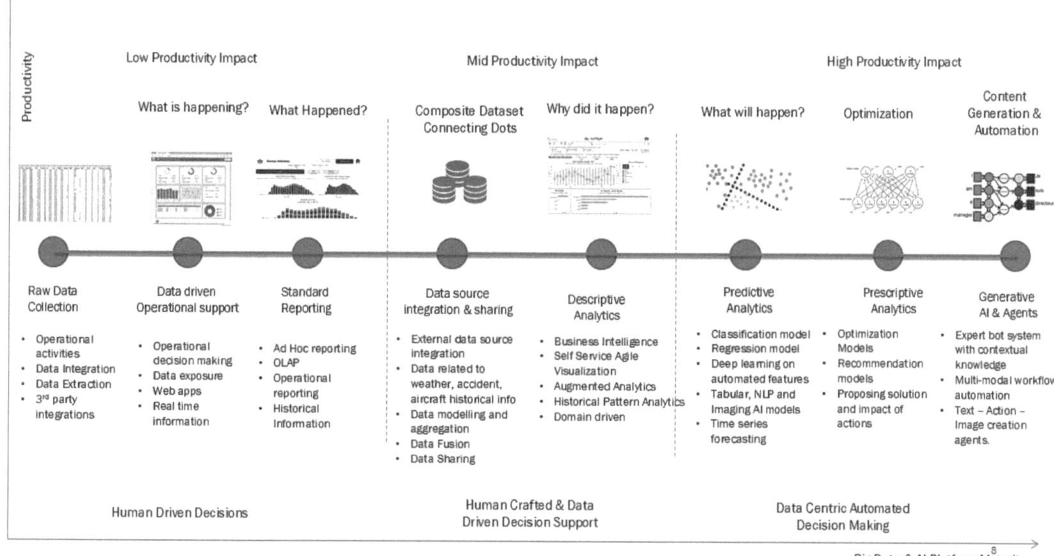

Figure 12-5. *An example data and AI roadmap for a business unit that can be achieved iteratively over three years*

Roadmap progress, delivery status, and required adjustments should be reviewed quarterly by the Data and AI Governance Council, comprising senior executive stakeholders. Early visibility and engagement at this level ensure timely endorsement, rapid resolution of bottlenecks, and sustained leadership commitment.

First 100 Days for a Leader

Before defining a data and AI roadmap, a newly appointed leader must undertake a thorough assessment of the organization's current maturity—across platforms, technology, and existing data and AI strategies. The first 100 days are critical for building trust, understanding the landscape, and establishing credibility before shaping the future roadmap.

Key Actions During This Period

- **Assess current maturity** - Review the maturity of data, analytics, and AI teams (low, medium, or high) using the analytics maturity model outlined in Chapter 6.
- **Understand the competitive landscape** - Evaluate competitor capabilities, positioning, and progress in data and AI adoption.
- **Align with business strategy** - Review the organization's three-year strategic plan and define clear goals and iterative focus areas accordingly.
- **Develop the data and AI roadmap** - Create a roadmap with quarterly milestones aligned to business strategy, investment priorities, and expected ROI.
- **Establish governance** - Set up a Data and AI Governance Council and an AI Enabling Board, comprising key business stakeholders, to drive accountability, transparency, and executive endorsement.
- **Build execution capability** - Hire, develop, deliver, and partner where necessary, while tracking progress on a regular basis.

This structured approach enables leaders to gain early momentum, build confidence across the organization, and lay the foundation for a sustainable and value-driven data and AI transformation.

Roadmap Adoption and Communication

Data and AI leaders must actively communicate the adoption journey of the roadmap and engage the entire organization in the simplest and most compelling way possible. Effective communication is essential to onboard and energize all stakeholders—from the executive team to frontline employees.

A well-presented roadmap should clearly articulate

- **Business outcomes** across the organization
- **Use case plans**, structured and grouped by delivery phases
- **Clear and precise quarterly timelines**
- **Required investment** and the expected return on that investment
- **Clear ownership** for each workstream
- **KPIs by phase**, covering value creation, adoption, and risk

A simple leadership test applies: if a leader cannot clearly answer the question, *"What value will we deliver in the next six months?"*, the roadmap is likely too technical and insufficiently focused on business impact. Figure 12-6 illustrates that AI investment should be structured across "now," "next," and "future" horizons, forming a portfolio that clearly reflects growth, outcomes, and progress.

Figure 12-6. *Two leaders talking about AI investment as portfolio*

Common Failures to Avoid

Measures of performance must reflect what matters most to the business.

—Kaplan and Norton

Designing a successful data and AI roadmap is inherently complex, which is why many organizations struggle with AI adoption. However, leaders can avoid common failure modes by applying the following strategic principles:

- **Avoid vendor- and hype-driven roadmaps** - Roadmaps should be guided by business value, not marketing trends or vendor influence.
- **Do not lead with tools or cloud platforms** - The roadmap must be anchored in decisions, outcomes, business needs, ecosystem readiness, and long-term vision—not technology selection.
- **Anchor data integration to use cases** - Integrating all data into a lake without clear use cases leads to waste. Roadmaps should be phased, with each phase tied to specific, high-value use cases.
- **Embed people and culture** - Without organization-wide involvement, training, and data literacy initiatives, even the best-designed roadmap will fail due to lack of engagement.
- **Drive adoption deliberately** - Low adoption can be mitigated by involving employees early and aligning leaders around the strategy. Analytics must be embedded into daily workflows rather than treated as ad hoc activity.
- **Balance governance and innovation** - Strong governance is essential during the foundational phase; however, excessive governance and bureaucracy in later phases can slow innovation.
- **Design for adaptability** - A roadmap must be flexible and continuously evolving. Overly rigid plans fail in the face of changing business priorities, resource constraints, and technological advances.

A successful data and AI roadmap balances structure with agility—enabling sustained progress while adapting to new challenges and opportunities.

Future-Proof Next Steps

A vision without a strategy remains an illusion.

—Lee Bolman

A well-designed data and AI roadmap should provide clear answers to the following questions:

- How do we measure success beyond AI model performance?
- How will teams work more effectively and efficiently?
- How do we maintain a healthy backlog of new product and service ideas?
- What data do we need next—and why?
- Which analytics initiatives will be launched next, and for whom?
- What are the adoption and usage rates of our analytics capabilities?
- How are we measuring efficiency gains enabled by data and AI?
- What level of investment is required over the next planning cycles, and what direct or indirect ROI is expected?
- What risks increase as we scale AI, and how are they being mitigated?
- What capabilities have become possible that were not before?
- What disruptive ideas will we bring to market in the next two cycles?
- How resilient is the roadmap if budgets tighten by 20%?
- Who owns the final decision when AI recommendations conflict with human judgment?
- What new skills must employees—and leaders themselves—develop?
- Where should we rely on partners, and which capabilities must we retain in-house?
- Which decisions will materially improve outcomes this year?
- How does this roadmap prepare the organization for technologies that cannot yet be fully predicted?

These are not merely diagnostic questions; they serve as guiding principles for designing a robust data and AI roadmap—one that independently and consistently delivers strategic clarity, resilience, and long-term value.

Chapter Summary

As the data and AI landscape continues to evolve, it is increasingly important for organizational leaders to establish a clear data and AI roadmap aligned with corporate strategy. Without this alignment, organizations risk pursuing hype-driven use cases that often result in wasted time, investment, and effort—ultimately leading to frustration and limited business impact.

Leaders must focus on aligning data and AI ambitions with enterprise strategy, translating strategic priorities into measurable, AI-enabled outcomes, and clearly distinguishing *AI aspiration* from *AI intent*. Equally important is setting realistic time horizons that balance short-term wins with sustainable, long-term advantage.

In this chapter, we have explored what a data and AI roadmap is, how to design one, where to focus, the key best practices to apply, and how to avoid common pitfalls.

CHAPTER 13

Conclusion: Leading with Confidence

> *Confidence in AI leadership does not come from having all the answers—it comes from asking the right questions, grounding decisions in data, and taking responsibility for outcomes.*
>
> —Satya Nadella

We are approaching the conclusion of this book. Its purpose has been to simplify data, analytics, and AI concepts for today's and tomorrow's business and technology leaders, while grounding these ideas in real-world scenarios and proven practices drawn from our own experience.

This final chapter serves as a reflection and consolidation of the key themes explored throughout the book. It revisits core concepts, discusses how leaders can lead with confidence in an AI-driven environment, highlights behaviors and practices to avoid—particularly those that result in toxic leadership—and outlines what successful implementation looks like in practice. The chapter concludes with a brief message from the authors on next steps.

This book is written for the senior executives seeking clear and comprehensive overview of the domain, leaders preparing to make strategic investments in data and AI, and technical professionals transitioning to leadership and digital transformational leads. The journey in this book started from data importance, cloud ecosystem, data and AI strategy designing, advanced analytics and AI ecosystem, different types of AI overview, and eventually data and AI roadmap designing and preparing for next steps.

R. Yasir and K. Shaikh, *Driving Business Transformation with Modern Data and AI Strategies*,
https://doi.org/10.1007/979-8-8688-2625-2_13

In this final chapter, we cover three closing topics:

- Leading with Confidence
- Things to Avoid "Toxic AI Leadership"
- Successful Implementation

Leading with Confidence

> *A successful data and AI journey is not defined by sophisticated models, but by consistent execution—where data informs decisions, people trust the outcomes, and value compounds over time.*
>
> —Andrew Ng

Data and AI are shaping the future of most organizations today. Increasingly, domain-focused companies are evolving into technology-driven, data- and AI-enabled enterprises. As a result, revenue models, competitive dynamics, and market landscapes are changing at pace. In this environment, data and AI leaders must lead with confidence.

Leading with confidence means consistently making sound, rational decisions in the best interests of both the organization and its people, while consciously avoiding common pitfalls. In the next two sections, we briefly address behaviors to avoid and outline what successful implementation looks like in practice. However, there are several core principles leaders should focus on to lead with confidence:

- **Understand the organization's current capabilities** - Assess where the organization sits within the analytics maturity model. If reliance on legacy systems remains high, prioritizing digital transformation before pursuing advanced analytics and AI will lead to more realistic and sustainable outcomes.
- **Anchor strategy to investment and ROI** - Data and AI strategies and roadmaps must be closely tied to funding and measurable returns. Planning should be both strategic and iterative.

- **Prioritize democratization** - The success of data, analytics, and AI initiatives depends heavily on broad participation. The more people are involved, the faster adoption, learning, and impact will occur.
- **Create a safe space for ideas** - Innovation should come from across the organization. Leaders must actively encourage contribution and ensure psychological safety for participation at all levels.
- **Avoid constant platform changes** - Resist switching platforms based solely on vendor recommendations. First, assess gaps and integration options. Where change is unavoidable, proceed iteratively and bring stakeholders along with transparency and honesty.
- **Address cost from the outset** - Cost considerations should be built into planning from day one. Leaders must clearly communicate where costs arise, why they are necessary, and how ROI can be achieved over time.
- **Embed data-driven accountability and transparency** - These principles should underpin all data and AI leadership efforts. Leaders must demonstrate accountability and transparency in their own decisions and operations, using data as the foundation.
- **Build teams, not heroes** - Sustainable success comes from building high-performing, well-aligned teams rather than relying on a small number of individual "superstars."
- **Champion responsible AI** - Responsible AI practices must be actively promoted and embedded. This safeguards the organization as regulatory expectations continue to evolve across countries and regions.

Together, these principles provide a practical foundation for confident, credible, and sustainable data and AI leadership.

Things to Avoid "Toxic AI Leadership"

The greatest risk in AI is not the technology itself, but leadership that treats AI as hype, ignores accountability, and sidelines people from the process.

—Peter Drucker

Over the years, we have observed a range of AI leadership styles. Figure 13-1 highlights examples of approaches that have proven ineffective for both leaders and their organizations. These scenarios are shared as learning points—illustrating behaviors to reflect on, learn from, and ultimately avoid.

Figure 13-1. Toxic AI leadership examples

The Hype-Driven Visionary

This leadership style launches into AI transformation while foundational elements—such as platforms, governance, data quality, and infrastructure—remain unresolved. While the narrative may sound compelling initially, the absence of a stable underlying system means the hype cannot be sustained. Over time, this approach results in wasted investment, lost momentum, and organizational frustration.

The PoC Collector

Proofs-of-concept (PoCs) and proofs of value (PoVs) are important, but only when they lead to production. Some leaders accumulate pilots as symbols of progress, running dozens of experiments without deploying solutions into real business environments. The result is visible activity but little measurable impact—innovation without outcomes.

Nepotism Hiring

In periods of market hype, we have observed leaders appoint individuals to data and AI leadership roles without the relevant experience, capability, or business alignment. Effective AI leadership depends on hiring the right talent with the right mindset. Experience, domain understanding, and credibility should always take precedence over familiarity or convenience.

The PowerPoint Strategist

Well-crafted slides, roadmaps, and vision statements have value—but presentations are not systems. In this leadership pattern, strategy looks polished on paper yet lacks execution, integration, employee involvement, and organizational alignment. Without disciplined delivery, even the most elegant plans fail to translate into results.

Vendor Dependency

Vendors play an important role in PoCs, validation, cost estimation, architecture design, and access to best practices. However, excessive reliance on vendors for end-to-end delivery can become costly and risky. Over time, organizations may lose intellectual property, fail to build internal capability, and erode their competitive advantage. Strong leadership requires a deliberate plan to balance vendor support with internal capability building.

The Cost Cutter

To move quickly, some leaders cut costs indiscriminately—particularly in areas such as model validation, monitoring, security, and governance. While this may appear to accelerate delivery in the short term, it often leads to silent failures, escalating technical debt, and repeated rework. Ultimately, shortcuts undermine trust, stability, and long-term value.

These examples are not critiques of intent, but lessons in execution. Avoiding these leadership traps is essential to building sustainable, credible, and value-driven AI capabilities.

Successful Implementation

> *Analytics and AI deliver value only when organisations move beyond experimentation and commit to execution, accountability, and scale.*
>
> —Rita McGrath

Successful data and AI implementation may appear complex, but when approached with the right mindset and a disciplined set of steps, it becomes far more structured and achievable. Effective implementation is characterized by six clear indicators, illustrated in Figure 13-2:

1. **Business-led focus** - Data and AI initiatives are consistently anchored in real business problems, supported by a strong, collaborative partnership between business teams and platform or technology functions.

2. **People enablement** - Employees are actively nurtured, well trained, and meaningfully integrated into the overall plan.

3. **Structured change management** - Data, analytics, and AI introduce new ways of working. Successful organizations recognize this and invest in thoughtful change management, including clear planning, timelines, communication, and training.

4. **Open innovation and feedback** - Ideas flow from across the organization, people remain engaged and motivated, feedback is welcomed, and delivered solutions increasingly address real problems.

5. **Iterative growth** - Progress occurs incrementally, with teams meeting realistic targets while building momentum and scaling impact over time.

6. **Demonstrated value** - The organization clearly recognizes the benefits of analytics and AI, observes positive ROI, and understands how these capabilities support sustained long-term performance.

Together, these indicators reflect a mature, balanced, and sustainable approach to data and AI transformation.

Healthy AI Development

Figure 13-2. *Healthy and successful data and AI implementation*

We hope you liked the overall content of this book. Hopefully you have learned something new and will be able to use the learnings from this book in your data and AI journey as a leader. We appreciate and thank you for all your support. Here is a simple message from both of the authors in Figure 13-3.

Figure 13-3. *"Thank you" message from the authors*

Index

R. Yasir and K. Shaikh, *Driving Business Transformation with Modern Data and AI Strategies*,
https://doi.org/10.1007/979-8-8688-2625-2

B

C

D

E

F

G

P, Q

R

U

V

W

X, Y

Z